D0603168

Exotic Indoor Plants

# Exotic Indoor Plants

## The Easy Guide to Buying and Growing Spectacular Varieties

**William Davidson**
*Contributors*
Clive Innes (Cacti and Succulents)
Ray Bilton (Orchids)

CHARTWELL
BOOKS, INC.

A QUARTO BOOK
Published by Chartwell Books Inc
A Division of Book Sales Inc
110 Enterprise Avenue, Secaucus,
New Jersey 07094



ISBN 0-89009-792-5



Art Director Robert Morley
Editorial Director Christopher Fagg
Editors Margot Patterson, Emma Johnson
Designer Joanna Swindell
Illustrators Edwina Keene, Simon Roulstone
Photography Ian Howes
Special thanks to Bridget Gibbs, Geoff Rogers
Filmset by QV Typesetting Limited
Origination by Hong Kong Graphic Arts Service Centre Limited,
Printed by Leefung Asco Printers Limited, Hong Kong

# Contents

# How to use this book

**Using this book** This book is laid out so as to give the maximum amount of information in the clearest possible way. The introduction gives general advice on growing plants indoors: what to look for when buying houseplants, how to care for them, how to propagate them, how to keep them free of pests and in good condition. Information on the different methods of indoor cultivation, as well as advice on building and stocking your own garden room, is also included.

The rest of the book is divided into three parts: a section on flowering and foliage houseplants, a section on cacti and other succulent plants, and a section on orchids. A short introduction precedes the last two sections and explains some of the special characteristics and cultivation requirements of cactus and orchids.

Plants are arranged alphabetically within each section. Each entry discusses briefly the general characteristics of plants within a genus and gives a more detailed description of the appearance and growth habits of selected species. A photograph and a chart summarizing how to care for the plant accompany each entry.

**Family name** Houseplants belong to many different botanical families. The family of each plant appears at the top of the page, but in a few cases there are entries containing plants from different families. These entries — Ferns, Carnivorous Plants, Succulents — are headed by a general group name.

**Generic name** Within each family the primary unit of classification is the genus. The generic name is the first name of any plant and is the main heading for each entry.

**Species name** Each genus can consist of a number of species. The name of the genus and the name of the species form the first and second parts of the Latin name of a plant, and are always printed in italic. Within a species, there may be varieties that differ in minor ways and which form the third part of a plant's full name. Varieties that occur in nature have Latin names; varieties that have been developed in cultivation are called cultivars and may have either Latin or vernacular names.

GESNERIACEAE

**Sinningia**

SINNINGIA

THERE ARE a number of sinningia species, most with brightly coloured flowers and foliage to match. The most common is the florists' gloxinia, *S. speciosa*, which is available for many months during the summer. Plants are low-growing and produce large, soft green leaves that are topped by brightly coloured trumpet flowers in many shades. Plants growing in 7in (18cm) diameter pots develop many more flowers than plants in smaller pots.

*Sinningia cardinalis* grows from a tuber and has most attractive foliage, emerald-green in colour and velvety in appearance. Flowers appear in clusters and are bright scarlet with a purple throat. A group of these plants in a large bowl can be a very impressive sight, and will be ample reward for the care required to grow them. In early autumn plants naturally shed their flowers and foliage, and this is a sign that watering should be reduced until such time as the soil is bone dry, in which condition the corm rests warm and dry over winter. In the spring, the corm should be planted into fresh soil to renew the growing process for another year.

**Light and position**
Find the lightest possible location for these plants, but avoid direct sunlight which can scorch the softer new leaves.

**Temperature range**
Cool Intermediate Warm
A room temperature of around 60°F (15°C) during summer is best. In winter keep the corms dry and frost free around 50°F (10°C). The maximum summer temperature should be 75°F (23°C).

**Watering**
In summer water generously two or three times a week. When growth has stopped, allow to dry out completely.

**Sinningias** have spectacular trumpet-shaped flowers and large velvety leaves. The scarlet red flowers of this gloxinia, *S. speciosa* (right), are just one of the many colours available. The mixed display of *S. speciosa* (above) shows the variety of flower shades that have been developed. All sinningias naturally die down in the winter, but if repotted in the spring, they will grow again.

100

**Avoiding problems** Light, temperature, water, feeding, etc., are critical to whether or not a plant succeeds. This easy-reference chart indentifies what conditions are necessary for your plant to prosper. The various symbols serve as a quick check-list, enabling you to see at a glance what kind of treatment a given plant should receive. The symbols are explained in detail, and information is further amplified in the captions.

**Crosses and ticks** A tick indicates that the plant benefits from a given condition and treatment, and a cross indicates that it will find it harmful.

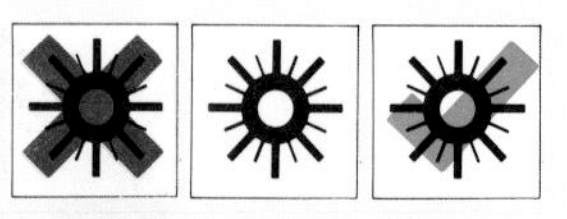

This symbol shows that the plant needs a bright position, but not direct sunlight. A plant that receives this mark could be placed near a window.

This symbol indicates full shade. Plants such as ferns need a very shady position, and are thus ideal for locating in a dark corner of a room.

**Light and position** This symbol indicates bright sunlight. A plant that needs bright sunlight could stand in a well-lit window, for example.

This symbol indicates a plant will benefit from partial shade. Place the plant in a fairly light room, but away from a window.

**Draughts** Except for a few species, most plants cannot tolerate draughts. Pay particular attention to this symbol.

SINNINGIA/SPATHIPHYLLUM

ARACEAE

## Spathiphyllum

SPATHIPHYLLUMS ARE prized both for their foliage and for their arum-shaped flower heads. Plants produce glossy green leaves on short petioles that sprout direct from soil level, forming into bold clumps of growth in time.

The most popular species is *S. wallisii*, which produces insignificant clumps of thin green leaves and white spathe flowers on short petioles. It is a neat plant for the windowsill and offers the prospect of flowers at almost any time of the year.

Much more spectacular and generally bolder in appearance is the hybrid *S.* 'Mauna Loa', which produces its large white spathe flowers on stems that exceed 24in (61cm) in length.

Both *S. wallisii* and *S.* 'Mauna Loa' need damp, shaded conditions. The temperature should be reasonably warm, around 60 to 70°F (16 to 21°C). Once established in their pots, these plants should be fed at every watering during the spring and summer months of the year. To make new plants, split clumps of growth into small sections, making sure that each piece has two or three leaves attached, and pot individually. Grow plants in loam-based soil.

**Spathiphyllums** are arum lily plants whose attraction lies in the contrast of their glossy green leaves and long-stemmed white spathe flowers with protruding central spadix. *S. wallisii* (above) has leaves growing in thick clusters and is a good plant for keeping on a windowsill, as it is slightly smaller than other species. Spathiphyllums need regular generous feeding in the spring and summer, otherwise the edges of leaves will become yellow and ragged.

SPATHIPHYLLUM

Light and position: Spathiphyllums like a sunny position but direct sunlight should be avoided.

Temperature range: Cool Intermediate Warm. Spathiphyllums should be kept at temperatures between 60°-70°F (15°-21°C). They do not like draughts and need a humid atmosphere.

Watering: The spathiphyllum should be watered with moderate amounts — the potting mixture should never dry out completely.

Feeding: Use a standard liquid fertilizer and administer every two weeks while the plant is growing.

Seasonal care: Winter Spring Summer Autumn. The plant grows fastest in summer and should receive greater quantities of water then. Avoid water-logging — worms in the soil may block up the drainage holes with their casts so check for these. Decrease food in winter.

Soil: The plants should be repotted every spring in a loam-based mixture. Ensure that they are properly drained.

101

**Name of plant** For easy reference, the generic names for the plants on these two pages appear here.

**Common name** The popular names for plants in a given genus appear at the top of the page underneath the generic name. In most cases, these common names apply to all plants in the genus.

**Picture** Photographs illustrate the plants discussed in the text, showing their color, shape and size.

**Captions** Captions identify the plants that appear in the photographs and amplify the material presented in the text.

**Charts** Charts provide readers with detailed instructions on how to care for particular plants. Observing these guidelines on light, water, temperature, etc., should enable readers to successfully raise exotic plants indoors.

**Temperature** Although they will not flourish, some plants may survive in temperatures other than those specified. The ideal temperature range is given for each plant. This may be cool (45°F/7°C to 60°F/16°C), intermediate (60°F/16°F to 65°F/18°C) or warm (over 65°F/18°C).

**Watering** The main methods of watering houseplants are **1.** applying water directly onto the soil, **2.** pouring water into the container

underneath the plant pot, **3.** spraying the plant with a plant spray, and **4.** immersing the pot (but not the whole plant) in water.

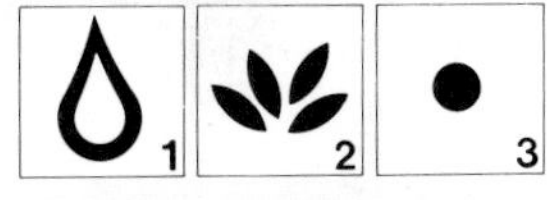

**Feeding** There are three ways of feeding houseplants. The symbols indicate that **1.** the plant should be given food in liquid form, **2.** as a spray on the leaves or **3.** in solid form, either as granules or a stick. It is important to feed the plant as recommended.
Most plants need food only during the growing season. Other plants, however, require varying amounts of food all year round.

**Seasonal care** This chart shows when plants require watering and feeding. The pale-blue color indicates when you should water; the droplet symbol shows when extra watering is essential

The feeding chart is very similar to the watering chart. The yellow areas indicate when feed should be given — the red dots show when it is essential.

**Soil** This section provides instructions on what kind of soil a given plant needs in order to thrive. There are many slightly differing formulas, but the two potting mixtures chiefly used are a soil-based mixture and a peat-based mixture.

# Introduction

PEOPLE TODAY are becoming increasingly adventurous about the sort of plants they choose to grow indoors — whether in a living room, garden room or conservatory. As interest has grown, professional plant hybridizers have responded by introducing, for general sale, indoor plants once thought of as exotic or rare, but now widely cultivated by amateur growers. Although some are more difficult to grow than others, all repay that little extra care by providing unusual and interesting foliage or flowers — and there is a particular satisfaction to be gained from successfully growing a delicate and beautiful specimen. This book is intended to give growers the information they need to maximize success and minimize failure in growing more exciting plants — from general care and maintenance to the specific needs of particular varieties. The alphabetical list of plants contains many suggestions which, I hope, will encourage amateur growers to try something a little out of the ordinary.

During the nineteenth century, naturalists such as Alexander von Humboldt (above) travelled to remote parts of the world in search of exotic plants (see opposite page). Those species they discovered were brought back and introduced into the grand conservatories of the day.

## The origin of exotic plants

Almost all the more exciting indoor plants that we know today originated in the tropics. During the nineteenth century there was a passion among botanists for plant-hunting in remote parts of the world. Famous plant hunters, such as Joseph Banks and Robert Fortune, brought back to Britain rare species which, duly noted by the Royal Botanical Society, were subsequently grown in the conservatories of the Victorian and Edwardian upper middle classes. The pioneering quest for rare

**Plant hybrids** Some of the most successful indoor plants are man-made hybrids that bring together the best attributes of the original strains. The example in the foreground shows *Fatshedera lizei*, an attractive hybrid of *Hedera helix* (top left) and *Fatsia japonica* (top right). The resulting hybrid has the leaf shape and hardiness of the hedera plus the more erect growing habit of the fatsia — an ideal combination.

and unusual plants has, over the years, developed into a flourishing international trade. Today, the householder need look no further than his local plant centers for species which, a hundred years ago, were to be found only in the depths of the tropical rain forest.

**Buying plants: what to look for**
This tropical heritage has an important bearing, not only on what to buy, but where to buy. When setting out to grow delicate plants it is of the utmost importance that the plant should be in good condition to start with. And, in order for the plant to be in good condition, the premises of the plant supplier should be something more than an inadequately heated and poorly-lit shed. It is important to find a shop that seems warm, well-lit and congenial.

The obvious place to start is the established, professional plant supplier, but in recent years department stores, too, have become an important source of plants for the amateur grower. And, surprising though it may seem, purchases from a top department store are often equal, even superior, in quality to plants bought in a plant shop. Department stores often go to considerable trouble, not only to get the right conditions to keep plants healthy, but also to provide trained staff who can offer customers proper advice on plant care. Moreover, as large-scale purchasers, department stores are able to demand high standards of quality from their suppliers.

You should give your retailer an idea of the conditions which the plant will meet in its new home. A good retailer will inquire about the light and the temperature in your home and will then suggest plants that are likely to do well there.

Last, but not least, a good plant supplier will carefully wrap the plant for the homeward journey. On a bitterly cold winter's day you will sometimes see a newly-purchased plant, its leaves blowing in the wind, clutched proudly by its new owner who is muffled to the eyes in protective clothing. Even a brief exposure to cold can irreparably damage a plant, and, if it is cold enough for an overcoat to be worn, you should insist that the plant is suitably wrapped for its protection.

These simple guidelines, no more than common sense, will nevertheless guarantee you the best chance of obtaining healthy plants in good condition. The advice given in the following pages is intended to help you keep your plants looking their best. The book is divided into three sections: a general section on houseplants, with special emphasis on those having ornamental and decorative foliage or flowers, and specialized sections dealing with two of the most popular families of exotic plants — cacti and succulents, and orchids. Each section gives general and specific advice on care and maintenance, together with a list of plants which, with proper attention, can be grown at home.

**Reviving a parched plant**
If a plant has not received a sufficient amount of water, the leaves wilt and they may drop off (above).

The first thing to do for a dehydrated plant is to loosen the top layer of soil (above). The water will then be able to permeate to the roots.

If the plant is very parched, it makes sense to spray the leaves with tepid water.

A plant should always be left to drain after watering.

**Signs of health** Buying a really healthy plant is the most important step to ensuring indoor gardening success. These beautiful plants of *Begonia hiemalis* 'Rieger' are literally bursting with health — the leaves are firm and glossy, the flowers are sturdy and bright, and the whole plant has a robust appearance. Take the opportunity to look at the surrounds of the plant shop, too. If they are clean and well maintained, chances are that all the plants on sale are in good health. But don't take your chosen plant home until you have checked out the detailed points raised in the annotations above — it could save you disappointment later on.

# General Care

ALMOST EVERY PLANT that is brought into the house will present some challenge to the plant grower. In the first place, no matter how good the environment you provide, it is not the stable greenhouse or hothouse conditions in which the plant has spent the early part of its life. Conditions in the greenhouse are carefully controlled: a moist atmosphere, if that is what the plant requires, good light, and the daily attentions of a skilled gardener who makes a living keeping plants in top condition. However, if you follow these guidelines in relation to your own houseplants then the risk of failure is very much reduced.

You can pick up some useful tips about the general care of plants from a professional plant grower. Firstly, a nurseryman will take precautions to ensure that the greenhouse is free from pests and disease. The soil he uses for potting will be steam-sterilized, and all pots will be either new or scrubbed clean before use. Almost all plants, and flowering plants in particular, need good light if they are to grow well. The professional grower, while ensuring that the plants have enough light, avoids exposing them to very bright sunlight. If necessary he will cover the glass with a material that provides some kind of shade. Finally, the greenhouse will always be heated to the correct temperature for the particular plants.

The nurseryman, having gone to the trouble of ensuring that plants are healthy, will carefully wrap and box plants so that they arrive at the home of the eventual purchaser in perfect condition — try to keep them that way. It may seem obvious to stress that the plant should be unwrapped as soon as you get it home, but this point is often neglected, with the result that the plant is deprived of the light that is so essential to its well-being. The plants concerned may have traveled hundreds of miles since leaving the nursery and may well have dried out in transit, so you should immediately check to see if they need water; some plants dry out at a surprisingly fast rate.

Given the amount of interest today in growing indoor plants for their own sake, rather than simply using them for decoration, it is not unusual to find rooms that have been entirely given over to plants. With controlled lighting, temperature, watering and humidity, it is possible to grow a very wide range of both flowering and foliage plants.

**Pots** Natural clay pots are attractive and provide a stable base for large plants. They allow the potting mix to 'breathe' through their porous sides. Lightweight plastic pots, available in many colors help to retain moisture in the potting mix.

**Potting mixes** Soil-based mixes, prepared from sterilized loam, provide firm support and longer-lasting natural nutrition. The lightweight 'soil-less' mixes, based on peat, are very convenient for indoor use.

**Accessories** Just as with outdoor gardening, you'll find such items as gloves, twine, clippers and scissors essential for good plant care.

**Pesticides** Aerosol sprays, powders, tablets and liquids are available to ward off pests and diseases. Always follow the label notes for proper and safe application.

**Plant foods** When the natural food value of the potting mix declines, use a liquid, tablet, granular or 'soil stick' fertilizer to keep plants healthy.

**Watering equipment** Use a watering can with a long, thin spout to reach into the centre of plant displays. A mist sprayer will help to keep humidity high around indoor plants.

**Essential equipment** Like most hobbies, indoor gardening needs a basic kit of tools and materials. These are usually on sale 'under the same roof' as the plants, making their selection an extension of the plant-buying process. This is to be encouraged because it is possible to match the plants with the most suitable equipment they require for continued health. Since most of the essential materials, such as potting mixes, are prepared and packaged for use in the home, even the most diffident of beginners should feel encouraged to give gardening a try.

**Grouping plants** together not only creates an attractive display but also helps the plants by providing group humidity.
**Room divider** Plants scrambling up a trellis (below) form an original and effective boundary between a dining area and lounge.
**Plant room** Most indoor plants revel in light conditions. In this kitchen/plant room (bottom) the bright blooms of geraniums contrast well with the cool greens of ferns and palms.
**Window group** Where space allows, a large window display of plants (bottom right) creates a superb room feature.

*Scindapsus aureus*
(Devil's ivy; Pothos)

*Nephrolepis exaltata*
(Boston fern)

*Dracaena marginata*
'Tricolor'
(Variegated silhouette plant)

*Saintpaulia ionantha*
(African violet)

*Hedera helix*
'Goldchild'
(Golden English ivy)

**Leaf Care** Dead leaves, such as the ones around the base of this cyclamen (right), should be pulled off regularly. However much care and attention they are given, dead leaves will not revive.

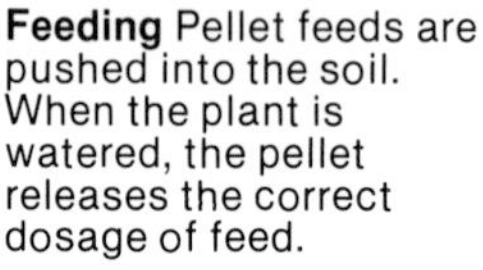

**Feeding** Pellet feeds are pushed into the soil. When the plant is watered, the pellet releases the correct dosage of feed.

**Fertilizer sticks** are pushed into the soil at the edge of the pot; they are designed to release nutrients over a given period of time.

**Liquid feeds** can be given to the plant when it is watered. Powdered feed can also be added to the water.

**Humidity** Many plants require more humidity in the atmosphere than is provided in the average home. If the atmosphere becomes too dry, the plant's rate of water loss increases, which causes it to wilt. You can prevent this by standing the plant on damp pebbles or gravel, or filling the space between the inner and outer pot with damp peat.

## Watering

If plants are on the dry side, pour water onto the surface of the soil, from a watering can with a small spout. Pour the water until you can see the surplus draining through the holes in the bottom of the pot. If the plant is excessively dry, then it should be submerged in a bucket of water. Hold the pot with your finger and place your thumbs on the soil before plunging it in. Leave the pot in the water until all the air bubbles have escaped. If the plant is very thirsty, this exercise can be repeated at every watering (perhaps twice or three times a week).

Rainwater is generally better for plants that object to lime, but it is not essential. It is important not to use very cold water, direct from the tap, when watering tender plants, such as saintpaulias. The best practice is to fill a can and leave it to stand in a heated room overnight, or to place it on a radiator for a few hours. In any event, you should avoid using water that is either very hot or very cold.

## Feeding

Your plant has been grown in a nursery where it will have been fed regularly, at least as necessary. If the plant has become accustomed to feeding, the practice must be continued when it is taken indoors, or it will suffer discoloration and general decline.

A very extensive selection of fertilizers, in various forms, is available from garden sundriesmen, and deciding what is most suitable for your plants is very often a question of trial and error. Fertilizer in liquid form is probably the best as the plant can absorb it more easily. You can buy powders that are diluted in water, so forming a liquid feed, or you can use slow-release fertilizers in the form of tablets or sticks. These are pushed into the soil in order to

**Positioning is the key** to displaying your plants to best effect. Plants with green foliage will do much better in poor light than plants with variegated or highly colored foliage, while nearly all flowering plants need good light if they are to do well.

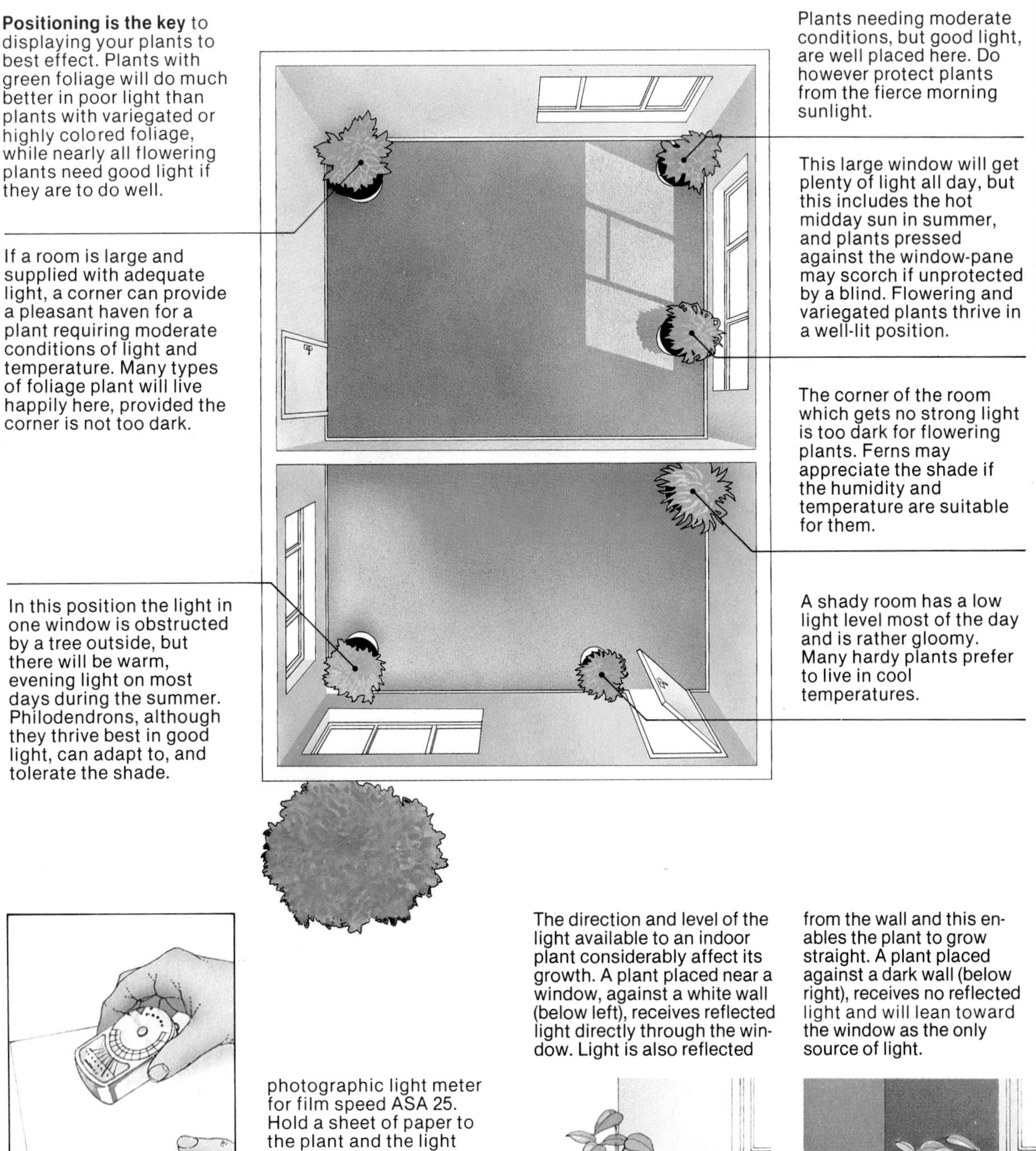

If a room is large and supplied with adequate light, a corner can provide a pleasant haven for a plant requiring moderate conditions of light and temperature. Many types of foliage plant will live happily here, provided the corner is not too dark.

In this position the light in one window is obstructed by a tree outside, but there will be warm, evening light on most days during the summer. Philodendrons, although they thrive best in good light, can adapt to, and tolerate the shade.

Plants needing moderate conditions, but good light, are well placed here. Do however protect plants from the fierce morning sunlight.

This large window will get plenty of light all day, but this includes the hot midday sun in summer, and plants pressed against the window-pane may scorch if unprotected by a blind. Flowering and variegated plants thrive in a well-lit position.

The corner of the room which gets no strong light is too dark for flowering plants. Ferns may appreciate the shade if the humidity and temperature are suitable for them.

A shady room has a low light level most of the day and is rather gloomy. Many hardy plants prefer to live in cool temperatures.

**Measuring light** intensity (above) A light meter can be useful if you are not sure how bright the light in a room is. Set a photographic light meter for film speed ASA 25. Hold a sheet of paper to the plant and the light meter to the paper. Adjust the dial of the meter according to the light reading obtained and check the f stop needed for a shutter speed of a quarter second. f64 or f32 indicates bright, direct sunlight, f16 bright light and f8 medium light.

The direction and level of the light available to an indoor plant considerably affect its growth. A plant placed near a window, against a white wall (below left), receives reflected light directly through the window. Light is also reflected from the wall and this enables the plant to grow straight. A plant placed against a dark wall (below right), receives no reflected light and will lean toward the window as the only source of light.

**Container sense** Strategic positioning of two different plants in the same pot (above) makes good sense — the large overhanging leaves of the rex begonias hide the bare lower stem of the upright *Cissus antarctica*. A colorful melee of plants and pots (right) makes a superbly informal feature in any room.

**Light work** If you are really serious about growing your indoor plants under artificial light,then arrange your set-up as shown above. Use fluorescent tubes — ideally ones that produce a balanced light output — and suspend them 6-24in (15-60cm) from your plants (depending on type). A pebble tray will help to maintain high humidity.

**Ordinary bulbs** If you illuminate your plant displays with ordinary incandescent bulbs, the result may look attractive but the plants may not receive sufficient light or the right sort of light to really prosper. Even so, as an evening supplement to daylight it's worth a try. Try to avoid burning the topmost leaves.

**Bowls of light** Fittings that combine lamps and plant containers can provide charming displays. Use them with shallow-rooted plants that benefit from some additional light in the evening, such as African violets. Keep a careful check on the potting mix to prevent it drying out too rapidly, and do not use too bright a lamp.

**Potting on** Carefully remove the plant, with soil attached, from its pot. The plant should be advanced to a new pot 2in (5cm) wider.

Place about 1in (3cm) of soil in the bottom of the new container, place the old pot inside and fill the space in between the two pots with more soil.

Press down the soil between the two pots and push the inner pot down inside the other very firmly.

The level of the soil between the pots should be at the rim of the inner pot. This empty pot can now be removed by twisting it free.

When the old pot has been removed, it will leave an impression in the soil inside the new container, into which the plant can be neatly placed.

Put the plant into the space left by the old pot, and press the soil around it. Finally, water the soil until the surplus water drains from the bottom.

feed the plant over a long period of time and are useful for plants in more inaccessible locations, or for houseplant owners who tend to be forgetful. There are also foliar feeds that the plant can absorb into its system through its foliage, and these are excellent for plants that have sensitive root systems, such as many of the smaller ferns.

### Conditioning

A gardener who is preparing borders for a show of summer bedding would not dream of taking plants direct from the greenhouse and placing them into garden soil — unless the temperature outdoors was very mild. Plants should be conditioned to accept changes in temperature; remove them from the greenhouse and place them in a cooler greenhouse or cold frame until they become hardened to the more extreme temperature. A similar practice is required for indoor plants that have been growing in strong greenhouse light — they should be gradually acclimatized to darker indoor areas.

The elegant Weeping Fig, *Ficus benjamina*, is a plant that appreciates good light, although not direct sunlight. It reacts to poor light by shedding its older leaves, so it is worth remembering, if you want to put this plant in a part of the house which is poorly-lit, it should be conditioned, by degrees, to accept a lower level of light. The same rule would apply if you were placing plants in cooler rooms — get them used to the change in temperature by reducing it in the same way that the gardener does with his summer bedding plants.

### Temperature

Temperature is critical when caring for plants indoors, but there is no way that most people can provide every plant they own with ideal conditions. Plants vary in their heating requirements — for example, ivies like to grow in coolish temperatures, while crotons and calatheas prefer warmth. If you are growing a wide variety of plants, you will have to aim for a happy medium.

Plants will generally accept an average room temperature between 60 — 70°F (16-21°C), and it is surprising how well they will do if there is adequate light, and a culture of reasonable standard is maintained.

### Light

To satisfy a plant's need for light, natural daylight can be augmented by utilizing artificial light in the evening. Some tougher plants can even be conditioned to survive solely on artificial light. For the latter purpose, warm white strip lights, operating for 12 hours in every 24, will be perfectly adequate.

## Maintenance

Keeping plants clean and tidy is an excellent practice, but they should not be fussed over constantly. Once their needs are attended to, plants are best left alone to get on with the business of growing. When the leaves of a plant have yellowed and died no amount of attention and encouragement will bring them back to life. However, a good clean-up at the start of the growing season, and again at the end of the season, is a good idea. Spindly growth should be removed, and any straggly pieces should be tied into position — longer canes can be put in if needed. Late autumn is usually a good time for pruning back overgrown branches of plants so that fresh spring growth will quickly come into flower.

Cleaning the naturally glossy leaves of indoor plants can improve their appearance, and there are many chemicals available for this purpose. Larger, tougher leaves, such as those of the Rubber plant, can be cleaned with a solution of tepid water with a little detergent added.

**A Wardian Case**
Wardian cases are miniature greenhouses. They are named after Dr Nathaniel Ward who discovered, by chance, that ferns need a humid atmosphere and protection from smoke and draughts in order to grow successfully. A keen entomologist, Ward was conducting an experiment on hawk moths, and he accidently included a seedling fern with a chrysalis that he had put into a sealed bottle, filled with moist earth. The fern flourished and Ward proceeded to build many different fern cases of varying shapes.

## Potting on

We hear much about potting plants on — when and how it should be done, what soil to use and so on. Almost any time is suitable, except for the middle of winter when plant growth has slowed almost to a standstill. Spring is probably the ideal time for potting on, but if plants are growing well and conditions are agreeable, there is no reason why they should not be potted on during other months. When large plants in relatively small pots have been purchased, it is sound practice to pot them on immediately, as the plant can starve before the spring comes around. These plants should have their root systems checked as soon as they arrive home and they should be repotted if the root development is excessive. When potting on, it is important not to advance the plant into a pot that is much larger than the one it is coming out of. Very large plants will generally require large pots, but once they are growing in a 7in (18cm) or 19in (29cm) pot they can be maintained simply by regular feeding. They will not need to be repeatedly potted on.

Although plants grow just as well (often better) in clay pots, since the clay retains moisture for a much longer period, plastic pots are light to handle and they drain better.

## Soil for potting on

There are now so many different brands of soil available that it is difficult to offer advice on what should be used. However, there is little doubt that almost without exception houseplants of both the foliage and flowering variety do better when grown in mixtures containing a high proportion of peat. In a heavy clay mixture, the roots of indoor plants become less active as they find it hard to penetrate the more compacted soil. If you use the tried and tested mixtures favoured by the old gardening school, it is wise to incorporate a good amount of sphagnum peat to lighten the mixture. A few plants will benefit from a heavier mixture — it will keep them more compact and will reduce the risk of the plants becoming top-heavy. An important point to remember when potting plants on is that the plant to be removed from its pot should be watered first. This will blend the old and new soil more effectively and reduce root damage.

## Top dressing

There is a tendency on the part of many indoor gardeners to constantly pot their plants on, with the result that many plants end up in pots that are ridiculously out of proportion to their size. As an alternative to potting on, you can 'top dress'. This is the practice of removing the hard crust and top two inches from the surface of the soil. A sharp stick should be used to loosen the soil and eliminate any seed and weeds at the same time. Once this layer of soil is disposed of, the stick can be used to loosen the surface of the remaining in soil before you place a handful or two of fresh soil in the pot.

1

2

3

4

5

6

**Creating a terrarium** Gardening in miniature has a special fascination, particularly planting up a terrarium. Many plants thrive in the humid atmosphere that builds up within the almost sealed glass container. Moisture given off by the plants condenses on the glass and is recycled. Maintenance is minimal — cleaning the glass and pruning is occasionally necessary.

**1** Terrariums are available in many shapes and sizes. This leaded-glass design lends an appealing 'antique' charm to the plants it displays.
**2** Fill the base of the terrarium with a layer of peaty potting mix at least 3in (8cm) deep. Some charcoal pieces and pebbles may be inserted first to assist drainage and to keep the mix 'sweet' for as long as possible.
**3** Tap out your chosen plants carefully from their pots and check the roots for healthy growth at the same time. Water each plant well before transferring it to the terrarium.
**4** Insert plants in pre-formed hollows in the potting mix, working from the back towards the front. For an intricate display always plan the arrangement on paper before planting.
**5** Use small plants that will not quickly outgrow the terrarium. This small-leaved fittonia (Little Snakeskin Plant) is an ideal choice.
**6** Fill in around the plants and ensure that all are firmly embedded in the potting mix before watering again.
**7** The final arrangement. The fine markings on the fittonia's leaves are echoed by the delicate fronds of a pteris fern. Height is provided by a small specimen of *Neanthe bella*.

7

# Pests and Diseases

IT IS ESSENTIAL for the grower of indoor plants to maintain a strict program of pest and disease control if he is going to prevent an epidemic that could devastate an entire crop. Despite the vast sums of money spent each year on pest control, aphids, red spider and mildew are always going to be a problem. In dealing with these pests, there is no substitute for vigilance and swift, effective action. If, for example, red spider mites are allowed to carry on feeding and breeding, they will reproduce at a phenomenal rate and will completely cripple the host plant before moving on to their next breeding ground. Similarly, if the white powdery spores of mildew are not controlled, they will quickly spread over the foliage and eventually kill the plant.

### Inspecting plants for pests

Although some pests enter through the open window, it is more likely that they were already on the plant when it was purchased. Inspect any plants that you are considering for purchase very carefully and reject anything that shows obvious signs of pests or disease.

Mildew can be recognized by the white powdery spots. These are usually found on the upper surface of foliage, but appear sometimes on flowers. Aphids are very common pests during the spring and summer months. They feed on the tips of young shoots, so always check the upper section of the plant.

**Inspecting roots** The plant must be taken out of its pot in order to have its roots inspected. Any roots that are brown and unhealthy-looking should be gently teased away from the central mass of roots. The outer skin should then be pulled gently to discover if the plant has root rot.

**Buying a plant** It is worth taking time when you buy a plant. A careful look at the plant's general appearance is essential and quickly reveals its condition. The leaves should be without blemishes and supple, and healthy in color. In particular, the undersides of leaves should be checked for signs of pests or disease. If possible, check the stems of the plant near the soil for signs of rot.

Whitefly can be both troublesome and difficult to get rid of once it has established itself, so keep a watch out for this pest on the undersides of foliage. Two flowering plants that are often hosts are the poinsettia and the hibiscus. Gently touching the leaves of either of these plants will cause the adult whitefly to immediately take flight.

Mealy bugs and scale insects can also be a nuisance; they get onto foliage and between the stems and leaves of plants. Scale insects can be very messy; their excreta falls onto lower leaves, producing a layer of black honeydew mold that is sticky and looks unpleasant. Both adult and young adhere to the undersides and stems of plants such as *Ficus benjamina* and give the appearance of being part of the plant. Scales can be removed with a fingernail, but if you detect scales when purchasing it is better to select a clean plant, as these insects can be a problem if present in quantity.

### Inspecting plants for disease

Inspecting the root system of the plant for problems when purchasing is not practical, but if root damage is at an advanced stage it will show on the leaves. To fully inspect plants that are about to be purchased, it is often necessary to remove the plant from the protective paper sleeve in which it is wrapped, since wrapping can conceal many plant defects. A few discolored leaves at the base of the plant are generally nothing much to worry about, but plants that have discolored leaves all over should be rejected. Leaves that are discolored around the margins indicate that the plant is either suffering from a root disease or has been overfed.

### Insecticide

When using insecticide, be sure to follow the manufacturer's directions to the letter. Experimenting is unadvisable as it can be very dangerous to use commercial insecticides that are not recommended for domestic use. Toxic insecticides should not be used anywhere other than in a properly controlled environment. Insecticides for treating indoor plants will have been tested and passed as safe for use indoors. Nevertheless, if plants are portable, it is wise to take them out of doors when spraying insecticide. When applying an insecticide in liquid form, be sure that

**Signs of ill-health** Sadly, indoor plants fall prey to a host of influences that sooner or later begin to tarnish the healthy glow that made you buy them in the first place. Sometimes it will be your fault; sometimes you can blame pests and diseases that 'came in through the window'. Whatever the cause, correctly identifying the symptoms is your first step to cure.

**Stem rot** The blackened base of this heptapleurum plant (above) is a sure sign of stem rot. Overwatering is the usual cause and recovery is unlikely.

**Undernourished** This beloperone leaf (above) looks distinctly unwell. The mottled appearance, browr tip and limpness point to a severe lack of nutrients in the soil. If proper feeding is resumed, the plant may respond.

**Potbound** This beloperone plant (above) is overdue for repotting. When roots run out of soil they grow round in circles.

**Cold and dry** Marantas thrive in warmth and moisture; this leaf (above) shows the signs that both are lacking.

**Leaves on parade** This collection of leaves (below) clearly demonstrates the classic symptoms of underwatering.

**Physical damage** Obvious signs of maltreatment are easy to recognize, but too late to reverse. This dieffenbachia leaf (above) has been chewed by pets and badly scorched.

**Overwatering** A Rubber Plant (above) assumes a drooping pose as it slowly 'drowns'.

**Cold and damp** This sickly codiaeum leaf (above) is the sad victim of a damp chill.

**Hygiene and Pest Control** Provided you keep your indoor plants clean, there should seldom be any need to use insecticides. Hardy plants with glossy leaves (above) can be cleaned by sponging the leaves with soapy water. The slightly hairy leaves of the African violet (top right) are delicate and must be treated gently. A soft brush can be used to remove surface dust -no liquid or chemicals should be used. An aerosol insecticide can be very effective provided it is used with care (bottom right) and should not be aimed directly at the plant.

all the foliage of the plant is treated and not simply the upper areas of the leaves. Most pests, such as red spider and white fly, will be concealed under the leaves, and it is important that the chemical used comes into direct contact with the pest. To avoid breathing in the fumes, a gauze face mask, or a handkerchief, should be placed over the mouth and nose, and you should wear rubber gloves when dealing with chemicals.

When the leaves are saturated, the plant should remain outside until they have dried off and there is no trace of any unpleasant smell. While plants are outside keep them out of direct sunlight, and do not allow them to become cold through exposure to low temperatures. In fact, when treating plant foliage with any sort of chemical, a leaf cleaner for example, it is essential to give it some sort of protection from strong sunlight and low temperatures.

### Aerosol insecticides

Insecticides in aerosol form can be very effective for many pests, but such insecticides should be used with care. The spray mist should not be aimed directly at the plant, since it is important to saturate the atmosphere around the plant. It is also important to apply the insecticide before you retire in the evening so that it can disperse before morning. Alternatively, the plants can be taken to a garage or shed for treatment. However, the atmosphere should be still to prevent the mist dispersing too rapidly.

### Systemic insecticides

Systemic insecticides are available that offer plants protection from pests over a long period of time. These are very easy to use and come in either tablet or stick form. Simply push the tablet or stick into the soil in the pot. The plant will draw the chemical up through its system, and probing insects will be killed off when they suck the sap from the plant. Systemic chemicals are ideal for larger plants that cannot be moved around and for plants in hanging containers that are not easily accessible.

### Hygiene

When all is said and done, the most effective pest control is hygiene. Good husbandry can make a great deal of difference to your plant's health; clean plants are much less likely to be pest-ridden than those that are neglected, have entangled growth or dead foliage. Insecticides should be used on indoor plants only when absolutely necessary and not simply for their own sake. You will find that recent arrivals of aphids on the topmost soft leaves of your plant, can be very easily removed by wiping them off carefully with a soft sponge that has been moistened in soapy water. Soapy water is an old-fashioned remedy for greenfly in particular, and in the country it used to be common practice to throw a bowl of soapy water over rose trees every other day.

Naturally, you must be a little gentler where smaller plants are concerned. Place a piece of polythene over the soil in the pot to prevent it from falling out, and then submerge the foliage of the small plant in the soapy water This treatment once or twice a year will give plants a fresher appearance and fewer pests.

Although most indoor plants fail because of indifferent culture rather than because of the presence of pests, it is always helpful to be able to recognize pests when they appear, so that the appropriate action can be taken. The following alphabetical list names the more common pests and diseases affecting indoor plants.

## APHIDS

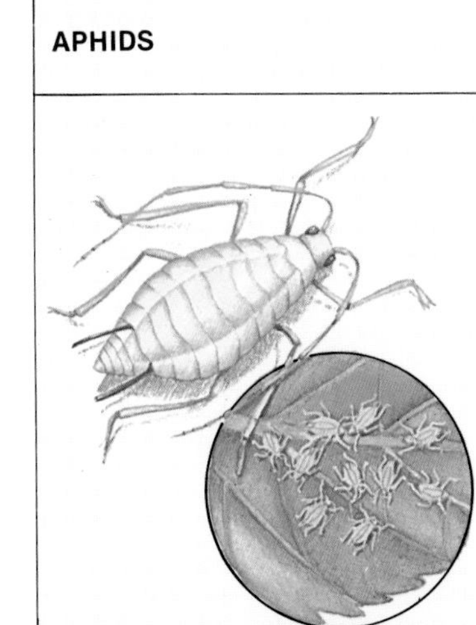

Aphids attack many different plants and can multiply at an alarming rate if left unattended. The young tips of growing plant shoots, such as ivy, are a favourite feeding place for this pest, but they may also be found on the undersides of plants. They are not difficult to see and their presence will generally be accompanied by a black sooty mold on leaves below where the pests are feeding. In the early stages a few pests can be wiped off the plant with a soft, damp sponge, but at a more advanced stage it is advisable to use an insecticide that is recommended for the treatment of aphids.

**Sooty mold** The black marks on this leaf (above) indicate sooty mold. This grows on sticky honeydew deposited by aphids and other pests.

## BOTRYTIS

Botrytis is a fungus prevalent in wet, warm and generally airless conditions. Signs of botrytis are large blotches of wet rot on leaf or stem that will quickly destroy affected plants if not dealt with immediately. Fungicide can be effective in controlling this disease, but the best preventatives are hygienic conditions and good culture.

**Fungus disease** Wet, rotting patches and fluffy gray mold on the cactus (above) and aglaonema (top) indicate botrytis. Cut out the infected areas and spray plants with a fungicide.

## DAMPING OFF

This is a problem that mainly affects young seedlings; mature potted plants do not generally suffer from it. An obvious symptom is a black discoloration at the base of the stem of the seedling, causing it to topple over and die. To obviate damping off, you should space seedlings a little further apart so that air can circulate around them. It will also help if the soil in which seedlings are growing is kept dry. You can purchase fungicide which will check stem rot in young plants, but be sure to follow the manufacturer's instructions carefully.

## LEAF MINERS

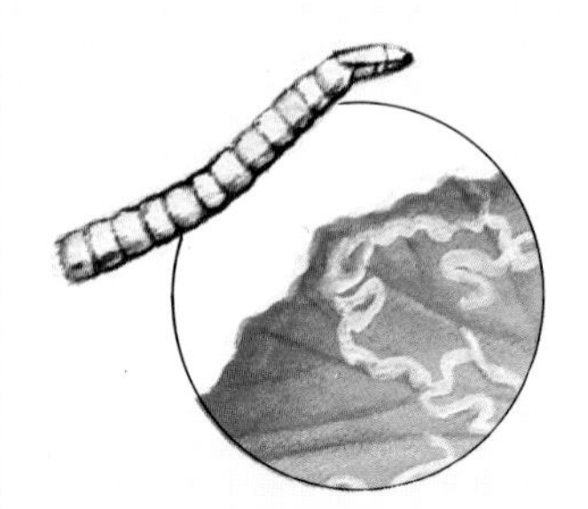

These are tunneling insects that get between the upper and lower surfaces of the leaves of many plants and leave a white trail behind them. The trail will also indicate where the pests are located on the leaf, and if there are only a few present it is easy enough to kill them by squeezing them gently between finger and thumb. Alternatively, there are numerous insecticides available for controlling leaf miners. If pests go unnoticed, the leaves become badly affected in time, and it is then wise to remove leaves and burn them.

**Leaf miner** This grub leaves a white trail as it burrows through the upper and lower tissue of a leaf (above). When the pest is found, pierce its body with a pin.

## MEALY BUGS

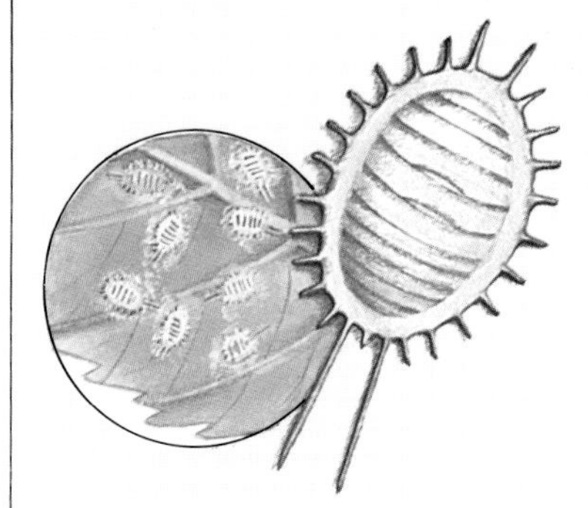

Mealy bugs are generally found on the more inaccessible areas of a plant. They get among the twining stems of plants such as stephanotis, where they are difficult to locate. Mealy bugs are very messy, and spraying the leaves of the plant with insecticide does not always eliminate them. The adult bug may be eradicated, but the young are more difficult to get rid of. They are wrapped in a waxy cotton wool-like substance that protects them from the elements and also from insecticide. One of the oldest yet most effective methods of ridding plants of young bugs is to wipe them off with a soft brush (an old toothbrush is excellent). If the brush is dipped in methylated spirit, the cleaning will be doubly effective. Adult bugs are easily seen and can be cleaned from the plant with a piece of cotton wool that has been soaked in methylated spirit.

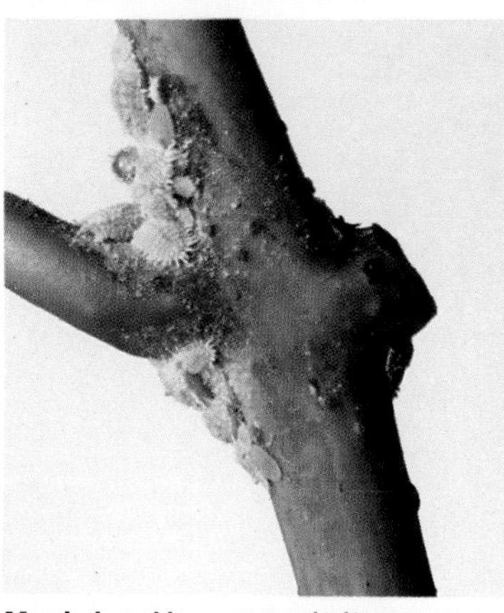

**Mealy bug** Young mealy bugs are wrapped in a cottony coating and cling to the plant. A thick cluster of them may appear on a stem.

## MILDEW

Mildew is another fungal problem which can be treated with fungicide if it is caught early enough. The appearance of powdery white circular spots on the upper surface of leaves is the first sign of mildew. If left unchecked, mildew will destroy the plant.

**Mildew** White powdery deposits on the leaves, stems or flowers indicate the presence of mildew. Plants with soft growth are particularly susceptible to this disease.

## RED SPIDER MITES

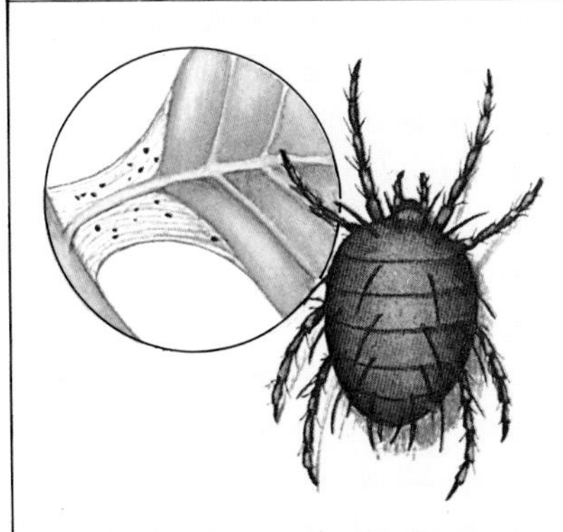

Although they are one of the smallest of plant pests, red spider mites are, without a doubt, the most devastating once they have got a hold on the host plant. Not easily detected with the naked eye, the adults are reddish in color while the younger ones are flesh-colored.

A damp atmosphere will deter red spider mites, which thrive in hot and dry conditions. Either group the plants together in a trough filled with peat or a tray that is covered with damp gravel, or spray a fine mist around the plants (except the flowering variety).

The first signs of red spider mite will be a pale yellowish-brown discoloration of green foliage around the margin of the leaf and a hardening of growth. Sometimes you will have to use a magnifying glass to locate the pests on the undersides of leaves.

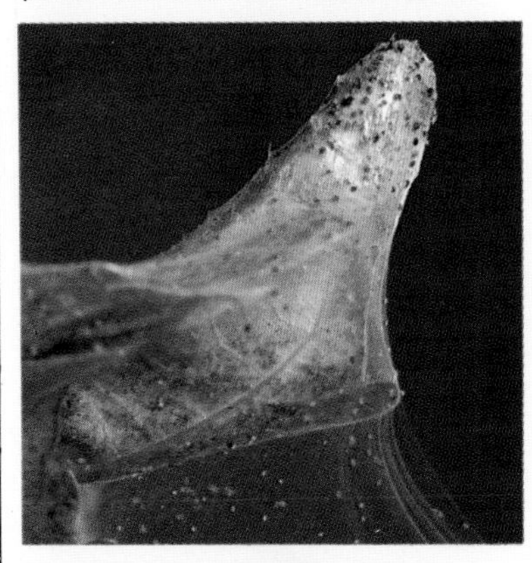

**Red spider mites** This acalypha (above) shows the tiny webs woven by red spider mites on the undersides of leaves.

## ROOT MEALY BUGS

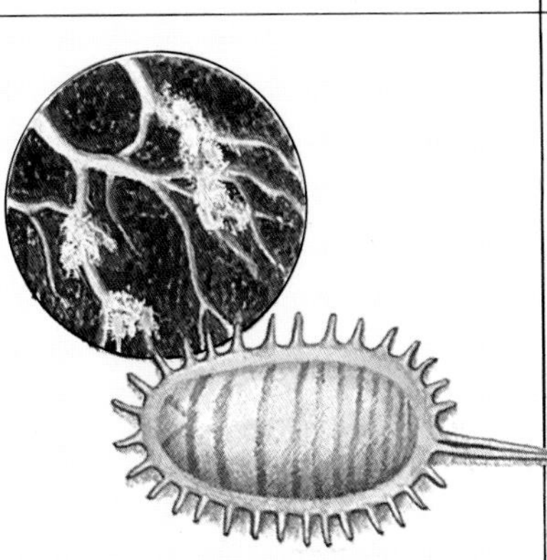

These pests inhabit the soil and show up as a white powdery substance aound the roots of the plant when it has been removed from the pot. A sign of their presence is a general debility of the plant. Root mealy bugs are much smaller than the ordinary mealy bugs, but they are similar in shape. You can control them by drenching the soil with insecticide.

**Root mealy bug** This cryptanthus (above) has been infested by root mealy bugs, small insects often covered with a fuzzy white coating. Cacti and succulents are particularly susceptible to this pest.

## SCALE INSECTS

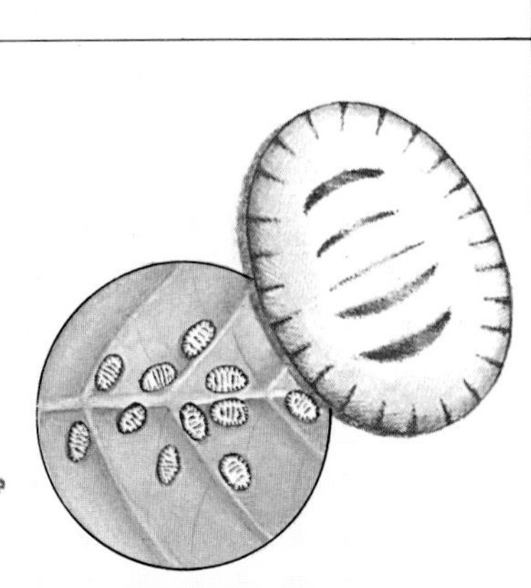

This is another messy pest which leaves a black sooty mold on the leaves underneath the feeding place. The adults are dark brown and the young are flesh-colored; both cling to the leaves and stems of plants like miniature limpets. Spraying frequently with a malathion solution will control them, but it is often better to don rubber gloves and sponge the plant with a solution of malathion liquid. Scale insects cling very tenaciously to their anchorage points and must be cleaned off very firmly.

**Scale insect** Plants with woody stems offer them camouflage, but when they appear on green foliage (above), these yellow or brown pests are easy to detect. Scale insects suck the sap from a plant, causing it to wither.

## SCIARID FLY

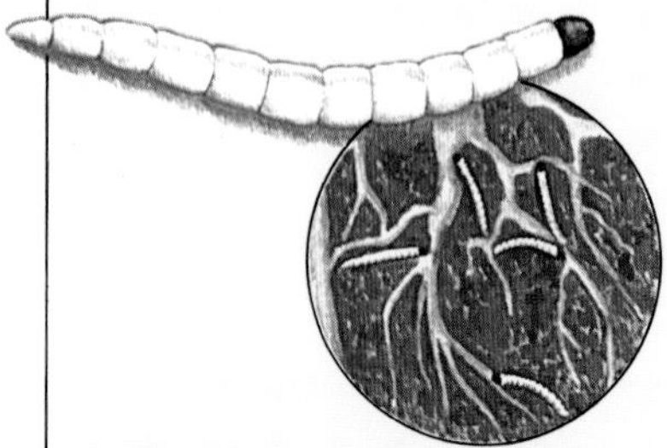

Sciarid flies, sometimes called fungus gnats, are soil-borne pests that sometimes appear if the mixture in the pot becomes stale. Maggots in the soil develop into small black flies and these jump around when the plant is watered. You can control this pest by watering the appropriate insecticide into the soil in which the plant is growing.

**Sciarid fly** This calathea (above) is a victim of sciarid fly. Maggots have attacked the roots of the plant, causing it to droop.

## SLUGS

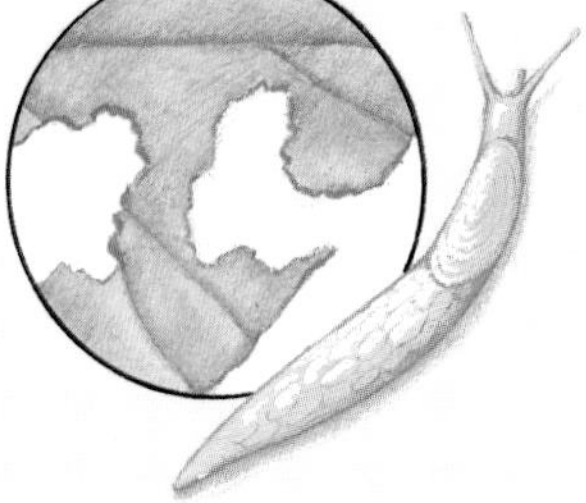

Large holes in the leaves of plants can often be traced to slugs, lurking among the lower growth at soil level. Locating and subsequently disposing of these pests is no problem. If you prefer not to remove them by hand, they can be killed off with slug pellets placed on the surface of the soil.

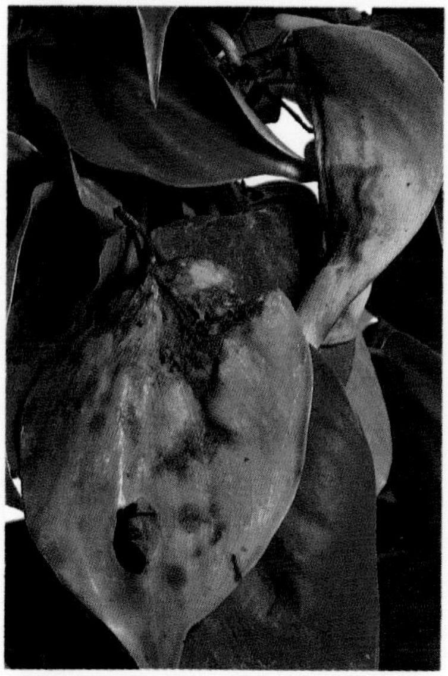

**Slugs** Slugs have eaten through the leaves of this philodendron (above). To eliminate these pests, apply a slug repellant to the base of the plant.

## SPRINGTAILS

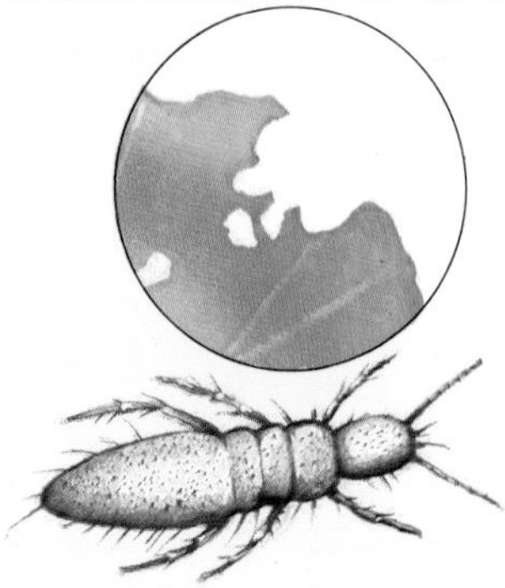

These are small white insects that jump around when the soil is watered. They do little harm, as they feed off decaying matter in the soil. Treat them by watering with insecticide, making sure that the water flows right through the pot.

**Springtails** These pests, which resemble small, cream-colored centipedes, gnaw at roots. The dieffenbachia (above) is infested with them.

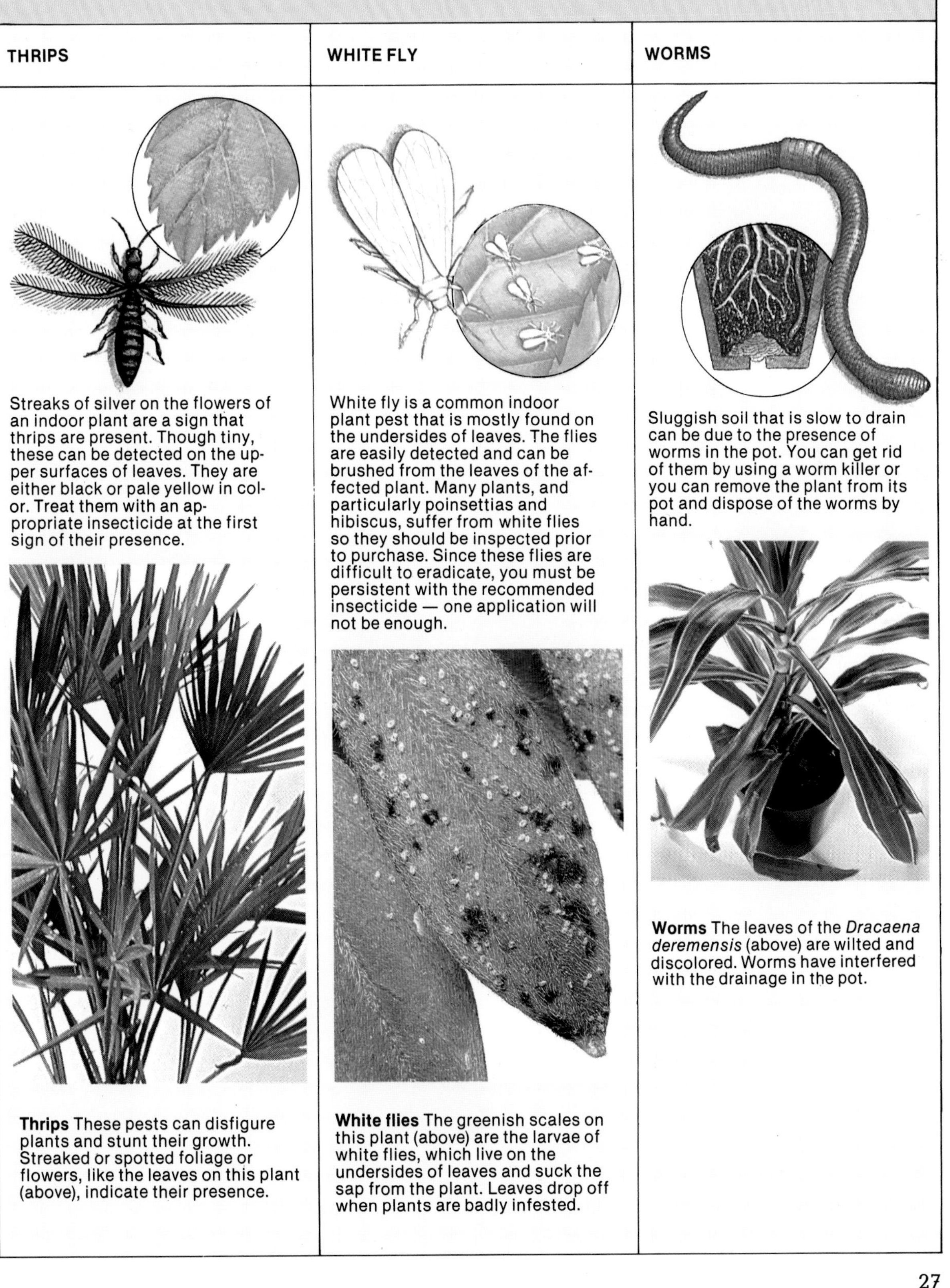

## THRIPS

Streaks of silver on the flowers of an indoor plant are a sign that thrips are present. Though tiny, these can be detected on the upper surfaces of leaves. They are either black or pale yellow in color. Treat them with an appropriate insecticide at the first sign of their presence.

**Thrips** These pests can disfigure plants and stunt their growth. Streaked or spotted foliage or flowers, like the leaves on this plant (above), indicate their presence.

## WHITE FLY

White fly is a common indoor plant pest that is mostly found on the undersides of leaves. The flies are easily detected and can be brushed from the leaves of the affected plant. Many plants, and particularly poinsettias and hibiscus, suffer from white flies so they should be inspected prior to purchase. Since these flies are difficult to eradicate, you must be persistent with the recommended insecticide — one application will not be enough.

**White flies** The greenish scales on this plant (above) are the larvae of white flies, which live on the undersides of leaves and suck the sap from the plant. Leaves drop off when plants are badly infested.

## WORMS

Sluggish soil that is slow to drain can be due to the presence of worms in the pot. You can get rid of them by using a worm killer or you can remove the plant from its pot and dispose of the worms by hand.

**Worms** The leaves of the *Dracaena deremensis* (above) are wilted and discolored. Worms have interfered with the drainage in the pot.

# Plant problem solver

| | Give the plant food | Water the plant | Reduce watering | Move the plant out of direct sun | Put the plant in better light | Repot in fresh soil or larger pot | Change the position of the plant | Protect the plant from draughts | Look for pests in leaves or soil | Look for caterpillars or earwigs | Examine the leaves for botrytis | Watch for signs of virus infection |
|---|---|---|---|---|---|---|---|---|---|---|---|---|
| Plant growing slowly | ● | | ● | | | ● | | | ● | | | |
| Wilting leaves | | ● | | | | | | | | | | |
| Mottled leaves | | | | | | | | | ● | | | ● |
| Browning on leaf margins | | | ● | ● | | | ● | | | | | |
| Flower heads dropping | | | ● | | | | ● | | | | | |
| Leaves bruised or broken | | | | | | | ● | | | | | |
| Leaves falling | | | ● | | | | | | ● | | | |
| Rotting in stems or leaves | | | ● | | | | | | | | ● | |
| Leaf color too pale | ● | | | | ● | | ● | | | | | |
| Small leaves/spindly growth | ● | | | | | | | | ● | | | |
| Leaves turning yellow | | | ● | | | | | ● | ● | | | |
| Holes in the leaves | | | | | | | | | ● | ● | | |

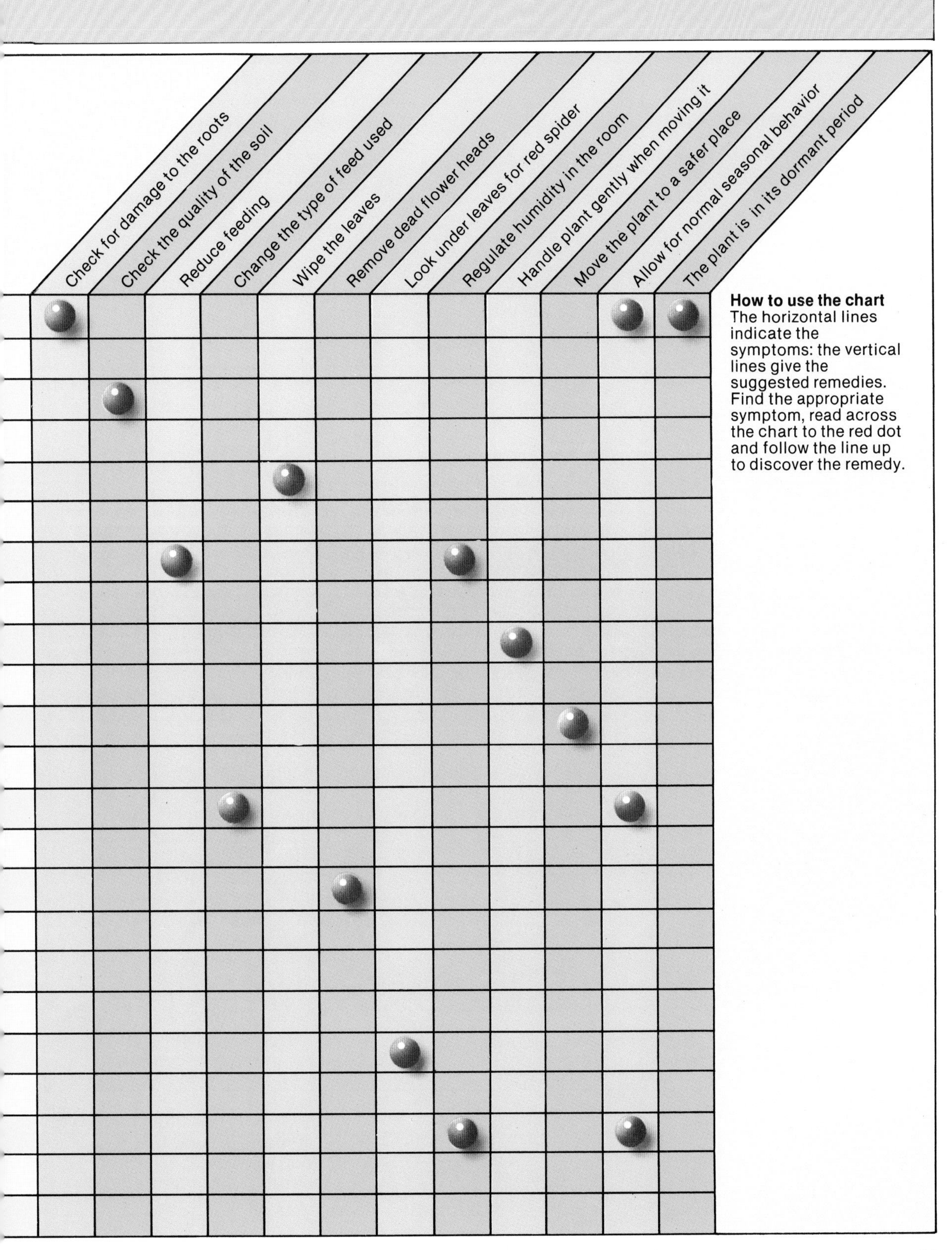


**How to use the chart**
The horizontal lines indicate the symptoms: the vertical lines give the suggested remedies. Find the appropriate symptom, read across the chart to the red dot and follow the line up to discover the remedy.

# Propagation

THE ABILITY TO MAKE new plants from all sorts of little bits and pieces — leaves, seed, stems or roots — is an admirable feat. Even in the nursery of the professional grower there is a feeling of reverence for the man or woman who bears the somewhat exalted title of 'the propagator'. However, propagating plants is often much simpler than it appears, and with indoor plants you can achieve a very high degree of success simply by following a few basic rules — provided of course that the right conditions for the propagation exist.

The first rule is never to use inferior material when propagating. Good cuttings and seed, plus clean stock, hygienic conditions and a moist, close atmosphere, should result in high germination. Keep a watchful eye for any signs of rot.

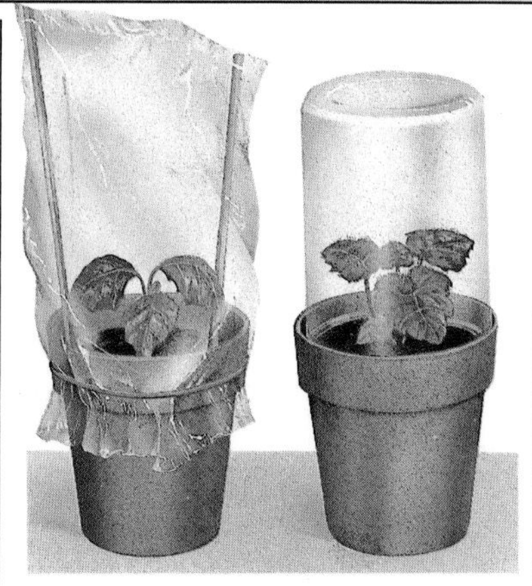

**Propagation** Plant cuttings need a high degree of humidity if they are to take root. Cover the cutting with a plastic bag (left) or invert a jam jar over the cutting (right).

## Simple propagation

You will need a sharp knife (a pair of scissors will do for cuttings such as *Ficus pumila*, or Creeping Fig), clean peat or peaty houseplant potting soil, a few clean pots and, if possible, a small heated propagator. Naturally you will also require some plant material to work with, and at the beginning the simpler the material the better. An easy plant to grow and to propagate is the saintpaulia (African violet). Propagators of these plants are convinced that leaves that are rounded in shape will propagate much more readily than those that are inclined to be pointed. However, the most important requirement when propagating plants is that leaves that are strong and healthy are used, while those that are weak and discolored are discarded.

**Propagators** The most basic propagator (left) is a seed tray filled with earth and covered with a perspex or plastic lid with vents in it. A more sophisticated propagator (right) incorporates a heated element which enables cuttings to become established more rapidly.

## Propagating African violets

To propagate the saintpaulia, the entire leaf is removed from the parent plant and cut cleanly back to the base (if stumps of leaf stalk are left attached to the plant, they will rot back in time and may cause botrytis). Once removed, the leaf stalk should be reduced to about 2in (5cm) in length, dipped in rooting powder and then placed in small pots filled with peaty household soil. Four or five leaves can be placed in small pots with the leaves facing inwards. The soil should be kept moist, and the pot can be enclosed in a polythene bag.

If the operation has been successful you should see the first signs of tiny leaves pushing through the soil in six to eight weeks. If the room temperature can be maintained at a constant temperature of 70°F (21°C), the rooting process will take less time than it would in cooler conditions. Once leaves are evident, the polythene can be completely removed and the cuttings allowed to developed sufficiently for the leaves to be showing well above the soil. At this stage the soil should be thoroughly watered and the cuttings removed by gently tapping the edges of the inverted pot on a firm surface. The root ball should gently slip out into your hand. At this stage the future appearance of the plant can be fashioned. If you want the plants to be well displayed, avoid potting the small clump of leaves intact into one larger pot. Instead, tease the soil away gently from the roots of the leaf cluster; you will then see that the clump is composed of a number of individual plants, or plantlets, each with two tiny leaves attached to a feeble central stem. If these tiny plants are gently pulled apart, they can be planted individually and centrally in small pots filled with peaty houseplant soil. Conse-

**Propagating an African violet** The easiest method of propagating saintpaulia (the African violet) is by rooting the leaves individually. These cuttings will produce plantlets which can, in turn, be propagated (see final five steps).

**1** Remove the entire leaf from a parent plant, cutting it back at the base of the leafstalk.

**2** Using a knife, cut the leafstalk back to approximately 2in (5cm) in length.

**3** Dip the end of the leafstalk in rooting powder before placing it in the soil.

**4** Insert the cutting, about ½in (1cm) deep, in small pots filled with peaty household soil.

**5** Four or five leaves can be placed in the pot or tray, with the leaves facing inwards.

**The second stage of propagation** After watering, the cuttings should be covered with a plastic bag to ensure humidity, or they can be enclosed in a propagator (see previous page). They should be left at a temperature of approximately 70°F (21°C) in bright, but slightly shaded light. After about 8-10 weeks a clump of plantlets will start to emerge from the surface of the soil.

**6** Gently remove the mother leaf, with the root ball attached, from the soil.

**7** The plantlets, rising from the base of the leafstalk of the mother leaf, should be about 2in (5cm) in height.

**8** Tease the soil away from the leaf cluster very carefully and gently pull the plantlets from the mother leaf.

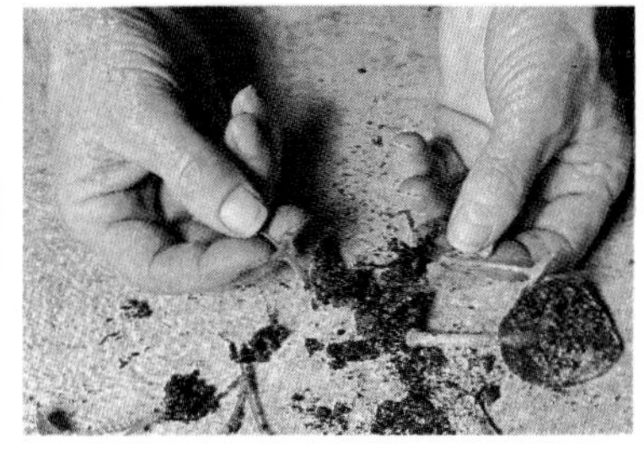

**9** Now you can see that the clump is composed of plantlets, each attached to a central stem. Pull these apart with great care.

**10** Insert each plantlet into a pot, filled with peaty household soil. Thereafter, treat them as adult plants.

**Propagating dracaena** Remove the mature plant from its pot and check to see if it has developed any thick fleshy roots. These are sometimes referred to as 'toes'.

Cut the 'toes' away from the root ball with a knife.

Chop the 'toes' into pieces, approximately 1in (2.15cm) long.

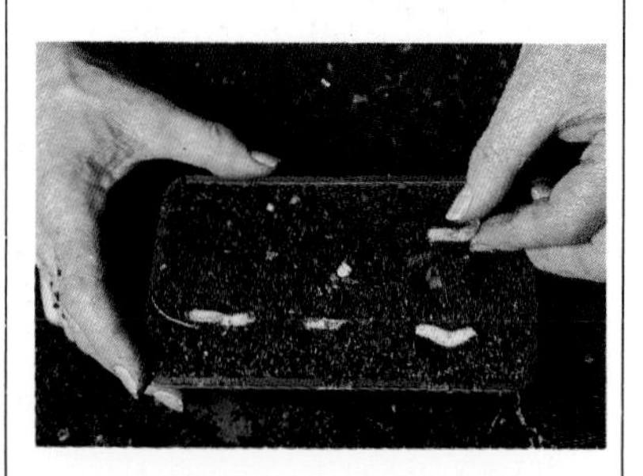

Bury the 'toes' an inch or so deep in peaty houseplant soil, leaving a gap in between each root.

quently when they grow and develop, all the leaves will radiate from a central stem, and when flowers appear they will stand cleanly away from the flat rosette of leaves. This method takes more time, but the end result is more satisfactory.

### Propagating other plants

Foliage plants with small leaves, such as the fittonia, will root fairly easily. Find a nice full plant with crisp foliage and remove a dozen or so shoots, 3-5in (8-13cm) in length, from the ends of the strands of growth. If you have chosen 12 cuttings, you should then fill three pots, 3in (8cm) in diameter, with a good houseplant potting soil. Give the soil a good watering once the pots have been filled. If the cuttings have been cut cleanly from the plant, they will be ready for insertion, and they should go four to each pot, evenly spaced. Depending on the size of the leaves of the cuttings, a greater or lesser number should be inserted, but in any event avoid overcrowing.

The severed ends of the cuttings can be treated with a rooting powder, but it is not really necessary if the plant is in good condition. However, to make doubly sure that roots are produced, you could enclose cuttings in a polythene bag to minimize transpiration. Place the cuttings and pot inside the bag. To prevent the bag sagging onto the cuttings, a small cane can be placed in the pot so that the top of the bag can be tied to it. Place the cuttings on a light, but not sunny, windowsill in a warm room. In about three weeks time you should be able to call yourself a propagator, because the cuttings will almost certainly have produced roots.

The lovely dark-green leaved Creeping Fig, *Ficus pumila*, can be treated in a similar fashion, but it will be necessary to take cuttings with four leaves and to remove the bottom one before firmly placing the cuttings in small pots. Probably the easiest of flowering cacti to root are Christmas and Easter cacti.

### Propagating from seed

The number of plants that may be grown from seed is constantly increasing, but there is very little to say about this method of propagation since all seed packets provide full instructions. However, one word of advice: If you require only a few plants for filling baskets and patio tubs, it is often better to buy small, reasonably mature plants in the spring, as a great deal of waste can result when sowing packets of seed.

### Refurbishing monsteras

Sometimes propagation is a matter of necessity rather than choice — for example when plants become overgrown. The Swiss Cheese Plant *(Monstera deliciosa)* has a tendency to push its way through the ceiling as it increases in height, at which stage it must obviously be cut back. Surprisingly, the firm top shoots of the plant, with some two or three leaves attached, will not be so difficult to root.

As monsteras increase in height, they shed their lower leaves and the lower section of the plant becomes sparse and unattractive. To refurbish the lower part of the plant, cuttings that are acquired as a result of removing the top sections of the stem can be inserted into the pot in which the plant is growing. Make a round hole of a reasonable size and fill with fresh potting soil that is peaty. Treat the cuttings with rooting powder and firmly push them into the prepared holes. Thereafter, spray the cuttings regularly so that they do not dry out. This will produce a much more attractive plant.

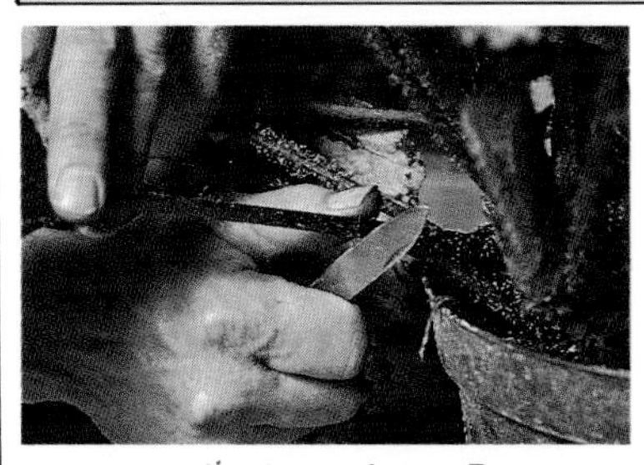

**1 Propagating begonia rex** Remove a mature, healthy leaf from the parent plant, using a sharp knife.

2 Hold the leaf steady with one hand and cut away most of the leaf stalk.

3 Cut half of the leaf into strips about ½ in (1.3cm) wide.

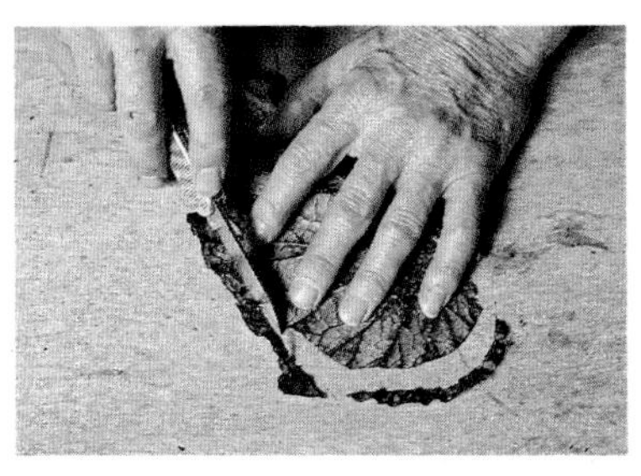

4 Now turn the other half of the leaf over and cut around the jagged edges, leaving a smooth outline.

5 Divide the leaf into sections about the size of an average postage stamp.

6 Lay the leaf pieces, the colorful side uppermost, on the tray of soil.

7 Leave a little space between each cutting in the tray.

8 Each section will root; when the new plant is well established it can be transferred to a suitable pot. This picture shows a healthy plant propagated from a single leaf section.

# Conservatories and Garden Rooms

THERE CAN SURELY BE no greater pleasure than creating and stocking your own garden room, where plants can flourish in conditions ideally suited to their needs. The main problem with growing exotic or tender plants indoors is that you cannot recreate the moist and humid conditions of their natural habitat — in a conservatory or garden room which is entirely given over to the plants, you can come closer to creating the right environment.

During the nineteenth and early twentieth centuries, the conservatory, with its palms, ferns and orchids, provided a natural adjunct to every elegant house. Many fine examples of the work of conservatory designers of the time still remain, although many more have long since disappeared.

At today's exorbitant prices, it would be difficult for all but a few to emulate the grand conservatory designs of the Victorian age, but there is no reason why similar results cannot be obtained with more modest constructions. If the modern conservatory is warm, light and adequately heated, then you should be able to grow palms, ferns and orchids just as successfully as the gardener of the past.

## Locating the conservatory

Siting the structure is not a major problem, as it is seldom a question of locating the conservatory in the ideal position. Most conservatories are simply tagged onto the house in a position that will be most practical. However, if there is a choice, then the conservatory or garden room should go on the sunny side of the house, as the plants will get the heat from the sun. Do, however, make sure that the plants receive adequate protection from bright sunlight so that they do not get scorched.

## Constructing the conservatory

The most important factors to consider when building a conservatory are height, ventilation, light and flooring. Many garden room plants attain a height of around 10ft (3m) and they will become distorted if they come into contact with the glass roof, so make sure your construction is tall enough to house them. Ensure at an early stage that the structure is adequately ventilated. Initially the

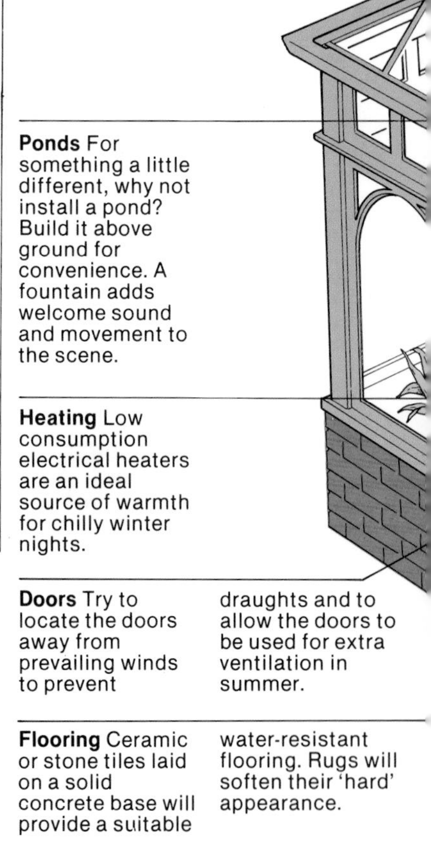

**The ideal conservatory** A place of peaceful beauty, a conservatory was the traditional plant-filled extension to Victorian houses. Today, its sumptuous elegance is still aspired to by many a green-fingered householder. If possible, build the conservatory on the sunny side of the house. In that position the only problem you should encounter is providing sufficient shade at the height of summer. Since the conservatory is designed to be a show-place for your plants, furnish it with style in mind, not utility. Then you can sit back and enjoy it as a welcome refuge from the cares of the world.

**Ponds** For something a little different, why not install a pond? Build it above ground for convenience. A fountain adds welcome sound and movement to the scene.

**Heating** Low consumption electrical heaters are an ideal source of warmth for chilly winter nights.

**Doors** Try to locate the doors away from prevailing winds to prevent draughts and to allow the doors to be used for extra ventilation in summer.

**Flooring** Ceramic or stone tiles laid on a solid concrete base will provide a suitable water-resistant flooring. Rugs will soften their 'hard' appearance.

**Conservatory pond** Water forms a focal point in any garden situation and so is an ideal addition to the conservatory. Water lily leaves float on the surface of this pond (left), with the stunning blooms of *Clerodendrum thomsoniae* adding a colorful accent among the fan palms and dieffenbachias around the edges.

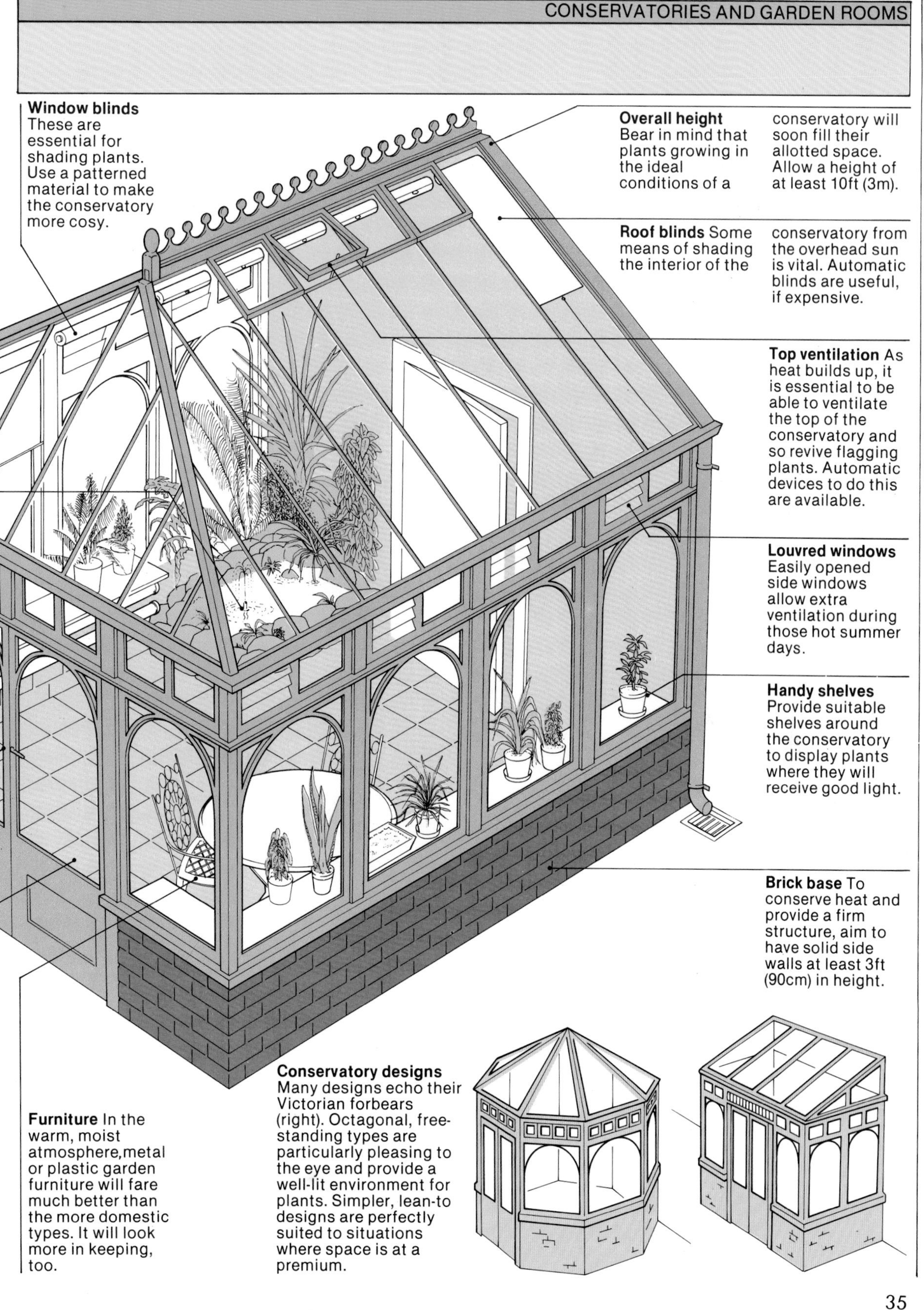
**Window blinds** These are essential for shading plants. Use a patterned material to make the conservatory more cosy.
**Overall height** Bear in mind that plants growing in the ideal conditions of a conservatory will soon fill their allotted space. Allow a height of at least 10ft (3m).
**Roof blinds** Some means of shading the interior of the conservatory from the overhead sun is vital. Automatic blinds are useful, if expensive.
**Top ventilation** As heat builds up, it is essential to be able to ventilate the top of the conservatory and so revive flagging plants. Automatic devices to do this are available.
**Louvred windows** Easily opened side windows allow extra ventilation during those hot summer days.
**Handy shelves** Provide suitable shelves around the conservatory to display plants where they will receive good light.
**Brick base** To conserve heat and provide a firm structure, aim to have solid side walls at least 3ft (90cm) in height.
**Furniture** In the warm, moist atmosphere,metal or plastic garden furniture will fare much better than the more domestic types. It will look more in keeping, too.
**Conservatory designs** Many designs echo their Victorian forbears (right). Octagonal, free-standing types are particularly pleasing to the eye and provide a well-lit environment for plants. Simpler, lean-to designs are perfectly suited to situations where space is at a premium.

principal concern is to conserve as much heat as possible and you are unlikely to give much thought to the opening of heat-losing ventilators. However, overheating a confined space during the warmer months of the year can be just as damaging to some plants as exposure to cold in winter, so be sure to have vents in the roof, and in the side walls, if possible. If the door of the building can be located away from prevailing winds, it can provide additional ventilation when the temperature is high.

Garden rooms must have sufficient light to enable the plants to grow properly, but there is a difference between good light and blisteringly hot sunlight streaming down on plants all day long. Plants that are close to the glass are particularly vulnerable. Therefore, when furnishing a garden room, be sure to provide some shade. Internal blinds that can be opened and closed as the weather conditions demand are an excellent idea, and enhance the atmosphere of the sitting-room-cum-garden room.

**Classic conservatory** In this superbly planted conservatory (above) it is possible to feel 'at one with nature'. Everything enhances the mood — the green canopy of vines, the mixture of plants, even the cane furniture.

Choosing suitable flooring can be difficult. If the plants are the main consideration, then you should have a solid floor, preferably tiled. However, if you plan to use the room as an occasional sitting area, colorful rugs on the tiled floor make a good compromise.

You may also want to consider including a fountain or pool in the garden room. If there is sufficient space for building a pond, be sure to give plenty of thought to its location, since it will be difficult and expensive to remove if you later change your mind about the site. It is probably best to opt for a pool that is built up from floor level, rather than dug and sunk into the floor. The sunken pool will inevitably be the more attractive, but the pool that is built up can easily be removed when it outlives its usefulness.

Finding space in a garden room for plants, furniture and people can be a problem during the summer months when the room is in peak demand. A patio outside the garden room is the ideal place to put some of the less tender plants when the weather is fine.

## Greenhouses

For a garden room to be really successful it should be combined with a more conventional greenhouse, set in another part of the garden. Thus you can bring on young plants to a certain stage in the greenhouse and then transfer them to the garden room. This also prevents you from forever falling over the pots and other paraphernalia that are an essential part of plant propagation. In addition, the greenhouse can serve as a hospital area for plants that have lost their sparkle and are not quite up to standard for the 'show-place' garden room. You can also prepare hanging baskets and other types of containers and give the plants a little time to settle before moving them into the conservatory.

# Hanging and Climbing Plants

IN RECENT YEARS the range of containers that can accommodate hanging plants of all shapes and sizes has increased. However, when you are aiming for a really bold display of color there is still much to be said for the old-fashioned moss-lined wire basket The only drawback with these is that when the container is watered, the surplus drains through onto the floor below, so an outdoor location is preferable when moss-lined baskets are in use.

When planting in a hanging basket, use soil that contains a reasonable amount of loam, as mixtures that are composed almost entirely of peat tend to dry out excessively — a common problem with plants that are suspended overhead. When the basket is past its best, the old soil should be disposed of and new soil used for the following season's plantings.

**Muted comfort** The juxtaposition of 'sensible' stone-flagged flooring and inviting sofas provides this garden room/conservatory (below) jwith just the right mix of beauty and utility. Natural clay pots containing palms, dracaenas and the odd flowering plant reflect the muted colors. Climbing plants soften the ceiling line.

As the basket is lined and soil is introduced, a few plants can be put in position around the sides of the container so that they will fill out the basket and trail down. Almost any of the conventional basket bedding plants will do for this purpose — hoyas, columnea, stephanotis and *Begonia semperflorens* will all give a splendid show.

There are many fine plants that may be put in hanging containers and suspended from the roof of the garden room. The more exotic ones will need to be kept at a temperature ranging from 50° to 65°F (13°-18°C). Throughout the colder months of the year, few plants will survive the combination of wet and cold conditions, so be especially careful not to overwater. Some of the best plants for indoor hanging baskets are mentioned below.

### Aeschyanthus speciosus

This species, commonly called the 'Basket Plant', is shown to best advantage in a hanging basket. It has fleshy leaves of a pale-green color and an abundance of trailing stems. The *Aeschyanthus speciosus* normally has a summertime flowering season which produces striking, tubular orange flowers.

### Begonia tuberhybrida

These are among the most spectacular of all flowering plants in pots, and there are many fine colored varieties to choose from. Besides the upright growing types, there are excellent pendulous forms that may be grown from tubers, available

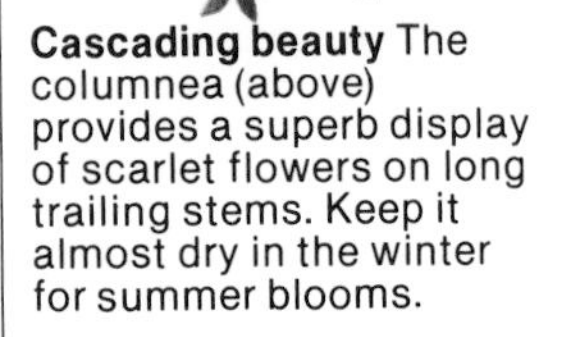

Cascading beauty The columnea (above) provides a superb display of scarlet flowers on long trailing stems. Keep it almost dry in the winter for summer blooms.

**Basket plants** The *Begonia tuberhybrida* (above) will grace any hanging basket with its exquisite flowers. Another good candidate for an eye-level, brightly lit location is the hoya (below). Grow it undisturbed; repot every two years.

in winter for planting in early spring. When well established, the young plants should be placed in hanging containers filled with loam-based soil.

### Columnea banksii

This species has changed little since it was introduced into the Victorian conservatories in the nineteenth century. The cascading flowers are a rich shade of orange and they will completely cover the plant if it is flourishing. To encourage later flowering, the plant should be in a cooler temperature, around 50°F (10°C), during the winter months. The soil should remain on the dry side.

### Hoya bella

This is a summer-flowering plant. It has pale to dark-green leaves, attached to wiry stems that fan out almost horizontally from the container in which it is growing. The branches do not hang pendulously as you would expect with a hanging plant, because the flower clusters form on the underside of the branches. The *Hoya bella* is a plant that should be suspended about head level so that the beauty of the waxy flower clusters and the delightful fragrance can be fully appreciated. Be sure to provide it with some shade in summer, avoid overwatering and be careful when applying insecticides.

### Climbing plants

Climbing plants are a particularly useful category of plants. Not only are many of them extremely attractive, adding decorative interest wherever they are placed, but climbing plants can also emphasize — or mask — architectural lines and serve as sun or wind screens. All climbing plants need some kind of support to which they can attach themselves. This may be either a trellis, bamboo cane or the wall of a garden room. If the latter, place climbing plants against a solid wall (most garden rooms will have at least one wall that is part of the house) rather than against walls that form the glass exterior of the garden room; the plants will appear to much better effect. Either prepare a border filled with good soil into which the climbing plants can be freely planted or extend the floor of the garden room to the base of the wall and establish the climbing plants in large containers. Small containers will be of little use since most indoor climbing plants produce an abundance of growth, and such plants cannot be sustained by the limited amount of nourishment contained in small pots of soil. The following plants are suggested for use as suitable climbing plants.

### Allamandas

There are a number of allamandas, mostly with rich-yellow trumpet flowers, that can be used as climbers in a room heated to 60°F (16°C). Attaining a height of 8ft (2.4m), *A. cathartica* has soft-yellow flowers and will need to be tied to a support.

**Hanging baskets** All stages of planting in a hanging basket are a pleasure to perform: The growing medium is easy to handle; the plants are small and the choice wide; and the final result can be truly hailed as 'all your own work'. This series of photographs demonstrates the essential steps in creating a hanging garden that will provide color and interest throughout the whole season. Several tyes of containers are available, ranging from pottery to wickerwork; some are solid plastic with built-in drip trays to make watering less of a hazard for people underneath.

**1** First line the base of the basket with a generous layer of damp sphagnum moss. This provides a firm foundation for the growing medium and plants.

**2** Add more moss and arrange it carefully around the sides of the container. This layer will form a semi-waterproof barrier and help to retain moisture.

**3** Make sure you bring the moss layer right up the sides to cover the wire framework. You can trim off any excess later when the planting is complete.

**4** Fill the center with peaty potting mix, liberally laced with extra drainage material such as perlite. Damp it first with a weak liquid feed.

**5** Insert each plant firmly in the mix, making sure that there are no air pockets around the roots. Have a layout in mind before you start.

**6** This heather, *Erica hiemalis*, is an ideal plant for a cool-season hanging basket; its tubular flowers provide color through the winter months

**7** Bolder splashes of color can be provided by planting pansies. These charming flowers are available in winter- and summer-flowering types.

**8** A red primula adds a contrasting shade to the emerging pattern. Be sure to keep these flowering plants moist for their relatively brief flowering period.

**9** When the planting is complete, trim the moss as necessary to tidy up the basket, and double-check that all the plants are firmly tucked in place.

**10** The finished result looks a little sparse but that is intentional; as the plants settle in and grow a little the gaps will disappear. Hang the basket at eye level for easy maintenance.

**Supporting plants** Plants can be supported in many different ways. A trellis (above) is an effective method of staking, or plants can be trained round a piece of plastic-covered wire (top right). Pieces of wood can be tied into decorative supports (right).

Not all indoor plants have to be grown in pots. The bromeliad (above) has been grown on a mossy log. When tying plants to a stake it is important to use the right material. Plain wire will corrode and may damage the plant; string may rot in time. Plastic coated or cardboard-covered wire is the best thing to use (below).

The rare variety *A.c. 'Grandiflora'* has flowers almost 5in (13cm) across.

The species *A. neriifolia* has woody stems that can be trained to a support (these are also very fine free-standing plants). The flowers are small, bright-yellow and trumpet-shaped. They do not have a particular season, but will flower throughout the year if conditions are moist, warm and shady. The soil should be wet all the time, and a moist atmosphere is also important for these plants.

**Clerodendrum thomsoniae**
This plant has thin leaves of mid-green coloring and clustered flowering bracts that are bright red and white in color. Although the stems are stout and woody, *Clerodendrum thompsoniae* is not a natural climber and will have to be trained to be seen at its best. It will reach a height of 8ft (2.4m) in time, but this vigorous plant is easily contained by pruning.

**Hoyas**
These are natural climbing and

trailing plants, as they have stems that twist and twine around everything in sight. They can grow several feet tall and are usually grown on indoor trellises, or wound around stakes. They are very easy to manage. Two fast-growing climbers are *H. carnosa* and *H. australis*, which are both summer flowering and produce clusters of star-shaped white flowers.

**Stephanotis floribunda**
Stephanotis is from the same family as the hoyas, and has the same twining habit. It has oval-shaped, dark-green leaves that are set opposite one another, and an overpowering and delicious fragrance that permeates every corner of the room. The flowers are creamy-white and are borne in clusters of five or more. They will appear at intervals over a lengthy period throughout the spring and summer months. If flower clusters are removed, they can be taken indoors and inverted in a dish of water, where they will last for several days.

**Plumbago capensis**
This is a plant that will grow quickly and produce lovely flowers throughout the summer and well into the autumn. Small leaves are attached to twiggy branches that will grow vigorously if conditions and culture are reasonable. The flowers are a lovely powder-blue in color. There is also a white form, *P. capensis 'Alba'*, but it is not quite so showy as the blue variety. If both varieties are planted together, the combination of the blue and white flowers is most attractive. Overactive growth of *Plumbago capensis* can be trimmed to shape at any time. At the end of the flowering season, you should cut the plant down to a foot or two from the base if it is very vigorous.

**Colorful climbers** No indoor plant display is complete without its fair share of climbing plants. *Clerondendrum thomsoniae* (above) is a vigorous twining plant that needs to be kept in check and properly trained to look its best. The delicate blue flowers of *Plumbago capensis* (right) are borne on straggly stems that benefit from being tied neatly to supports.

**Golden trumpet** This common name echoes allamandas' bright-yellow flowers.

Even this young specimen is bursting with bloom. As it matures, the plant will need a suitable support and plenty of warmth and sunlight to develop fully. Superb for a large plant window.

# Containers

AN EXCELLENT WAY to display plants is in mobile, free-standing tubs. There is a wide range to choose from, made from many different materials. The plant containers that are now fitted with castors can be pushed around and rearranged quite easily, either singly, or in groups, for a bolder effect. These containers should be completely watertight, but when watering the plants, check that there is no build-up of water in the bottom of containers that have no means of drainage. This can be difficult with plants growing in soil, and it may be necessary to insert a piece of tubing into the soil to drain liquid at the bottom of the container. You can then use a cane to check if here is an accumulation of water and, if there is, it can be siphoned out.

### Self-watering containers

Many of the better containers have self-watering devices. The self-watering unit has a base on which the soil rests and a water reservoir between the soil and bottom of the container. Water is drawn from the reservoir via a nylon wick and the water level in the base is controlled by means of an indicator. The water-level indicator must remain at minimum for at least one week between each topping-up operation so that the soil becomes properly aerated. The major benefit of these units is that plants can be left unattended for a period of up to a month without needing water.

Almost any kind of indoor plant can be grown with comparative ease in these containers if both temperature and light are correct, but it is better to grow more mature plants, rather than very small ones. Mature palms, philodendrons and ficus plants are among the best subjects, with plants such as aglaonemas and dieffenbachia to fill the base.

**Plant containers** Indoor plants can be grown in a wide range of containers (above). The original — and some say still the best — are the clay pots. Plastic pots are suitable for many plants and decorative 'pot hiders' are available in a plethora of styles and materials.

**Self-watering pot** This ingenious pot (above) allows you to leave plants unattended for some time. Moisture reaches the soil from a basal water reservoir (1) by means of a nylon wick (2).

## Hydroponic growing

The practice of growing plants in water, with only a nutrient added, has become increasingly popular in recent years.

Commercial gardens usually handle the first stages of water cultivation. When plants are a good size and showing strong, firm roots, the plant is taken from its pot and all the soil is removed by washing it clean under running water until no toxic particles of soil remain. The plant roots are then surrounded with clay granules in a pot with open sides before being placed in a trough of gently flowing water in a warm greenhouse. The granules are there simply to support the roots, and the plant will start to grow on its more succulent water roots in about two months time. After this period, the plant is usually considered sufficiently established to be sold.

You will find that most water-culture units have an indicator similar to the self-watering planter. It is important that the water level remains at the minimum mark for at least one week before the container is recharged. This ensures that the roots are well aerated — an important requirement for all plants that are growing with their roots restricted to pots.

To sustain the plant, a special slow-release nutrient is placed in the water. The nutrient is activated and made available to the plant as the water goes through its various chemical changes. In order for a chemical change to take place, the water surrounding the plant should come from the domestic water supply.

If you follow the directions that come with the plant and offer reasonable cultural conditions, the plants that are grown by water-culture methods will generally be of much better quality than similar plants grown in soil.

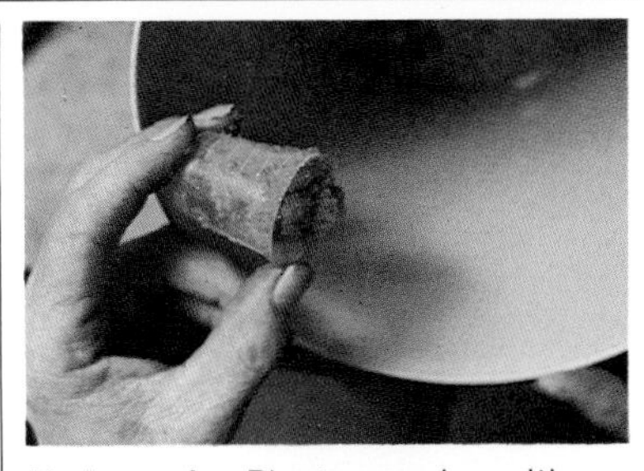

**Hydroponics** Plants growing with their roots in water need a special type of slow-release fertilizer. First add a dose of this to the outer container.

Next pour in a layer of the expanded clay granules to provide support for the inner pot containing the plant. Add water to dissolve the fertilizer.

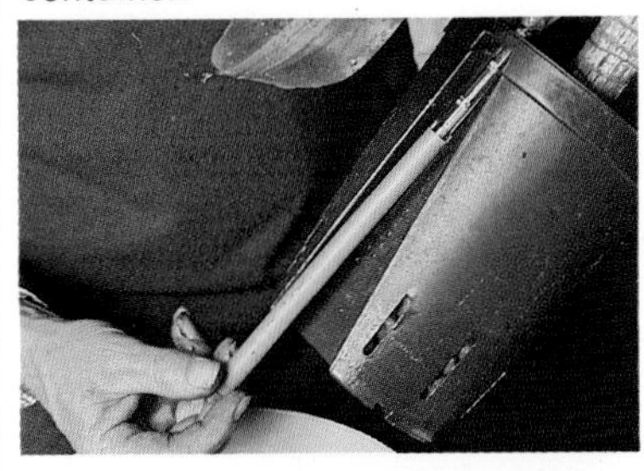

The inner pot houses a water-level indicator that extends to the base of the outer pot. Slits allow roots to grow out into the fertilizer solution.

Insert the planted pot in the centre, resting its base carefully on the layer of granules, with the rim just below the level of the outer pot.

Finally, pour in more granules to fill the space between the two pots (above) and provide a tidy top surface.

The finished pot (right), in this case sporting a stately *Yucca*, has a neat appearance with the all-important water-level indicator, a vital clue to its hydrocultural status. When the float in the indicator falls to the minimum level, leave it there for about a week before adding more water. This will allow the roots a beneficial 'breather'. The fertilizer should keep the medium-sized plant well-nourished for about six months. It works by releasing the nutrients in balance with the plant's needs; an ordinary fertilizer would provide too much 'food' all at once. Hydroponic displays are useful for reception areas and offices.

# The Plant Finder

A colorful three-part guide to over 100 exotic plant species. The first part provides information on the flowering and foliage varieties, the second deals with cacti and succulents, and the third covers a selection from the orchid family. For easy reference, each division is arranged in A-Z order, according to the genus of the plant.

A healthy example of *Belperone guttata* (opposite page), commonly called 'Shrimp Plant' on account of its shrimp-like bracts.

# Abutilon

ABUTILONS ARE free-growing plants with either green or variegated foliage and pendulous bell flowers that appear in the summer. These are easy plants to care for if given adequate light, and may be planted out of doors during the summer months of the year. Older plants can be hard-pruned in the autumn, and it is usually best to discard abutilons after two or three years. Propagate from top sections of stems about 5in (13cm) in length.

The two species commonly grown for indoor use are *Abutilon thompsonii* and *Abutilon sevitzia*. *A. thompsonii* (sometimes called *A. striatum*) has a reddish-orange bloom and grows to a height of 5ft (1.5m). It requires ample water and feeding during the growing season, and needs good light to retain its bright foliage color.

*A. sevitzia* attains a maximum height of 6-7ft (1.8-2.1m) when grown in a pot of sufficient size, but can be kept to more manageable dimensions if pruned regularly. Pendulous apricot-colored flowers bloom in summer, but the species' principal attraction is its green and white foliage.

**Abutilon** Colorful foliage is a principal feature of these plants, but bright light is necessary to ensure that coloring does not revert to green. As cool conditions will not be unduly harmful, plants can be placed out of doors during the warmer months of the year and can make fine central features in more elaborate bedding islands and borders. At the end of the summer, plants can be trimmed back to a more manageable shape. They will do better over winter if the soil is kept dry and no feed is given.

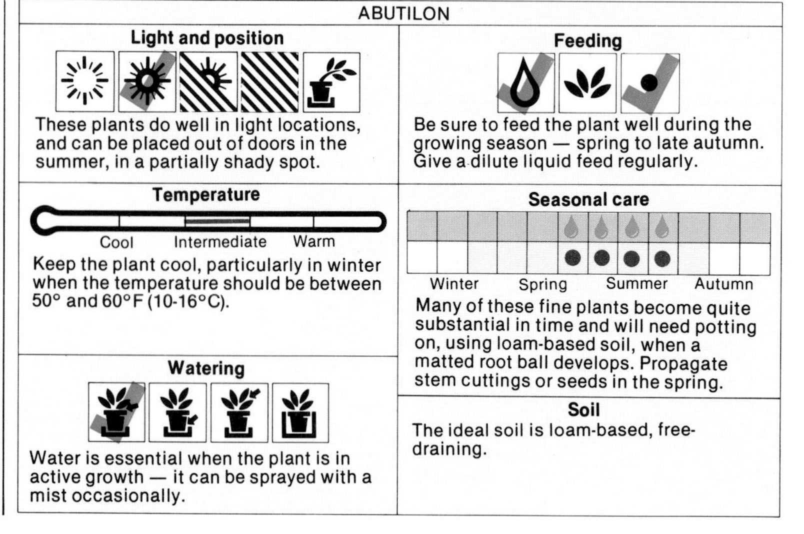

# Acalypha

THIS GENUS includes decorative plants with highly-colored foliage in the numerous varieties of *A. wilkesiana,* and with interesting and pendulous bracts in *A. hispida.*

The wilkesiana varieties are not too difficult to manage if temperature in the region of 65°F (18°C) can be maintained and a sharp eye is kept for red spider mites on the undersides of leaves. These plants are grown entirely for their exotic foliage coloring which is usually mottled and highly colored, ranging from red to yellow to deep bronze. Many of the varieties of wilkesiana have a mixture of many colors in a single leaf. If plants are grown in good light, they will have much better coloring and will also be more compact. Plants grown in pots around 8in (20cm) in diameter will grow to about 3ft (91cm) in height with similar spread.

With drooping rattail of red bracts that may be 18in (46cm) or more in length, *A. hispida* is impressive when well grown, but it is not the easiest of subjects. Large leaves are pale-green in color and coarse in appearance. They are not of great significance, although they do help to set off the vivid coloring of the bracts when they appear.

Rich, loam-based soil is essential, and pots not less than 7in (18cm) in diameter will be needed for plants that are intended to become specimens of larger size. Moist conditions and regular feeding are important, and watch for red spider mites, especially around the young leaves that are forming at the tips of each branch.

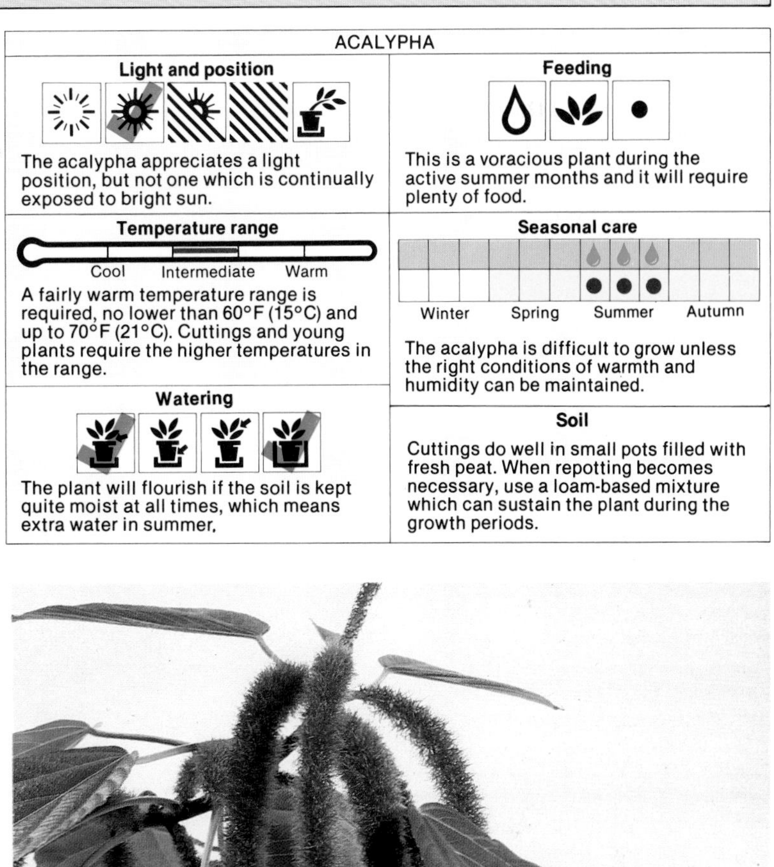

ACALYPHA

**Light and position**

The acalypha appreciates a light position, but not one which is continually exposed to bright sun.

**Temperature range**

Cool Intermediate Warm

A fairly warm temperature range is required, no lower than 60°F (15°C) and up to 70°F (21°C). Cuttings and young plants require the higher temperatures in the range.

**Watering**

The plant will flourish if the soil is kept quite moist at all times, which means extra water in summer.

**Feeding**

This is a voracious plant during the active summer months and it will require plenty of food.

**Seasonal care**

Winter Spring Summer Autumn

The acalypha is difficult to grow unless the right conditions of warmth and humidity can be maintained.

**Soil**

Cuttings do well in small pots filled with fresh peat. When repotting becomes necessary, use a loam-based mixture which can sustain the plant during the growth periods.

**Acalypha hispida** (main picture right), with its drooping tail-like red bracts, is a particularly striking plant despite its dull-colored leaves. By contrast, *A. wilkesiana* (inset) is grown for its decorative foliage, for in several varieties there are many colors in a single leaf.

GESNERIACEAE

# Aeschynanthus

Basket Plant

THESE ARE natural trailing plants that produce an abundance of branches to which are attached leathery leaves that are a metallic glossy green in color. To show them to their best advantage, grow plants in small hanging pots or baskets and confine the planting to one variety of aeschynanthus per pot, rather than combining different varieties or including other kinds of plants.

Cuttings root with little difficulty if placed in a warm propagator. It is best to place five or six cuttings in pots 3in (8cm) in diameter, and to then put three of these plants in a small hanging basket. The result will be a full plant with lots of cascading branches.

*Aeschynanthus lobbianus* is one of the most popular species and perhaps the easiest to obtain. During mid to late summer, the branches will carry lovely dark-red flowers emerging from interesting cup-shaped calyxes that are a sooty red in color. Red flowers have a yellow throat, and make for a very attractive plant. There are numerous other species that all have similar habits of growth with attractive and quite varied flower coloring.

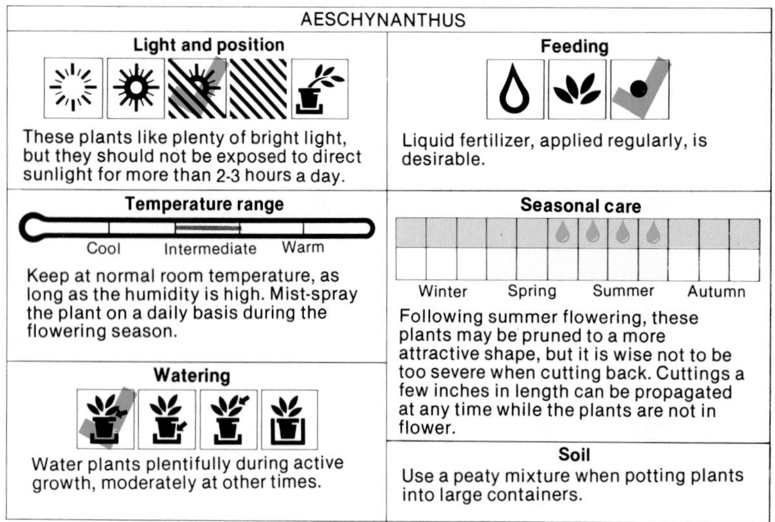

**Aeschynanthus lobbianus** (top above) is ideal for hanging baskets. The beautiful red and yellow flowers (detail above) appear in mid to late summer.

# Aglaonema

THERE ARE numerous species of aglaonemas. Almost all have attractive mottling and grow as tight clumps of growth, which makes them ideal for planting under other subjects when indoor-plant displays are created. Aglaonemas do especially well in low-light situations where there is a reasonably moist atmosphere and the temperature is in the region of 60-70°F (16-21°C).

The most popular variety is *A. crispum* 'Silver Queen', which is an American hybrid often used in plant decorations on the continent of Europe. As the hybrid name suggests, the greenish-grey leaves have a silver sheen to them.

*A. pseudo bracteatum* is a much bolder plant that will attain a height of some 30in (76cm) and has long spear-shaped leaves that are attractively variegated in cream and green.

For bolder groupings of plants, there are few better subjects than *A. roebelinii,* which has silver-and-green leaves that give an overall gray appearance. Plants develop into large clumps that might well measure 3ft (91cm) high and 3ft wide in 10in (25cm) pots.

AGLAONEMA

**Light and position**

The aglaonema will tolerate poor light with no ill effects, but must not be exposed to direct sunlight.

**Temperature range**

Cool Intermediate Warm

This plant must not be placed in cold conditions. A warm room anywhere between 60°-70°F (15°-21°C) is suitable, but an aglaonema will grow more vigorously if the temperature is higher.

**Watering**

Aglaonemas should be watered regularly so that the potting mixture stays moist.

**Feeding**

Established plants should be given a liquid feed each time they are watered if they are to flourish.

**Seasonal care**

Winter Spring Summer Autumn

If kept in suitable conditions, aglaonemas tend to stay healthy. They are susceptible to oil and gas fumes however, and should not be exposed to them. Aglaonemas should be kept away from windows and draughts.

**Soil**

A peaty mixture is needed for aglaonemas, and repotting should be avoided in winter if possible.

**Aglaonemas** are compactly growing foliage plants. *A.crispum 'Silver Queen'* (above) and *A.trewbii* (below) are two popular species.

APOCYNACEAE

# Allamanda

ALLAMANDAS ARE very attractive flowering plants with dark-green leaves and rich-yellow trumpet flowers. They are natural climbing plants but thrive only in the room heated to not less than 60°F (16°C).

With soft-yellow flowers, *A. cathartica* will attain a height of some 8ft (2.4m) and will need to be tied to a support – the variety *A.c.* 'Grandiflora' has flowers almost 5in (13cm) wide, but is something of a rarity.

With woody stems that can be trained to a support (it is also a very fine free-standing plant), the species *A. neriifolia* produces small bright-yellow trumpet-shaped flowers that have no particular season. Foliage is not particularly attractive, but the plant will flower for almost the entire 12 months of the year if moist, warm and shaded conditions are provided. The soil should always be wet, and moisture in the atmosphere is also important. These plants must be fed regularly. Propagate tip cuttings in early spring in a mixture of equal parts peat moss and coarse sand.

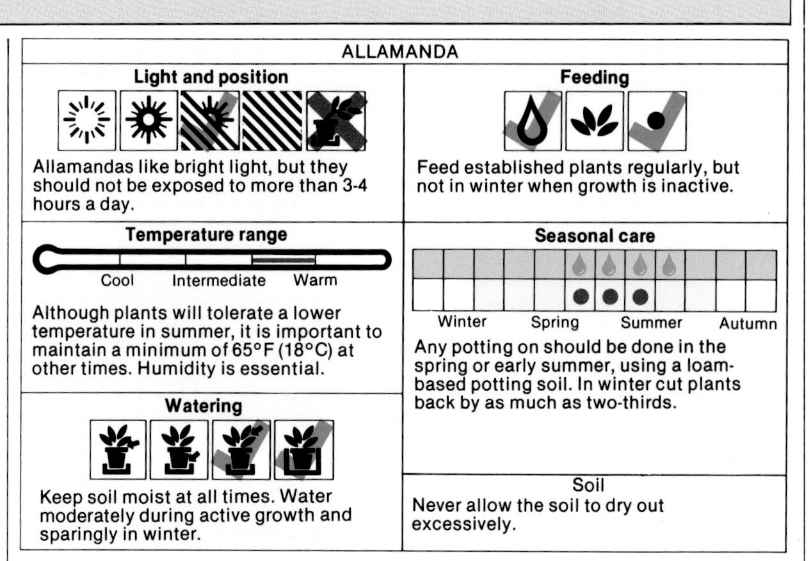

ALLAMANDA

**Light and position**

Allamandas like bright light, but they should not be exposed to more than 3-4 hours a day.

**Feeding**

Feed established plants regularly, but not in winter when growth is inactive.

**Temperature range**

Cool Intermediate Warm

Although plants will tolerate a lower temperature in summer, it is important to maintain a minimum of 65°F (18°C) at other times. Humidity is essential.

**Seasonal care**

Winter Spring Summer Autumn

Any potting on should be done in the spring or early summer, using a loam-based potting soil. In winter cut plants back by as much as two-thirds.

**Watering**

Keep soil moist at all times. Water moderately during active growth and sparingly in winter.

Soil

Never allow the soil to dry out excessively.

**Allamandas** are shrubby or climbing plants which grow vigorously in warm, moist, shaded conditions. Many species need to be trained to a support, and they are seen at their best when growing against the wall of a garden room or greenhouse. Like all allamandas, *A. cathartica* (below) produces clusters of eye-catching trumpet-shaped yellow flowers (detail right).

# Anthurium

THIS GENUS includes three species that one is likely to find in plant shops: *A. andreanum, A scherzerianum* and *A. crystallinum*. The first two have spectacular waxy flowers while the latter is principally a foliage plant.

*Anthurium andreanum* is one of the aristocrats of the plant world. It produces large spathe flowers held well above the leathery leaves on petioles 3ft (91cm) or more in length. Since these flowers, when cut, will last for up to six weeks in water, they are a particular favorite of florists.

*A. scherzerianum* produces smaller flowers in greater quantity. The bright-red spathe flowers bloom in the early months of the year. Larger flowers may need a supporting cane. *A. scherzerianum* is an easier plant to care for than *A. andreanum,* but will need humidity, warmth and reasonable light to do well. In some plants the flower stems tend to be weak and may require a supporting cane to appear to best effect.

The third plant in this genus, *A. crystallinum*, has large heart-shaped leaves. Primarily dark-green in color, they are heavily veined and quite magnificent. The spathe flower is very insignificant by comparison.

*A. crystallinum* is really a plant for the specialist who can provide it with the 70°F (21°C) plus temperature and high humidity it needs. It must be moist at all times, and the soil in which the plant is growing should be very free-draining, to the point where the water disappears through the soil as soon as it is poured onto the surface. To this end, plants will grow better on a 'raft' — a small slatted wood structure with raised sides. The outside is lined with moss, keeping peaty, open soil in position.

**Anthurium** flourish in warm and humid conditions which offer some shade. They will flower throughout the year if the conditions are right. Although these plants need to be permanently wet at their roots, it is inadvisable to stand the pots in water, as this can lead to root rot and general deterioration of the plant. Rainwater, at room temperature, is better than cold tap water. Winter feeding is unnecessary, but at other times feed at every watering with weak tomato fertilizer.

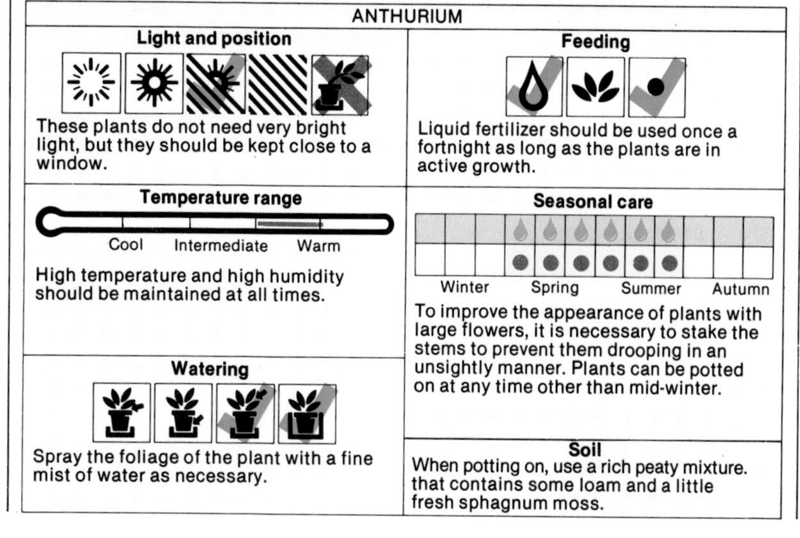

# Aphelandra

THIS GENUS includes about 80 species of shrubs and plants, but only a few are grown indoors. Grayish-green foliage has silver markings; colorful yellow bracts are produced at the top of each growing stem and compensate for the small, rather unimpressive flowers.

The popular species *Aphelandra squarrosa* is usually seen either in the variety *A.s.* 'Louisae' or *A.s.* 'Dania'. *A.s.* 'Louisae' is indigenous to Brazil and attains a height of some 30in (76cm) when grown as a pot plant. The firm leaves are a fine mixture of silver and green, and the bracts when they appear are rich yellow in color and long-lived. The flowers of this aphelandra are quite insignificant when compared to the colorful bract.

*A.s.* 'Louisae' is generally sold in 5in (13cm) pots and must be watered very freely, as it produces an extraordinary amount of thick fleshy roots. Frequent feeding is also important, and is best done at every watering; don't be concerned about exceeding the manufacturer's dosage recommendations. Aphids during the summer months and scale insects at any time can be a problem.

*A. squarrosa* 'Dania' has a compact habit of growth and bright-green foliage with silver markings topped by yellow bracts throughout the summer. When potting, use a loam-based soil; this will sustain the plant over a longer period of time than a soil-less mixture.

**Aphelandras** have attractive foliage and spikes of colorful yellow bracts with rather insignificant flowers. *A.squarrosa* (right) is a popular species. The oval leaves (below) are striped with silver, giving the plant its common name of Zebra Plant.

### APHELANDRA

**Light and position**

The aphelandra does not require full light in order to flourish successfully. Good light is needed, but not full sun.

**Temperature range**

Cool Intermediate Warm

Warm temperatures of 65°-70°F (18°-21°C) are essential and this is a plant which is particularly vulnerable to a cool environment. A humid atmosphere is also appreciated.

**Watering**

The aphelandra must be watered regularly, although overwatering may encourage botrytis.

**Feeding**

This plant produces a mass of roots and is a heavy feeder. Liquid fertilizer should be supplied through the soil.

**Seasonal care**

Winter Spring Summer Autumn

The only real variation in the treatment of this plant is after the flowering, when it can be kept at the cooler range of its preferred temperatures and given less food and water while it rests. It is not a plant which can survive neglect.

**Soil**

Pot on an aphelandra soon after purchasing, using a potting mixture with a high proportion of loam.

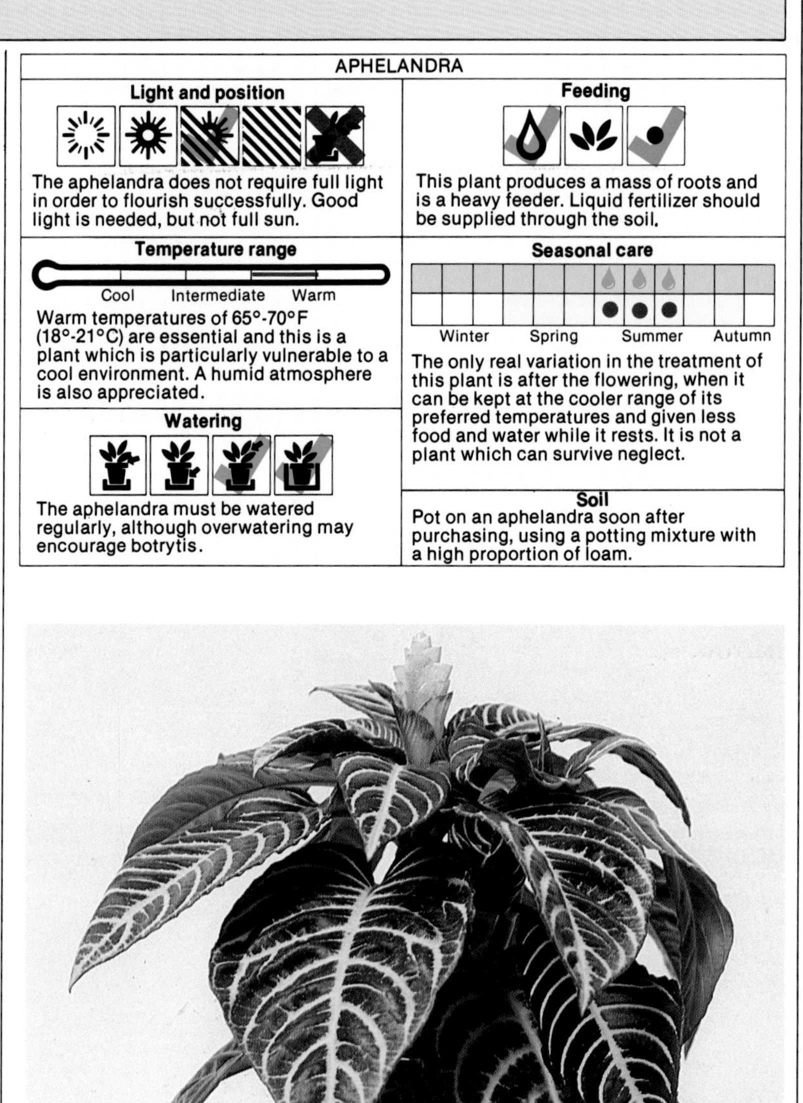

# Beaucarnea

THERE IS only one houseplant in the *Beaucarnea* genus. A relative newcomer to the European indoor-plant scene, *Beaucarnea recurvata* is a tough plant that will tolerate much ill-treatment (though not low temperature) without being unduly affected.

*B. recurvata* is indigenous to Mexico. Its comon name in America is Bottle Palm; in Europe it has become known as the Pony Tail plant. The first name refers to the bulbous bottle base that older plants develop, while the name Pony Tail derives from the way in which the stiff, recurving leaves bend over in a way that is not unlike the tail of a well-endowed pony. Leaves are narrow, brittle, dark glossy green in color.

This species is accustomed to growing in very arid conditions. Water plants well during the spring and summer, but because they hold moisture in their bulbous stems, give little or no water during the winter. No fertilizer is necessary during the summer, but mature plants must be fed at weekly intervals during the summer months. Mealy bug can occasionally be a problem.

**Beaucarnea recurvata** (above) is a tough plant with an unusual appearance. The stiff, brittle leaves grow up out of a bulbous base, giving the plant its two common names of Pony Tail and Bottle Palm. This houseplant suffers from few problems and is undemanding as long as it is kept at a reasonable temperature.

BEAUCARNEA

**Light and position**

Grow plants in bright indirect light; some direct sun is beneficial.

**Feeding**

Plants do not demand much feeding. Provide a weak liquid fertilizer in spring and summer.

**Temperature range**

Cool Intermediate Warm

Beaucarneas will flourish in average room temperature. A minimum temperature of 50°F (16°C) is necessary in winter.

**Seasonal care**

Winter Spring Summer Autumn

These are easy-care plants and require little attention. Repot them in spring if necessary.

**Watering**

Water thoroughly, then leave until compost is moderately dry. Do not overwater.

**Soil**

Use a loam-based compost.

# Begonias

THE PENDULOUS white flowers of *B. solonanthera* are delicately fragrant, but it is the only member of the vast begonia family that offers this bonus. Yet, while lacking in fragrance, the begonia family gives us almost everything else that one can desire from plants, including exotic foliage and brilliant flowers. There are delicate and hardy begonias, begonias for the sun and begonias for the shade, upright growing kinds and those that sport an amazing cascade of briliant color.

*Begonia cleopatra.* This is a neat and attractive plant with leaves that are almost star-shaped in appearance. Plants develop into compact mounds of growth that are little more than 15in (38cm) in height with coloring that is a lovely shade of bronzy green. Pink flower clusters on foot-long (30cm) stalks appear in late spring and early summer.

*Begonia fuchsioides.* As the name suggests, this plant has flowers that resemble those of the fuchsia. Flowers are bright-red in color and grow in great profusion for a long period over the summer months. Leaves are small and dark glossy green, and are produced in abundance.

*Begonia haageana.* Also known as *B. scharffii*, this plant has leaves the color of beetroot when beetroot has lost its red color and developed that odd mixture of yellow, green and brown. The leaves are covered with fine hairs and clusters of pink flowers appear on stems that tend to droop.

*Begonia lucerne.* Also known as *B. President Carnot*, this is one of the tallest of the cane-type begonias and probably the best of them. Brownish-green leaves are silver-spotted and appealing but the greatest attraction is the immense drooping clusters of pink flowers that flourish during the spring and summer months.

*Begonia manicata* has colorful bronzy-green leaves that are rounded in shape, topped with a wealth of delicate, pale-pink flowers that almost completely obscure the foliage.

*Begonia rex.* These are grown almost entirely for their strong and interesting foliage rather than for the insignificant flowers. The range of leaf colors encompass silver, dark-brown and many shades of red and green.

Although good light is required, the plants should not be exposed to direct sunlight. Unlike the majority of plants with colorful leaves, they lose none of their brilliance when grown in weaker light.

*Begonia 'Rieger'* is a very popular plant that was developed on the continent during the past decade. The plant has dark-green glossy leaves and flowers in many colors, from white to yellow, orange and red. This is the easiest of any flowering begonia to care for.

*Begonia solonanthera.* This is a natural hanging plant that is set off to best effect when two or three small plants of the same variety are placed in a medium-sized hanging basket. Pale-green leaves on numerous stems will trail over the side of

**Begonias** have a wide range of patterned foliage and brilliantly colored flowers. *B. tuberhybrida* (below left) is available in many varieties, each with different colored flowers. The pink-flowered *B. haegaena* (below center), is easy to manage. *B. lucerne* (below right) is one of the tallest species.

the container and will soon be followed by clusters of white flowers, which will continue for many months. Flowers continually shed petals and brown husks, so the plant is somewhat messy. There are compensations, however; this is one of the few scented begonias available.

*Begonia 'Tiger'.* This plant produces lots of small leaves and is neat and compact, which makes it ideal for the inside windowsill. The background color of the foliage is a bronzy green, and there are lots of chocolate-brown blotches over the leaf. The pale-pink flowers are comparatively insignificant.

*Begonia tuberhybrida* is among the most spectacular of all flowering houseplants, and when grown by the specialist for show purposes can be quite stunning. Leaves are oval and dark-green; flowers are white, orange, pink, red or yellow. Plants may be grown from seed, but it is usually better to begin with tubers. If one can afford to purchase named varieties, do so, for the end result will generally be much superior to tubers that are obtained as a mixed bunch.

**Begonia 'Rieger'** (above) is a very popular houseplant producing bright blooms and growing easily indoors. **Begonia Tiger** (below right) is a compact plant prized for its unusual foliage.

BEGONIA

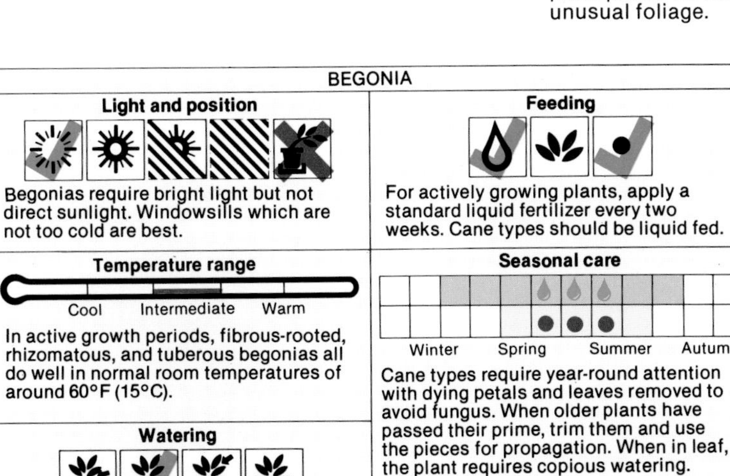

**Light and position**

Begonias require bright light but not direct sunlight. Windowsills which are not too cold are best.

**Temperature range**



In active growth periods, fibrous-rooted, rhizomatous, and tuberous begonias all do well in normal room temperatures of around 60°F (15°C).

**Watering**

Begonias do not like dry air. During active growth, water moderately allowing the top inch (3cm) of soil to dry out.

**Feeding**

For actively growing plants, apply a standard liquid fertilizer every two weeks. Cane types should be liquid fed.

**Seasonal care**



Cane types require year-round attention with dying petals and leaves removed to avoid fungus. When older plants have passed their prime, trim them and use the pieces for propagation. When in leaf, the plant requires copious watering.

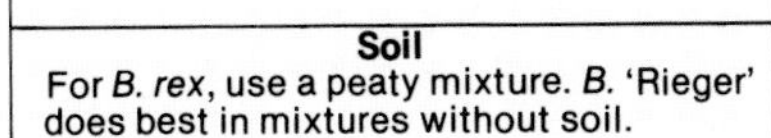

**Soil**

For *B. rex*, use a peaty mixture. *B.* 'Rieger' does best in mixtures without soil.

ACANTHACEAE

# Beloperone

THE ONLY PLANT in this genus widely grown indoors is the world-renowned plant, *Beloperone guttata.* Commonly called the Shrimp Plant, it is a bract-forming plant that offers a great profusion of color almost all year round, though fewer bracts appear in winter. Thin, insignificant green leaves are attached to wiry stems that will attain a height of some 6ft (1.8m), but branches can be trimmed to a more compact shape at almost any time. The actual flowers are off-white in color, but add little to the plant's appearance and can be a nuisance since they fall in all directions. The bracts, however, are a rich autumnal shade on top and an attractive lime green on their undersides. They have a distinctly shrimp-like appearance, hence the plant's common name.

*B. guttata* needs full sun and rich loam-based potting soil.

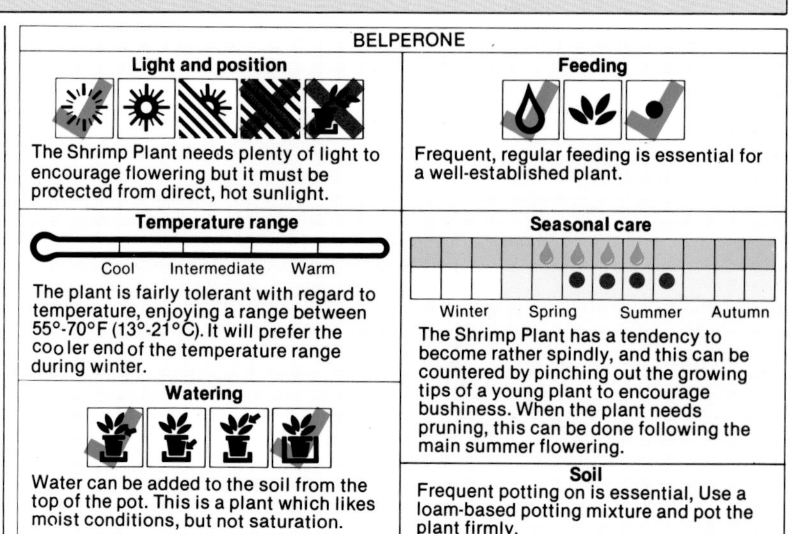


Keep plants moist, and feed at every watering after they have become established in their pots. In the plant's early stages of development, remove bracts as they appear in order to promote stronger growth. Prune to shape leggy and unattractive growth. Cuttings of young shoots a few inches in length will root at almost any time, but remove any bracts that may be attached to the cutting. No pests seem to attack the plant.

**Beloperone guttata** (above) is a tall bushy plant which grows leggy if not cut back to retain its shape. The noticeable feature of this popular houseplant is the reddish overlapping bracts (right) which resemble shrimps in appearance.

# Bougainvillea

Paper Flower
Paper Vine

**Bougainvilleas** are climbing plants whose brilliant colors are a feature of Mediterranean countries. Their striking characteristic is the clusters of bold-colored papery bracts which surround the insignificant flowers. *B. glabra* (above and detail left) is one of the species that can be grown in pots, provided it has sufficient light.

FOR ANY PERSON traveling in temperate regions the most striking plant encountered must surely be bougainvillea, commonly called Paper Flower. Colourful, papery bracts usually appear in clusters of 10 to 20 and can persist for several weeks. Leaves are small and oval; bracts surround tiny, cream-colored flowers.

One of the best species for use indoors is *Bougainvillea glabra*. Paper-thin bract flowers are growing red and produced in profusion; the small green leaves aı e insignificant in comparison. Several variegated forms of this plant are available. *B.g.* 'Harrisii' has green leaves streaked with creamy white; *B.g.* 'Sanderana Variegata' has leaves edged in the same creamy white. Numerous other bougainvillea species exist, with flower colors ranging from white through orange to yellow, pink and purple.

In spite of their bright coloring and exotic appearance, bougainvilleas are not difficult plants to care for, needing full light and generally airy conditions. Although seen in Mediterranean countries, bougainvilleas are fine plants for the cool conservatory, where they can be trained against a wall or ceiling so that cascading flowers are seen to best advantage.

Growth can be pruned to shape after flowering, and it will not be difficult to propagate new plants from firm pieces of stem about 6in (15cm) in length. Dormant over winter when no water is needed, plants should remain dry until new growth is evident. Then pot on, using a loam-based soil.

Bougainvilleas need bright light, with several hours of direct sunlight each day during the growing period. Keep plants cool during the winter, but do not let the temperature drop below 50°F (10°C).

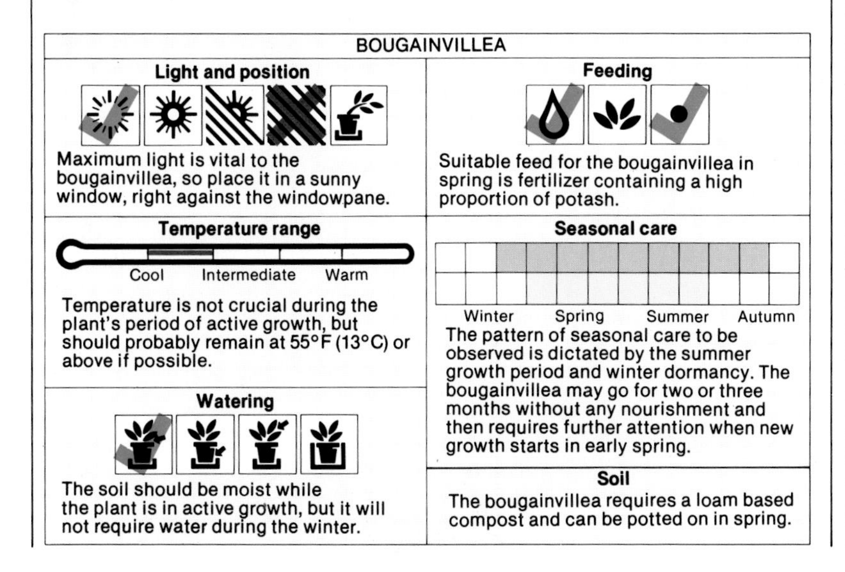

BOUGAINVILLEA

**Light and position**

Maximum light is vital to the bougainvillea, so place it in a sunny window, right against the windowpane.

**Feeding**

Suitable feed for the bougainvillea in spring is fertilizer containing a high proportion of potash.

**Temperature range**

Cool Intermediate Warm

Temperature is not crucial during the plant's period of active growth, but should probably remain at 55°F (13°C) or above if possible.

**Seasonal care**

Winter Spring Summer Autumn

The pattern of seasonal care to be observed is dictated by the summer growth period and winter dormancy. The bougainvillea may go for two or three months without any nourishment and then requires further attention when new growth starts in early spring.

**Watering**

The soil should be moist while the plant is in active growth, but it will not require water during the winter.

**Soil**

The bougainvillea requires a loam based compost and can be potted on in spring.

# Bromeliads

BROMELIADS ARE perhaps the most fascinating of all tropical plants, and are indigenous to South America.

Almost all are easy to care for and will tolerate considerable neglect. Many plants in the family are epiphytes and make their precarious anchorage in trees, depending on the elements and passing birds for much of their nourishment and moisture. Some of the plants, such as the many and varied cryptanthus, are terrestrial and grow among the rocks and fallen trees at ground level. Others are virtually weeds.

The larger bromeliads produce rosettes of leaves that overlap at their base and make perfect water reservoirs. Flowering bracts appear from the center of these urns - some to stand out from the leaves, others to barely emerge from the water in the urn. Heavy dew or rainfall will fill these urns when plants are growing in habitat. Because plants can derive their water requirements from this source, they are able to withstand the most difficult conditions. These urns also provide water for the many birds and small animals that frequent tropical trees, and whose droppings provide a certain amount of nutrition for the bromeliad plants.

**Watering bromeliads** Larger bromeliads should have water poured directly into their urn. This reservoir is formed by the overlapping bases of the rosette of leaves.

Although bromeliads vary in size from tiny tillandsias to majestic vriesias, all are similar in their requirements. Most are within the scope of the reasonably competent gardener. Those plants that form water urns should have the urn filled to capacity all the time; very little water should actually be poured into the soil. The water in these urns will become stagnant in time, especially after plants have produced their bracts, so tip the old water away periodically and replenish the urns with fresh water, preferably rainwater.

**Bromeliad tree** An established bromeliad tree (above) is an attractive addition to any indoor setting. (Opposite page) This one shows the variety of genera that can be included, each plant firmly secured in a fork or angle of the branch.

Smaller tillandsias are particularly good plants to place on a bromeliad tree. They are very durable and will come to no harm provided the tree is sprayed over with water occasionally. Another fine bromeliad to place on the tree is *Bilbergia nutans*, or Queen's Tears, which produces pendulous bracts of spectacular coloring at regular intervals throughout the year.

For the finest-looking tree possible, it is best to include other plants as well as bromeliads. The soft-green foliage of small ferns provides a contrast to the tillandsia. The miniature ficus, *F. pumila*, is another good plant for a bromeliad tree. The firm, oval-shaped leaves will twine around the branches of the tree.

Moist sphagnum moss is wrapped around the base of each rosette, covering any roots.

Pieces of cork bark are placed around the moss base and the whole thing is then attached to the branch of the tree with reel wire.

## Aechmea

THIS GENUS provides numerous majestic plants, many of which are used often for decorative purposes. The bright cream-and-green foliage and striking rosettes of growth produced by *Aechmea caudata* make it one of the best display plants. The plant's orange bracts are lovely, but are only occasionally produced.

Perhaps the best-known of all the bromeliads as far as decorative plants go is *A. fasciata* (also called *A. rhodocyanea,* or *Bilbergia rhodocyanea*), which has large powdery silver-gray foliage and superb pink-colored bracts from which appear small intensely blue flowers. The leaves are broad and upright and have black spines along their margin, and the bracts remain colorful for several months, making this one of the finest of all exotic indoor plants. With softer leaves of wine-red coloring, *A. fulgens* is a pleasing plant that produces small bracts. *A. chantinii* has vicious spines along the margins of the leaves, so must be handled with care.

## Ananas

THE ONLY BROMELIAD that is of any commercial value to the world is the ananas, which provides us with the pineapple of commerce. Most ananas are not grown indoors, but *A. comosus* develops small pineapples when roots are confined to pots, though the result is a very insignificant little fruit. The hard green leaves are not particularly attractive, but there are variegated forms of ananas, *A. bracteatus striatus* being one, that have special value as decorative plants, both for their striking foliage and for the majestic appearance that the plant assumes when the bright-pink pineapple fruit is produced. All the ananas are easy-care plants, but they are inclined to become rather large, with spiteful spines along the margins of leaves, and need ample space in which to grow.

### Billbergia

THE MORE COMMON *B. nutans* (Queen's Tears) and the broader-leaved *B. windii* are among the most tolerant of indoor plants, putting up with much mistreatment without too many ill effects. Flowering bracts are highly colorful and naturally pendulous, so plants are seen at their best when they are raised on a pedestal or planted in small hanging containers. The foliage is not of any great merit, but flowers are likely to appear at any time. Both *B. nutans* and *B. windii* make thick clumps of growth that can be separated to make additional plants at any time other than when in flower.

*B. pyramidalis concolor* is a plant that is reluctant to produce offsets for propagation and is consequently rarer. This is a more tender plant than *B. nutans* and *B. windii,* and has longer tubes of leaves from which appear bracts of the most spectacular coloring, a combination of crimson-red, purple and blue. The bracts are also broader and more upright than those of *B. nutans,* and in common with other bilbergias, the bracts are short-lived. One common name for the plant is Summer Torch.

### Cryptanthus

PLANTS IN THIS GENUS have thick fleshy leaves that form rosettes in the shape of flat stars. In their natural habitat, they grow at ground level. They do well in shallow pans or pots provided with drainage material and holding soil that is very open and free to drain. Plants rarely, if ever, reach any great size and, in fact, lose much of their appeal when they have formed into heavier clumps of foliage. The best method of growing them is to regularly split the bolder clumps and to use the offsets for propagating fresh plants.

*C. bromelioides tricolor* has bright-pink and cream-colored foliage and pushes its leaves up much higher than most cryptanthus. As a result, the plant appears less star-like than other cryptanthus. With very small rosettes that are olive-green in color with contrasting bands, *C. bivittatus* 'Minor' is one of the smallest plants in the entire bromeliad family. Small rosettes become very crowded in their pots, and it is quite common for individual rosettes to be virtually pushed out of the way by other developing rosettes. One result is that they can be found rooting into almost anything that will give them a reasonable foothold.

The aristocrat of this genus must be *C. fosterianus.* The leaves are very fleshy and are shaped like large flat stars. The remarkable marking on them has given the plant the common name of Pheasant Leaf. This plant is generally difficult to obtain, but it belongs in every good collection of bromeliads. The species *C. zonatus* is similar in color, with leaves that are gently waved, but it lacks the distinction of the Pheasant Leaf.

### Guzmania

WITH ROSETTE-FORMING foliage that is less vicious than many of the larger-leaved bromeliads, guzmanias are well worth acquiring. *Guzmania lingulata* is an epiphytic species. It has metallic-green leaves, red and yellow bracts and yellow-white flowers. Another easy-care plant that is in this genus is *G. monostachya*, which produces slender rosettes of yellowish-green leaves in large free-growing clumps with stiff multicolored bracts.

A product of Belgium, where much has been done to popu-

**Billbergia pyramidalis** (above) and *B. nutans* (below) have spectacular bracts from which emerge spikes of flowers. But, as with all billbergias, they do not last long.

**Ananas** (above) is not a particularly attractive bromeliad, but it is interesting for the fact that the genus is the source of pineapple fruit, and some species develop tiny fruit when grown in a pot.

**Cryptanthus** plants usually have leaves that form flattish, star-shaped rosettes. Three decorative species are *C. tricolor* (above right), *C. zonatus* (below right) and *C. 'Foster's Favourite'* (far right).

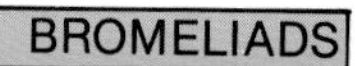

**Aechmeas** include some of the largest and most magnificent bromeliads. The showy pink bracts of *A. fasciata* (left) last for several months. *A. fulgens* (inset) shows wine-red coloring and has scarlet bracts with purple flowers.

larize bromeliads, G. 'Omar Morobe' has a somewhat insignificant bract, but more than compensates with foliage that is bright-pink and cream in color. Rosettes should mature to a reasonable size before you pull them from the parent plant and root them in an open mixture as individual plants.

**Neoregelia**

BY FAR the most popular species of neoreglia is *Neoreglia carolinae tricolor.* Plants make flat cartwheel rosettes of splendid coloring, with the added attraction that the center of the plant around the water reservoir changes to the deepest red as bracts form just below water level. Bracts are insignificant, and the parent rosette dies after it has produced its bracts. The old rosette is cut away when it has lost its attractive appearance. The small offsets that appear at the base of the plant should then be removed and rooted as individual plants.

**Tillandsia**

PLANTS IN THE *Tillandsia* genus range in size from tiny lichen-like plants to plants with very large rosettes of leaves. Almost all are easy to care for and can go for weeks on end with no water or feeding whatsoever – many seeming to exist virtually on air. Most tillandsias grown as houseplants have little or no roots and will do best on a bromeliad tree or fixed to a piece of cork bark and tied with a little sphagnum moss.

*Tillandsia cyanea* has recurving rosettes of hard green leaves, and spectacular pink bracts that produce bright-blue petunia-like flowers.

*Tillandsia usneoides,* commonly known as Spanish Moss, consists of threadlike stems covered with minute grey scales. When growing in the wild, it hangs from trees and rocks in great curtains of grey, choking the life of everything around it. Under controlled conditions, however, Spanish Moss can be a very striking addition to a bromeliad tree.

**Vriesia**

THERE ARE many splendid plants in this genus, all of them forming large rosettes of leathery leaves with an attractive pattern and coloring.

The best-known is *V. spendens,* which produces a brilliant-red bract that is spear-shaped and stands proudly away from the leaves, which are banded green and brown in color. Bracts are long-lived and plants require good light in which to grow. The urn formed by leaves must always contain water. Only the minimum of water should be given to the soil, and feeding is not necessary. Plants will not flower until several years old.

Other vriesias, such as *V. hieroglyphica*, or *V. fenestralis*, which has a netted pattern to its leaves, produce very large and majestic rosettes of leaves that may be 3ft (91cm) or more in diameter. However, these are plants for the connoisseur and will not often be available for sale.

**Guzmanias** have softer foliage than many of the larger bromeliads. *G. lingulata* (top) and *G. 'Omar Morobe'* (above) are two attractive species.

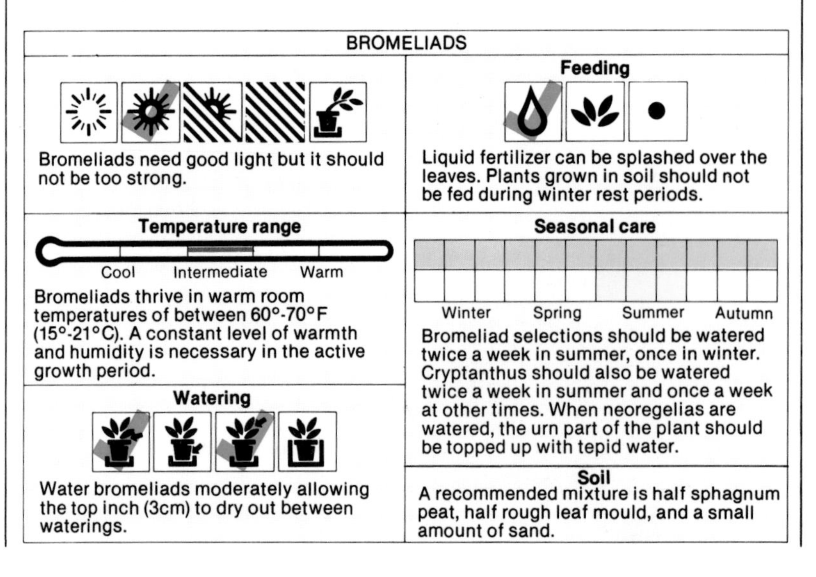

**Neoregelia carolinae 'Tricolor'** (above) is a plant which will grow to 2ft (60cm) in width. Its rosette of cream-striped leaves will turn brilliant red at flowering time and remain so for months if the center is kept full of water.

**Tillandsia** plants (below) are highly suited to bottlegardens. They have huge rosettes with colorful flowers.

**Vriesia splendens** is a fine plant. Its principal feature is the erect sword-like bract that emanates from the rosette of leaves. The yellow tubular flowers that emerge from the bract are of little consequence. In common with many species of bromeliad, the leaves of this one overlap at their base and form a rosette that is a water-tight urn. The urn should at no time be allowed to dry out, although it is advisable to dispose of existing water and to replenish with fresh water periodically.

ARACEAE

# Caladium

Angel-wings
Elephant's-ears
Heart of Jesus

THE CALADIUMS have large heart-shaped leaves which are supported on petioles 12 or 18in (30-51cm) in length that sprout from soil level. There are many different species, and their foliage ranges in color from white to very deep red with many mottled shades in between.

Few plants in nature can compete with the caladiums when it comes to foliage color, and an added attraction is that leaves are so thin they are translucent in some species, notably *C. candidum*. The latter is the most popular plant and one that is readily available during the summer months of the year when caladiums are in their prime. Caladiums have the common name of Angel's Wings, which suits *C. candidum* in particular, with its white coloring and prominent green venation.

To succeed, these plants need a light but not sunny location in a temperature not less than 65°F (18°C). Humidity helps caladiums flourish. Plants are normally available in the spring and early summer and are sold in 5in (13cm) pots in which they can remain if a regular weekly feed is given. Toward the end of the summer, plants will die down naturally and should then be gradually dried off until such times as the soil is completely dry. After the plant is completely defoliaged and the soil is dried out, the plant should be stored in a warm, dry place until early spring, when it should be watered and brought into the light to start the new season.

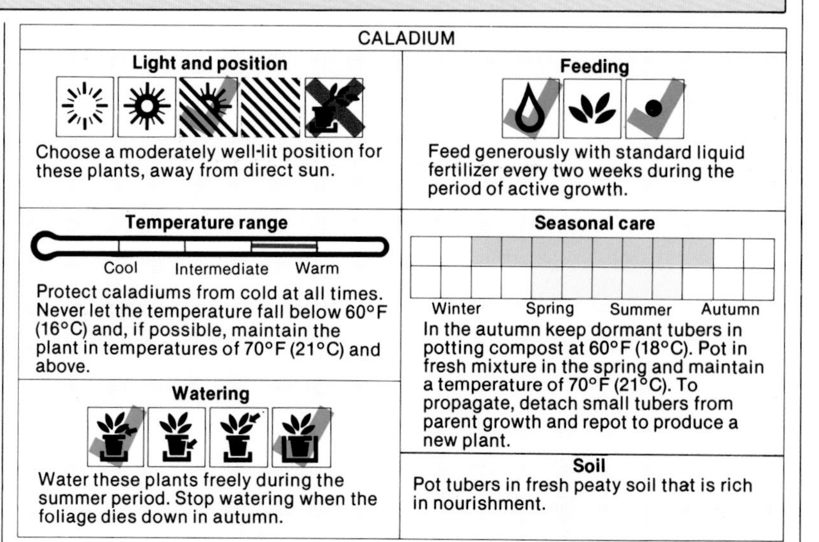

**Caladiums** are decorative plants with extremely delicate-looking foliage. The large heart-shaped leaves are papery thin and vary widely in color, from pale creamy white to pink and deep red. *C. 'Silver leaves'* (right) is one of many hybrids. As in most plants of this genus, the pattern on the leaves largely follows the leaf veining.

# Calathea

MOST CALATHEAS are grown for their colorful foliage, and all are tender plants needing a minimum temperature of 60°F (16°C) and light shade in which to grow.

With upright leaves that are colorfully patterned on their upper surface and maroon in color underneath, *C. insignis* is a bold and striking plant that will require all the experienced gardner's skill to do well.

The Peacock Plant, *C. makoyana*, has crowded leaves that are paper-thin and carried erect on long petioles. Its bronze-colored leaves are heavily patterned with many contrasting shades of color make this an this plant especially desirable.

*C. ornata* has upright but more elongated leaves. Close-set, colorful stripes extend from the midrib of the leaf to its outer edges — stripes become paler in color as the plant ages.

*C. roseo-picta* is one of the finest of the more compact calatheas. The background coloring of olive-green has a metallic sheen that sets off perfectly the rosy-red lateral stripes.

*Calathea crocata* is one of the few calathea species that have attractive flowers. The foliage, however, is less appealing than other calatheas'. The bracts are bright orange; leaves are dark green, and ovate in shape.

**Calatheas** are challenging houseplants, grown for their strikingly patterned foliage. *C. makoyana* (above left) and *C. roseo- picta* (above right) show the variety of leaf color and patterning.

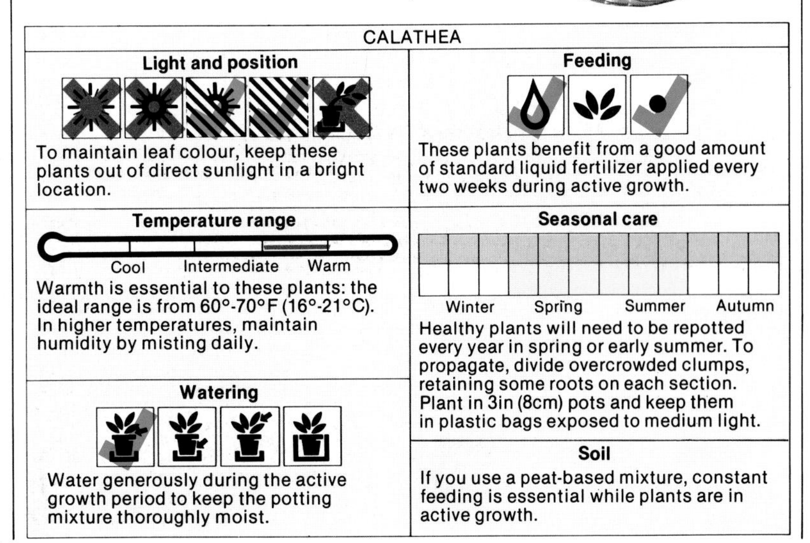

# Callistemon

ONLY ONE SPECIES of the genus *Callistemon* is grown indoors. Indigenous to Australia, *C. citrinus* is a strong-growing plant. Its common name of Bottlebrush refers to the cylindrical flowers that are formed in the shape of a flue brush and are bright red in color. Leaves are narrow and bright-green; stems are woody and plants are evergreen, with flowers developing at the apex of the many branches during the summer months. *C. citrinus* reaches a maximum height of 5ft (1.5m).

During the summer months, plants will benefit if placed out of doors in a sunny, sheltered position. Pruning is seldom necessary, but removing the growing tips of young plants will encourage plants to branch as they age. New plants may be raised from seed, and by rooting cuttings about 4in (10cm) in length. Cuttings should be prepared from firm stems taken after plants have flowered. These plants should be potted on in early spring into only slightly larger containers. A soil-less mixture will be suitable if plants are adequately fed, but a loam-based potting medium is preferable.

CALLISTEMON

**Light and position**

Callistemons need several hours of direct sunlight daily in order to flower well.

**Feeding**

Feed with liquid fertilizer once every two weeks while plants are in active growth.

**Temperature range**

Cool Intermediate Warm

Normal room temperature is fine while plants are in active growth. Keep plants cooler during the resting period, at a temperature of 45 to 50°F (7°-10°C).

**Seasonal care**

Winter Spring Summer Autumn

Take cuttings in early summer. Cut back plants as soon as flowering is over. During the growing season, water plants well, but do not allow pots to stand in water.

**Watering**

Water plentifully while plants are in active growth, keeping them just moist during the dormant period.

**Soil**

Use a soil-based mixture composed of equal parts soil, sand and either peat moss or leaf-mould.

**Callistemon citrinus** (above top) is the only species of this genus of Australian evergreen shrub to be grown indoors, although the taller *C. speciosus* (above) may occasionally find its way into larger conservatories. The bright-red cylindrical flower spikes consist largely of stamens and so give rise to the common name of 'Bottlebrush'.

# Carnivorous Plants

**Dionaea muscipula**, the Venus's Flytrap (above), is the most popular of the carnivorous plants.
The Venus's Flytrap has pairs of hinged lobes wih toothed edges at the end of its leaves which snap shut around visiting insects.

THERE ARE MANY odd plants in nature, but few as unusual as the carnivorous plants. These plants have various ways of trapping within their foliage flies and other creatures, which they digest and use as nourishment.

The Venus's-flytrap, *Dionaea muscipula*, is the plant that is most commonly offered for sale as a subject for indoor decoration. The leaves of the Venus's flytrap are equipped with teeth along their margins and a trigger mechanism that is activated by any insect that chances to land on the upper surface of the leaf. The leaf folds together with the teeth interlocking, making it impossible for the prisoner within to escape. When flies are less plentiful, plants may be fed by placing on the leaves minute pieces of meat or fish. The plant will digest them in the same way it would a fly.

The Venus's-flytrap must have a close, humid atmosphere if it is to succeed. It may be necessary, then, to provide a microclimate within a Wardian

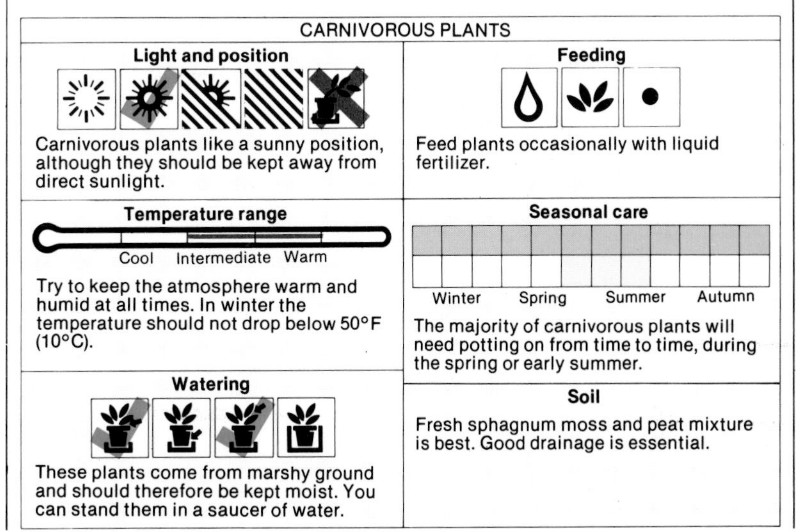

case of some kind. This could easily be a box filled with damp moss topped by a sheet of glass. To make a box, choose fresh, clean sphagnum moss. Wet it before making a bed about 5in (13cm) deep in the bottom of the box. Bury the pot in the moss up to its rim, so that the plant derives the maximum benefit from the surrounding moisture. (It goes without saying that while the plant is in the box the moss should at no time dry out.) The atmosphere must be moist, and the temperature should be 65°F (18°C) and above — the higher the temperature the better, if the air is moist.

Perhaps the most spectacular of the carnivorous plants are the nepenthes, which are commonly named Pitcher Plants. Green leathery leaves are not especially attractive, but from their extremities they produce strands of growth on which pitcher-like vases are attached. The bottom of the pitcher contains pepsin liquid in which insects drown when they are attracted inside; the cover of the pitcher enables the plant to shed rainwater and keeps the water from spilling into the bottom. There are numerous varieties of this plant, and all of them need the same humid and warm conditions

In their natural habitat, almost all of the nepenthes are natural climbers, and in greenhouses they can be very exotic when suspended in baskets from the ceiling so that the pitchers hang freely away from the main part of the plant. It is not possible to confine these large plants to propagating cases, so a greenhouse or conservatory heated to a minimum of 65°F (18°C) is necessary.

**Nepenthes**, the Pitcher Plants, have a very unusual appearance with pitcher-like vases hanging from the ends of leaves. *N. hookeriana* (above) shows the special pitchers which contain liquid in which insects drown and are digested.

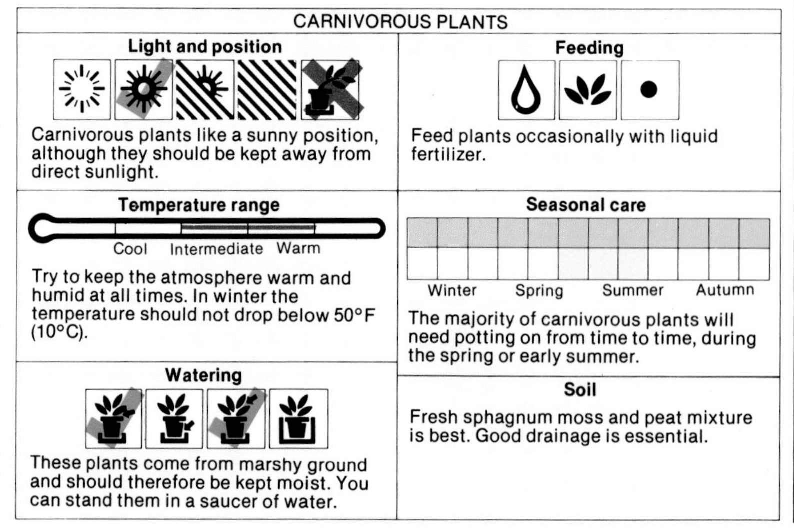

# Clerodendrum

THE ONLY SPECIES in the *Clerodendrum* genus that is grown as a houseplant is *Clerodendrum thomsoniae.* Leaves are mid-green in color; clustered flowering bracts are bright red and white.

*Clerodendrum thomsoniae* is best seen to advantage placed against a wall. But although the stems are stout and woody, the plant is not a natural climber and will have to be trained. It will attain a height of 8ft (2.4m) in time, but this vigorous plant can be easily contained by pruning.

To do well, plants need a minimum temperature of 60°F (16°C) and a light but not sunny position. Take cuttings following flowering in the autumn. They should be 6in (15cm) in length with two pairs of leaves. A temperature of not less than 60°F (16°C) and a close, moist atmosphere are necessary to root this difficult subject.

CLERODENDRUM

**Light and position**

These plants will not flower without bright light. However avoid direct sunlight through glass.

**Feeding**

Apply a weak liquid fertilizer once every two weeks.

**Temperature range**

Cool Intermediate Warm

During active growth these plants can be kept at room temperature — in winter they require a cooler atmosphere of 50°-55°F (10°-13°C).

**Seasonal care**

Winter Spring Summer Autumn

Propagate in spring, and after four months move the plant into a soil-based potting mixture. Cut the plant back by at least half in winter.

**Watering**

Water well during the growing period, always keeping the soil moist. The plant should never stand in water.

**Soil**

Loam-based soil should be used for large plants; peaty soil for smaller ones.

**Clerodendrum thomsoniae** (below) is a pleasing shrubby or climbing plant that needs to be either pruned vigorously or trained to a support. The attractive flowers (detail right) appear in spring and contrast well with the green leaves.

# Codiaeum

Croton
Joseph's Coat

CROTON LEAVES can vary considerably in shape, from broad to needle-like, from round to pointed leaves, but almost all have spectacular coloring — predominantly red, orange or yellow set against a pale-green background.

Plants are normally offered in 5in (15cm) size pots, but when well managed they can grow as high as 8ft (2.4m) with a spread of 4 to 5ft (1.2 to 1.5m). However, this would be exceptional and plants would have to grow in a greenhouse heated to not less than 70°F (21°C). Indoors, these plants will be of more modest size and will be more difficult to care for. In fact, they are the sort of foliage plants that the beginner should avoid — a little experience of plants is needed to manage crotons.

Red spider mites find the croton a particularly palatable morsel, and will frequently be found on the undersides of leaves and around the fresh growth at the top of the plant.

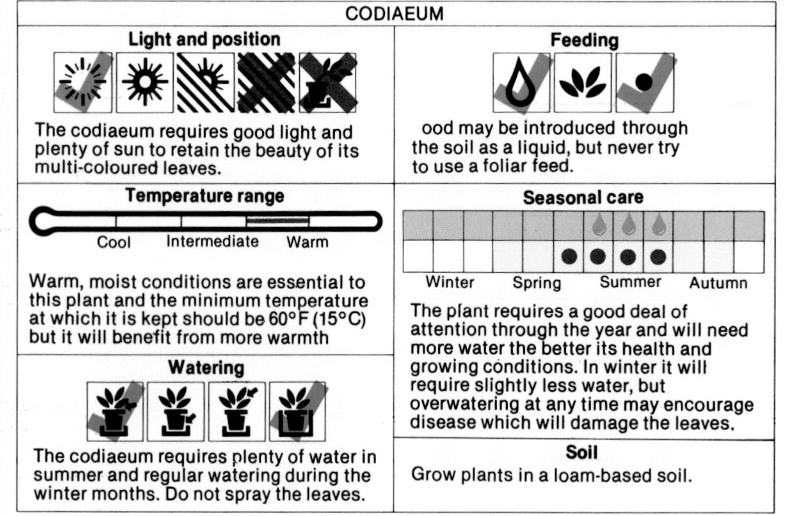


Codiaeum leaves come in many different shapes and colors. Those of *C.* 'Mrs Iceton' (above left) are oval and red and green; those of *C. holufiana* (above) are elongated and more yellow. The leaves shown below are examples of foliage variation. **1.** *C. craigi*, **2.** *C. 'Eugene Drapps'* and **3.** *C. reidii*.

# Columnea

THESE ARE beautiful flowering plants that don't enjoy the popularity that they deserve — perhaps because it's mistakenly thought that they are too delicate for room culture. But the long-established species *Columnea banksii* has been popular for many years and grows with little difficulty. No pest troubles this plant, which has been a favourite since the Victorian era.

*Columnea banksii* has oval, fleshy leaves attached to trailing stems that are supple when young, getting firmer with age, and dark-green in color. Cascading flowers are a rich shade of orange and will completely cover the plant if it is doing well. Cuttings of tips or stem sections will root with little trouble. For best effect, put three or four cuttings into small hanging baskets.

The limp, pendulous stems of *C. gloriosa* are soft and the plant is generally more tender than *C. banksii*. The oblong leaves are small and covered in reddish hairs. Flowers are bright-red with a yellow throat and generally appear in early summer, but for no apparent reason will often oblige later in the year also. Since *C. gloriosa* is slightly more tender, one should try to maintain a temperature of not less than 65°F (18°C). There is also a very attractive variegated form. It is shy of flowering and grown almost entirely for its white-and-green foliage.

Perhaps the most spectacular of all the columneas is *C. microphylla*, which has minute pale-green leaves that are attached to slender, pendulous stems. These may reach 6ft (1.8m) in length. When plants are in flower in mid-summer, they present a great cascading sea of orange and yellow – the outer part of the flower being orange while the inside is yellow.

**Columneas** are attractive trailing flowering plants. *C. banksii* (right) produces a cascade of rich orange flowers against a background of neatly paired leaves on trailing stems. The open flowers of the plant (detail below) have given the plant the common name of Goldfish Plant, as they resemble the open mouth of a fish.

### COLUMNEA

**Light and position**

The columnea requires a position with good light, to encourage flowering, but shaded from direct sunlight.

**Temperature range**

Cool Intermediate Warm

Few plants care for a wide temperature range of periods of excessive heat or cold. A suitable range for the columnea is 60°-70°F (15°-21°C).

**Watering**

Water the plant regularly during the summer growth period, giving slightly less in winter.

**Feeding**

Established plants should be fed about once a week in summer when they are active, once a month during winter.

**Seasonal care**

Winter Spring Summer Autumn

The columnea is quite easy to care for. The foliage can be trimmed to shape at any time when the plant is not in flower, but this is not essential to its health. The autumn is the time to tidy the plant and cut out any dead material. Beware of overwatering at all times.

**Soil**

When transferring cuttings to a hanging basket, use a loam-based potting mixture.

ACANTHACEAE

# Crossandra

**Crossandra infundibuliformis** (above) is the only species of this genus which is grown as a houseplant. It is a shrubby plant with glossy leaves, but tends to grow straggly with age. The cultivar *'Mona Walhed'* (left) has attractive flowering bracts.

THE ONLY crossandra grown indoors is *Crossandra infundibuliformis.* It is generally sold as a compact little plant, with its orange-colored bracts just coming into flower over the glossy green leaves, but it will eventually attain a height of some 6ft (1.8m), by which time it will be very straggly and much less attractive. Cutting it back will help to retain its attractiveness, but once plants have shown the tendency toward legginess they never regain their early appearance. The best solution is to take cuttings from growth ends and to start afresh. Give plants good light but not bright sun.

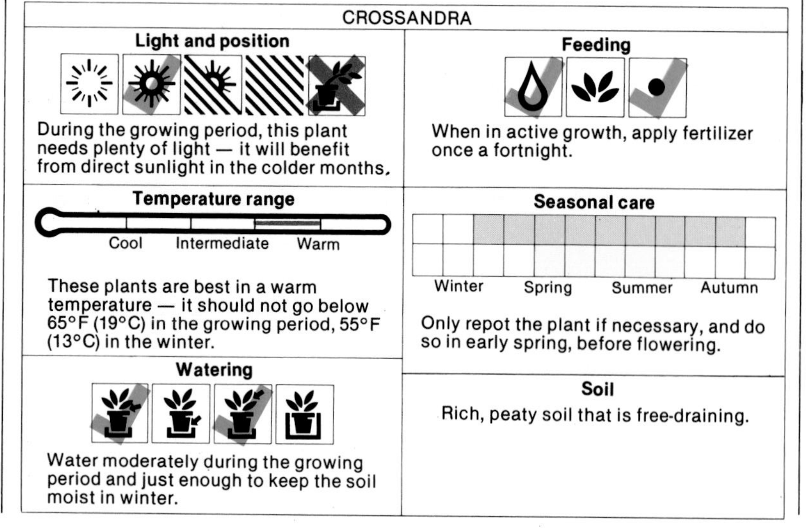

# Cyperus

Umbrella Sedge

CYPERUS PRODUCE leaf-like bracts and grass-like flower heads surmounting thin, narrow stems. They thrive in wet, boggy conditions and are perfect plants for the person who is heavy-handed when watering, as they will actually flourish if their plant pots stand in water.

*Cyperus alternifolius* has thin, green leaves at pot level and produces tall, flowering stems that have secondary leaves displayed in the shape of an umbrella – hence the species' common name of Umbrella Plant. The plant can reach a height of 10ft (3m) if growing in pots of 10in (25cm) diameter.

**Cyperus** are elegant grass-like plants which actually flourish if over-watered. The tall stems of *C. alternifolius* (above right) are topped by leaf-like bracts (detail above).

*Cyperus diffusus* (sometimes called *C. albostriatus*) is a better plant if space is limited. It attains a maximum height of 3-4ft (91cm-1.2m) and produces a much greater number of stems per pot than *C. diffusus*. Heads have up to 24 narrow bracts; flowers are pale brown. Plants will grow readily from seed, or established clumps of growth may be divided at any time of the year to produce individual plants. Flower heads with a piece of stem attached can also be rooted with peaty soil.

### CYPERUS

**Light and position**

The Umbrella Plant can be grown equally well in full, bright sunlight or slight shade.

**Feeding**

Because the plants sit in water, the best way to feed is with fertilizing tablets pushed well into the soil.

**Temperature range**

Cool | Intermediate | Warm

The Umbrella Plant will tolerate most temperatures between 50°-70°F (10°-21°C), provided there are no extreme fluctuations. In winter the temperature shoud not go below 50°F (10°C).

**Seasonal care**

Winter | Spring | Summer | Autumn

Throughout the year, the Umbrella Plant needs a constant source of water to keep the roots saturated. If kept in dry, heated environments, the water level should be checked frequently. The plants can be propagated by division in spring.

**Watering**

Being aquatic, the Umbrella Plant must be grown in pots placed in a shallow pan of water.

**Soil**

The soil should have a high loam content to prevent it from disintegrating in the water. Pieces of charcoal can be added to the soil to keep it fresh .

# Dieffenbachia

Dumb Cane

**Dieffenbachias** are handsome, variegated foliage plants. They are slow-growing and compact. A number of species are available, varying in leaf patterning from well mottled as in *D. exotica* (above) to almost entirely creamy white, edged with green as in *D. camilla* (above right).

NO COLLECTION of tropical subjects could possibly be complete without some representation from the many dieffenbachias. Leaf coloring ranges from very dark green to almost pure white, with many plants bearing very beautiful mottled shades in between.

Some of the more majestic dieffenbachias may attain a height of 6ft (1.8m). Perhaps the most splendid of these plants is *D. amoena* 'Tropic Snow', which has large dark-green leaves with striking greenish-white mottling. *D. amoena* is similar in appearance but with slightly softer leaves, and the mottling in the center of the leaves is not so striking.

The more compact plants for the windowsill have seen many improvements in recent years, particularly in the *D. exotica* varieties. The latest in this strain is *D. camilla*, which has a green margin leaf with a center that is entirely creamy white. In contrast, *D. oerstedii* has leaves that are a blackish-green all over, except for the midrib running through the center of the leaf, which is a fine shade of ivory white.

DIEFFENBACHIA

**Light and position**

Place a dieffenbachia in a fairly light position, but shaded from direct sun.

**Temperature range**

Cool Intermediate Warm

A dieffenbachia will live in a temperature of 60°F (15°C) but would probably prefer nearer 70°F (21°C). In higher temperatures it is important to keep up a good level of humidity.

**Watering**

Moisture is required all year round, but the plant can be watered less in winter than in summer.

**Feeding**

While the dieffenbachia is producing new leaf growth, feed with every watering, using weak, liquid fertilizer.

**Seasonal care**

Winter Spring Summer Autumn

Propagation is most successful from stem cuttings, placed in peat and sand and kept moist and in a high temperature of 70°-75°F (21°-23°C).

**Soil**

Repot in summer, using an open potting mixture containing loam and peat.

# Dizygotheca

THIS GENUS comprises fragile-looking tropical plants that may reach 5-6ft (1.5-1.8m) in height, with a spread of 20in (51cm).

*Dizygotheca elegantissima* (also known as *Aralia elegantissima*) is a very slender plant. The leaves of older plants are almost black in color, but when young they are coppery-red. Very slender and delicate, they have an almost filigreed appearance. However, as the plant ages, the leaves gradually change color and become much coarser. Older leaves radiate in palmate fashion with stiff petioles that are attached to a solid woody stem. Overall, the plant presents a fine canopy of greenery.

This is not the easiest of plants to manage, but when properly cared for, it can be one of the most attractive of all foliage plants. It is an excellent plant to use in groupings.

To do well, *Dizygotheca elegantissma* needs light shade in temperatures of around 65°F (18°C). Be careful when watering that the soil does not remain soggy for long periods of time. Dizygothecas are slow-growing and need to be potted on only once every two years. Use a soil-based potting mixture for this.

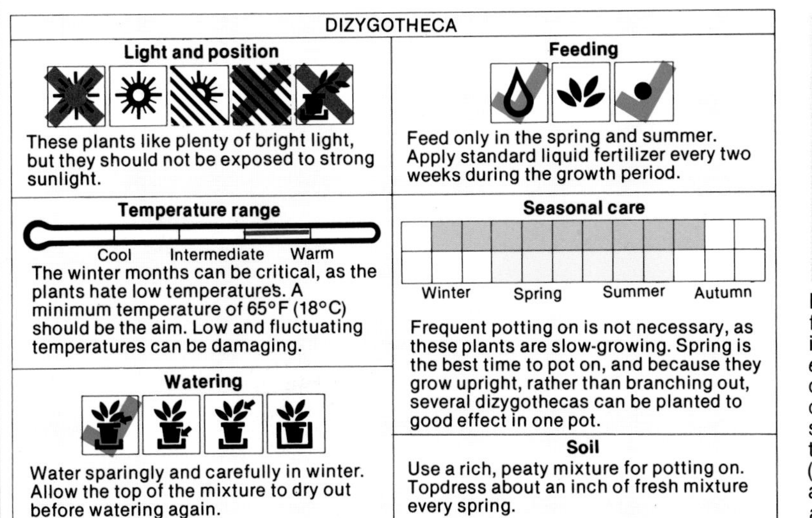

DIZYGOTHECA

**Light and position**

These plants like plenty of bright light, but they should not be exposed to strong sunlight.

**Temperature range**



The winter months can be critical, as the plants hate low temperatures. A minimum temperature of 65°F (18°C) should be the aim. Low and fluctuating temperatures can be damaging.

**Watering**

Water sparingly and carefully in winter. Allow the top of the mixture to dry out before watering again.

**Feeding**

Feed only in the spring and summer. Apply standard liquid fertilizer every two weeks during the growth period.

**Seasonal care**



Frequent potting on is not necessary, as these plants are slow-growing. Spring is the best time to pot on, and because they grow upright, rather than branching out, several dizygothecas can be planted to good effect in one pot.

**Soil**

Use a rich, peaty mixture for potting on. Topdress about an inch of fresh mixture every spring.

**Dizygothecas** are delicate-looking foliage plants, with leaves divided into radiating leaflets. *D. elegantissima* ( top) shows the characteristic very dark-green coloring of a healthy plant. This species has deeply toothed margins to the leaflets, giving the leaves (detail above) an almost filigreed appearance. Plants are slow-growing, and need careful management.

# Dracaena

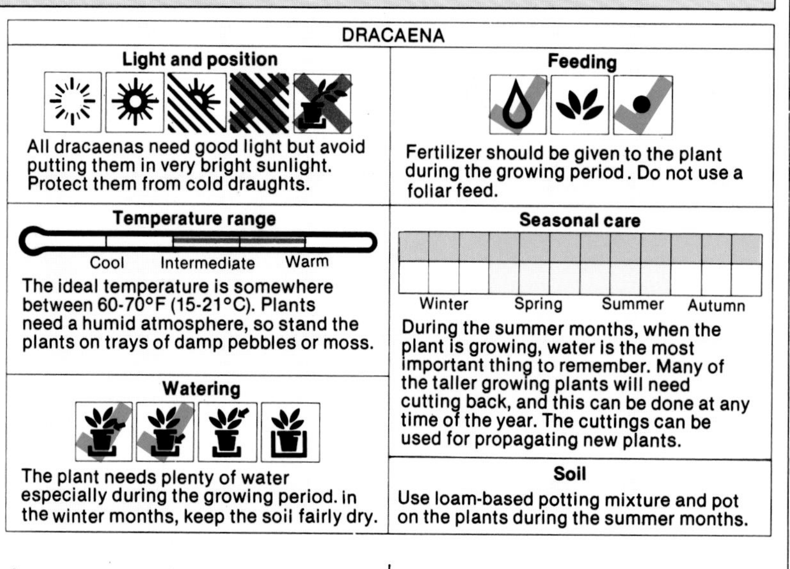


ONE OF THE MOST attractive dracaena is *D. terminalis,* whose bright-red color is matched by no other foliage plant.

*D. marginata* is perhaps the easiest dracaena to raise. It is an upright grower with dark-green leaves that have a dull-red margin. Stiff stems may be 10ft (3m) tall in time, but you can remove the top section of the plant at any time to check upward growth.

Also of upright habit, *Dracaena deremensis* has broad dark-green and dull-white variegated leaves that curl their bases around stiff, upright stems that attain a height of some 10ft (3m). This fine plant is not difficult to care for in a location that offers reasonable warmth and light. There are numerous cultivars. One of the finest is *Dracaena deremensis 'Souvenir de Schriever'*, which has leaves that are a rich golden-yellow, tinged with pale-green.

With broad recurving leaves that are mustard in color, *D. fragrans* is of bold habit and produces glossy rosettes of topmost leaves that are attractively set off against duller-colored lower foliage. There are several cultivars of this plant, with striped foliage of varying shades of color — from creamy white to bright yellow.

**Dracaenas** are a large and varied group of palm-like plants. *D. marginata* (below left) is one of the most upright species with a fountain of narrow arching leaves colored green with cream and red margins. *D. terminalis* (below) is of contrasting appearance with broader, stouter-looking leaves. Young plants of this species have green leaves, but they turn a brilliant red as they mature.

# Episcia

EPISCIAS ARE excellent flowering as well as foliage plants. Leaves are oval and hairy; flowers are brightly colored and dainty. Episcias are commonly called Carpet Plants because of their creeping stolons.

*Episcia cupreata* is a striking plant that can be encouraged to trail as it ages. The leaves are all shades of silver and pale-green, and the small flowers are an intense shade of red. The combination is very appealing when plants have developed into fairly large clumps — in hanging baskets, for example. This tender plant will not take kindly to lower temperatures, and needs a minimum temperature of 65°F (18°C).

*Episcia dianthiflora* is an easier plant to grow and should fall within the scope of almost all indoor-plant growers. Pale-green leaves are formed in rosettes and are attached to rapidly growing pendulous branches that are much enhanced when gleaming white flowers appear from within the foliage. The plant is commonly named Snowflake Flower because of the tubular flowers that are prettily frayed around their margin. These are fine hanging plants that grow and propagate easily.

**Episcias** are grown both for their attractive trailing foliage and for their small, often brightly colored flowers. *E. dianthiflora* (right) is the easiest species to manage, rewarding the grower with dainty white flowers with unusual frayed margins (above).

### EPISCIA

**Light and position**

Bright light is desirable, with a few hours of direct sunlight a day. If humidity is high, reduce the amount of direct sunlight.

**Feeding**

Apply liquid fertilizer at every watering. Do not give any feed in winter.

**Temperature**

Cool Intermediate Warm

These plants do best at temperatures between 60°F (16°C) and 85°F (29°C). They require high humidity and do very well in terrariums.

**Seasonal care**

Winter Spring Summer Autumn

Frequent potting on is not necessary — you need only repot when the roots appear to fill the pot.

**Watering**

Water as necessary throughout the growing period, but never stand the plant in water. In winter water sparingly.

**Soil**

Use a rich peaty mixture with some loam.

# Ferns

FERNS come from many different plant families and genera. Not all ferns are easy to care for indoors, but there is little doubt that their soft greenery makes them almost indispensable to the home gardener who is interested in creating attractive indoor plant arrangements.

Because ferns have comparatively weak root systems that may be damaged if fertilizer is given at strong dosage, plants should be fed with a weak solution of fertilizer each time the plants are watered. An alternative way of feeding ferns is to use a foliar feed in place of the more conventional fertilizers that are introduced to the plant via its roots.

Many ferns at the time of acquisition will be too large in proportion to the pot in which they are growing; this is due to the rapid growth that most ferns produce in a heated greenhouse environment. Inspect the plant immediately upon receipt, and repot it if necessary. Use a moist peaty mixture that will allow roots to move unrestricted.

Since the leaves of many fern plants are delicate and can easily be damaged by insecticides, no attempt should ever be made to clean the foliage in any way other than spraying with tepid water. For a good spring-cleaning, invert the pot, holding a hand over the soil. Immerse the foliage of the plant in water and gently move the plant around to get rid of dust.

### Adiantum

PROBABLY THE most popular fern is the adiantum, or Maidenhair Fern, which is available in numerous varieties. These plants produce neat mounds of soft greenery. Leaves are thin and triangular-shaped and are attached to stiff stems that are black in color.

### Cyrtomium

THIS GENUS includes *Cyrtomium falcatum*, whose glossy green foliage resembles that of holly — to such an extent that the plant has become known as the Holly Fern. *Cyrtomium falctum* is a very tough plant that will do well in situations that offer reasonable warmth, moisture and shade from direct sunlight. This and numerous other ferns can be put to good use as additional plants in pots whose occupants have lost much of their lower foliage.

**The adiantum's** (above) feathery foliage and hardy habit make it a favorite indoor plant.
**Bird's Nest Fern** (right) is another easy-care plant, and has shiny, upward-growing fronds.

### Nephrolepsis

NEPHROLEPSIS are particularly good ferns for decorating one's home or office. Plants produce bold clumps of greenery and are seen to best advantage when grown in hanging baskets. Depending upon the size of the container, individual fronds will vary in length from 10in (25cm) to about 30in (76cm). The various forms of *Nephrolepsis exaltata* are particularly suitable when bolder displays are required.

### Platycerium

THE MORE COMMON name for *Platycerium alcicorne* is the Stag's Horn Fern. The plant produces main fronds — in shape similar to the horns of a stag — and what are known as anchor fronds. In the wild, these anchors wrap themselves around trees in order to support the plant. Indoors, plants will grow in a more natural fashion if you wrap sphagnum moss around the root ball of the plant and affix plants to a section of cork bark. Water by submerging the plant and its bark anchorage until it has had a thorough soaking.

**The illustrations** on this page show the enormous variety of ferms that exist. The pellaea (top) is bushy with fronds of button-like pinnae. The cyrtomium (middle) has fronds resembling holly and, unusually, can stand dry air and draughts. Platycerium (bottom) is the most distinctive of all ferns. Known as the Stag's Horn Fern, it produces broad anchor fronds from which emerge spore-producing main fronds shaped liked stag's antlers.

**Pteris** (above) has many species all with intricate lacy fronds. Shown here is *P. cretica albolineata*, with attractive, variegated fronds. **Nephrolepsis** (left) has long, elegant fronds in a dense clump. Because of their hanging growth, these plants are particularly suitable for decorative use.

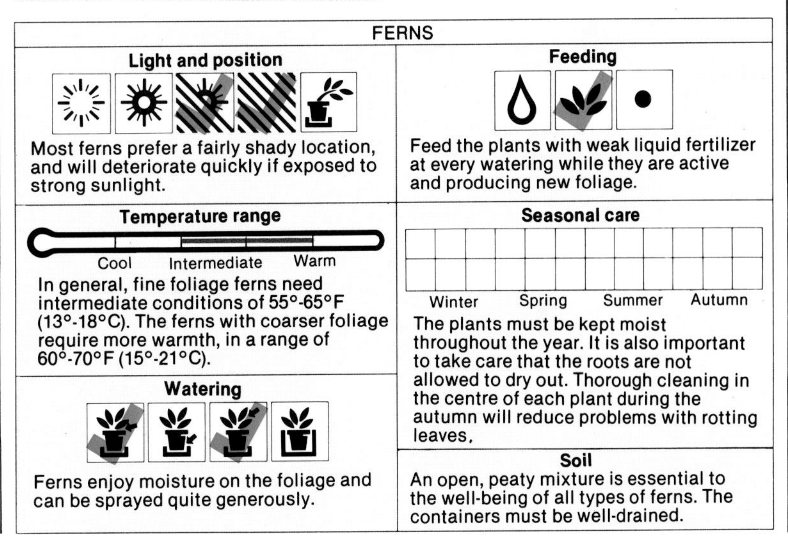

FERNS

**Light and position**

Most ferns prefer a fairly shady location, and will deteriorate quickly if exposed to strong sunlight.

**Feeding**

Feed the plants with weak liquid fertilizer at every watering while they are active and producing new foliage.

**Temperature range**

Cool Intermediate Warm

In general, fine foliage ferns need intermediate conditions of 55°-65°F (13°-18°C). The ferns with coarser foliage require more warmth, in a range of 60°-70°F (15°-21°C).

**Seasonal care**

Winter Spring Summer Autumn

The plants must be kept moist throughout the year. It is also important to take care that the roots are not allowed to dry out. Thorough cleaning in the centre of each plant during the autumn will reduce problems with rotting leaves.

**Watering**

Ferns enjoy moisture on the foliage and can be sprayed quite generously.

**Soil**

An open, peaty mixture is essential to the well-being of all types of ferns. The containers must be well-drained.

# Ficus

THIS GENUS includes over 800 species. A number of these are grown indoors, where they are prized for their evergreen foliage. Probably the best-known houseplant in the genus is the long-established Rubber Plant, but there are many other, less common species that are no more difficult to grow.

Ficus plants need good light — but provide plants with protection from direct sunlight — and copious watering. Always pour enough water onto the surface of the soil for you to see surplus water drain through the holes in the bottom of the pot. Let the soil dry out to a reasonable degree before giving further water. The drying-out period will aerate the soil, maintaining roots in much better condition.

Ficus plants have vigorous root systems and should usually be fed with a good fertilizer from the moment they are acquired. Water immediately upon receipt, and remove plants from their pots to inspect root development. If there is a tight mass of roots, do not delay in transferring the plant to a slightly larger container. Pot on, using a loam-based potting mixture.

All ficus plants with naturally glossy leaves will benefit from having their foliage cleaned periodically with a water-moistened sponge. Chemical leaf cleaners will keep leaves shiny, but excessive use will damage plants.

Pests are not a great problem, but some of the ficus species are susceptible to scale insects. These can be eradicated by using one of the many insecticides that are available, or by washing the plant clean with a firm sponge. When washing the plant, you must apply the sponge with some pressure to remove the scales from their anchorages.

*Ficus benjamina*, which is commonly referred to as the Weeping Fig, is one of the best ficus plants for indoor use. Leaves are glossy and massed on pendulous branches. *Ficus benjamina* 'Hawaii' is a hybrid of *Ficus benjamina*. It is a very attractive plant with brightly variegated foliage, which weeps in spectacular fashion on more mature plants. Though less weeping in habit, the variety *F. benjamina* 'Golden Princess' is also a fine plant that is more erect in habit and has foliage that is a little less colorful than *F. b.* 'Hawaii'.

Aptly given the common name of Fiddle Leaf Fig on account of the large green leaves that have the shape of a violin body, *F. lyrata* is a glossy leaved plant that is seen at its best when there is ample space for its spreading branches. The leaves have prominent yellow veins and are attached to brown woody stems, which will in time attain a height of some 10ft (3m) when roots are confined to pots.

The Creeping Fig, *F. pumila*, has small rounded leaves that are dark-green in color and are attached to wiry stems that will climb or trail. Although leaves are small, this is a fine plant for growing on a wall trellis.

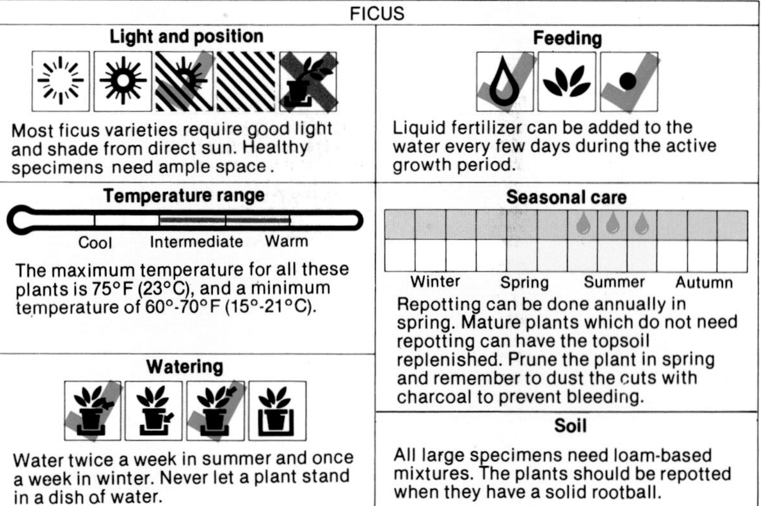

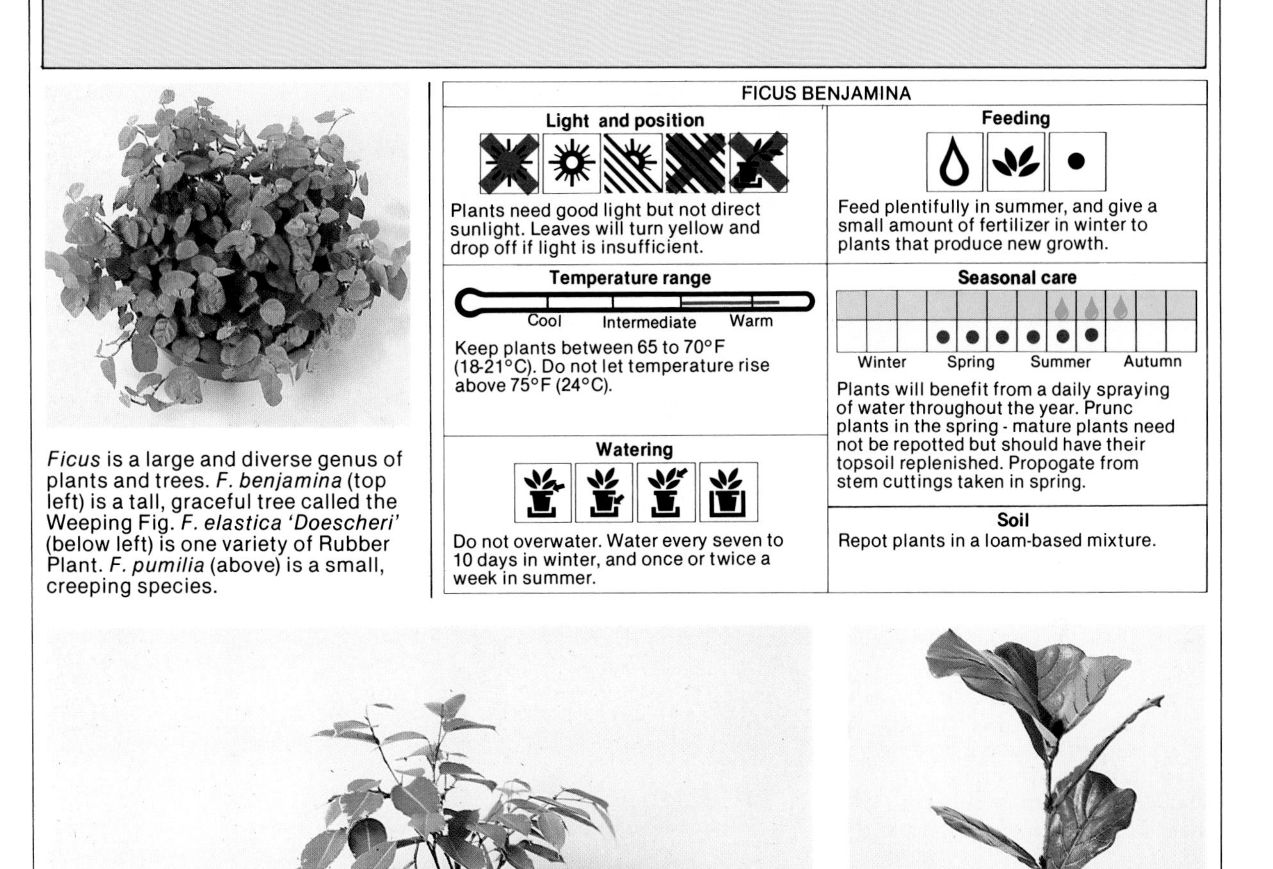

*Ficus* is a large and diverse genus of plants and trees. *F. benjamina* (top left) is a tall, graceful tree called the Weeping Fig. *F. elastica 'Doescheri'* (below left) is one variety of Rubber Plant. *F. pumilia* (above) is a small, creeping species.

## FICUS BENJAMINA

**Light and position**

Plants need good light but not direct sunlight. Leaves will turn yellow and drop off if light is insufficient.

**Feeding**

Feed plentifully in summer, and give a small amount of fertilizer in winter to plants that produce new growth.

**Temperature range**

Cool Intermediate Warm

Keep plants between 65 to 70°F (18-21°C). Do not let temperature rise above 75°F (24°C).

**Seasonal care**

Winter Spring Summer Autumn

Plants will benefit from a daily spraying of water throughout the year. Prunc plants in the spring - mature plants need not be repotted but should have their topsoil replenished. Propogate from stem cuttings taken in spring.

**Watering**

Do not overwater. Water every seven to 10 days in winter, and once or twice a week in summer.

**Soil**

Repot plants in a loam-based mixture.

**Ficus benjamina 'Golden Princess'** (left) is a less weeping variety than *F. benjamina*, with attractive,variegated foliage. The common name of *F. lyrata* (above) is the Fiddle Leaf Fig, which is easily understood by looking at its violin-shaped leaves (detail below).

# Fittonia

FITTONIAS ARE creeping plants indigenous to tropical rain forests. Leaves are small, oval, with fine colored veins. Plants produce small yellow flowers but these seldom bloom indoors.

There are perhaps three species one can find in a good plant shop, and all of them are compact and low-growing. All of them can be a problem indoors if the temperature is inadequate; 65°F (18°C) and above is essential. Roots should be kept moist but not wet.

The paper-thin leaves of *F. verschaffeltii* have a base color of olive green, but what makes the plant so attractive is the multitude of red veins, which makes the leaves seem entirely red in color. Shaded, moist conditions are required, and weak feed only. When potting on, use peaty soil and shallow pots, not pots of full depth.

Very similar in habit and requirements to *F. verschaffeltii* is *F. argyroneura*, which has attractive veined leaves in silver. More popular on account of its neat habit and slightly easier culture is *F. argyroneura Nana*, a lovely plant for bottle gardens and confined moist areas. It is troublesome in winter if temperatures fall too low, but it is very easy to propagate and pests are not a problem.

**This plant** (above) illustrates the low, creeping growth typical of all fittonias. Because of their spreading habit, fittonias appear to advantage when growing against a background of taller plants in a bottlegarden.

**Fittonias** are small-leaved foliage plants. The thin green leaves of *F. verschaffeltii* (above) appear to have a net of red drawn over them, as the leaf veins are colored red. The leaves of *F. argyroneura* (right) are veined in silver, but apart from this, the two species are very similar in their appearance and requirements.

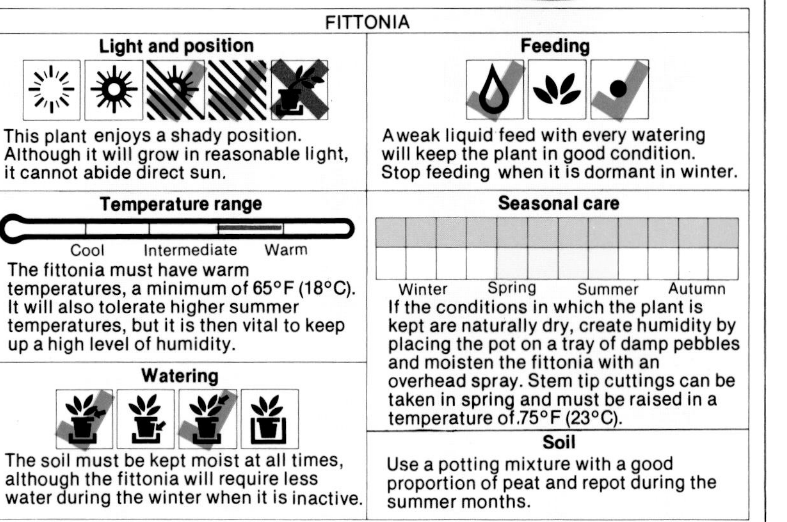

FITTONIA

**Light and position**

This plant enjoys a shady position. Although it will grow in reasonable light, it cannot abide direct sun.

**Feeding**

A weak liquid feed with every watering will keep the plant in good condition. Stop feeding when it is dormant in winter.

**Temperature range**

Cool Intermediate Warm

The fittonia must have warm temperatures, a minimum of 65°F (18°C). It will also tolerate higher summer temperatures, but it is then vital to keep up a high level of humidity.

**Seasonal care**

Winter Spring Summer Autumn

If the conditions in which the plant is kept are naturally dry, create humidity by placing the pot on a tray of damp pebbles and moisten the fittonia with an overhead spray. Stem tip cuttings can be taken in spring and must be raised in a temperature of 75°F (23°C).

**Watering**

The soil must be kept moist at all times, although the fittonia will require less water during the winter when it is inactive.

**Soil**

Use a potting mixture with a good proportion of peat and repot during the summer months.

# Heptapleurum

Parasol Plant
Green Rays

HEPTAPLEURUMS WERE introduced only in the last decade, but there are now many variations on the original *H. arboricola*. Plants grow as tall as 6ft (1.8m), but can become bushy if encouraged. Leaves have seven or more leaflets radiating from the tips of the long stalks. Heptapleurums are very similar to scheffleras and are often sold under that name.

*H. arboricola variegata* has bright-yellow leaves splashed with green and forms into a neat, rounded bush if growing tips are periodically removed. *H. arboricola* 'Capello' is of more upright habit and has pale-cream and green leaves.

There are also variations on the purely green forms of *H. arboricola* that have attractive rounded leaves. *H. a.* 'Geisha Girl' has slender green stems with shiny dark-green leaves. *H. a.* 'Hong Kong' has glossy green leaves but is a more compact plant.

Heptapleurums are easily grown from cuttings. New plants can also be grown from single leaves with a piece of stem attached.

**Hepatapleurums** are relative newcomers to indoor cultivation. The tall *H. arboricola*, or Parasol Plant (right) is the original species, with its glossy green leaves. *H. arboricola variegata* (above) is a bushier plant,with yellow leaves splashed with green.

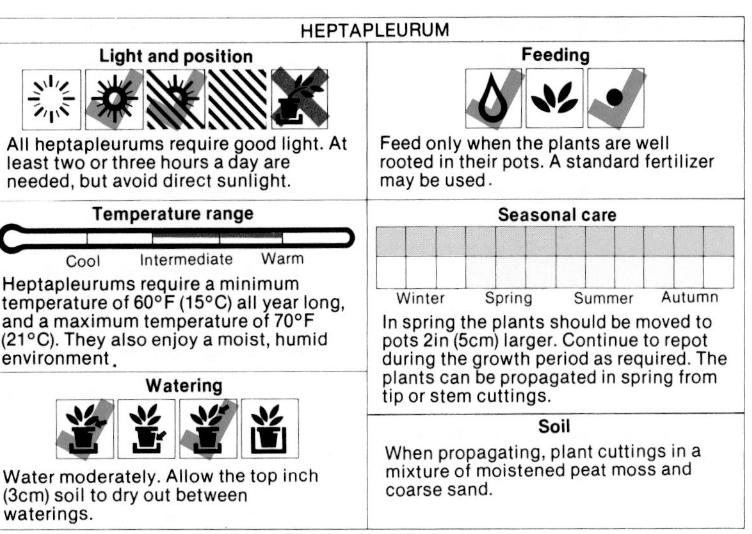

HEPTAPLEURUM

**Light and position**

All heptapleurums require good light. At least two or three hours a day are needed, but avoid direct sunlight.

**Feeding**

Feed only when the plants are well rooted in their pots. A standard fertilizer may be used.

**Temperature range**

Cool Intermediate Warm

Heptapleurums require a minimum temperature of 60°F (15°C) all year long, and a maximum temperature of 70°F (21°C). They also enjoy a moist, humid environment.

**Seasonal care**

Winter Spring Summer Autumn

In spring the plants should be moved to pots 2in (5cm) larger. Continue to repot during the growth period as required. The plants can be propagated in spring from tip or stem cuttings.

**Watering**

Water moderately. Allow the top inch (3cm) soil to dry out between waterings.

**Soil**

When propagating, plant cuttings in a mixture of moistened peat moss and coarse sand.

# Hibiscus

**Hibiscus** are shrubby flowering plants with enormous trumpet-shaped flowers with protruding stamens. *H. rosa-sinensis* (above) is the main species grown indoors. Cultivars have been developed with double or single flowers in a wide range of brilliant colors, such as the orange and red-flowered plants shown above. Each new flower only lasts for about a day, but new buds appear all the time during the flowering season.

HIBISCUS ARE GROWN for their bright funnel-shaped flowers. These come in many colours, and there are single and double forms. Individual flowers last for little more than 24 hours before they fade and die, but in light and sunny locations there is a continiual supply of fresh buds followed by flowers.

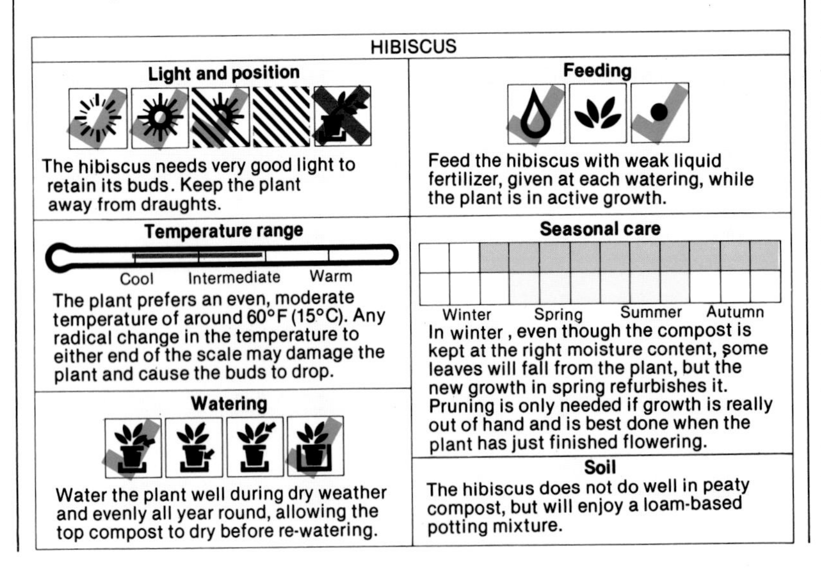


*Hibiscus rosa-sinensis* is the species usually grown indoors. It has gained steadily in popularity and is now an important flowering plant for the middle months of the year. Much of the species' new-found popularity has been due to the selection of more appealing varieties with dark–green foliage and brightly colored flowers. However, some of its success is also owing to the introduction of growth-retarding chemicals that are now available to the commercial grower. When applied in correct dosage, these growth depressants prevent plants stretching to their full length. The result is plants that have many more leaves on short stems, as opposed to fewer leaves on longer stems.

Hibiscus are resilient plants. Winter temperature can drop to 50°F (10°C) as long as the soil is kept on the dry side. In spring, plants may be potted on for the new season in a loam-based potting mixture.

# Hoya

HOYAS ARE naturally climbing plants that twist and twine around everything in sight. Their common name is Wax Flowers because of the waxy star-shaped flowers that bloom in clusters.

Hoyas are very easy plants to manage. They need good light and careful watering, especially in winter when growth is less active. Possibly the greatest difficulty is keeping the twisting branches under control.

The two species grown indoors are *Hoya bella* and *Hoya carnosa*. *Hoya bella* has pale to dark-green leaves that are attached to wiry stems that fan out almost horizontally from the container in which it is growing. The branches do not hang pendulously as one would expect from a hanging plant, because the flower clusters form on the underside of the branches. With the branches fanning out as they do, the exquisite waxy flower clusters are seen to perfection.

*H. carnosa* has dark-green leaves and white to pale-pink flowers that bloom in clusters of 10 to 30. There are two variegated-leaved cultivars: *H. c.* 'Exotica' and *H. c.* 'Variegata'.

**Hoyas** are pretty climbing plants with sweet-smelling, star-shaped waxy flowers. They are vigorous growers and even the dwarf species *H. bella* (top) needs care to keep its fanning branches under control. The flower clusters of *H. bella* (above left) hang from the underside of branches, making this a plant to suspend at head level so that its beauty and fragrance can be fully appreciated. *H. carnosa variegata* (above) is a variety with pink-edged leaves.

HOYA

**Light and position**

Three to four hours of sunlight a day is desirable for healthy growth, but shade the plant from the hot midday sun.

**Feeding**

During active growth, feed with a liquid fertilizer once every two weeks.

**Temperature range**

Cool Intermediate Warm

Keep these plants at room temperature. The temperature should not drop below 55°F (13°C) at any time. In spring and summer maintain a humid atmosphere.

**Seasonal care**

Winter Spring Summer Autumn

Hoyas in pots can be potted on each spring, as necessary. Trailing hoyas need only be moved once very two years.

**Watering**

Water moderately during the growth period. Use a spray-mist regularly, except when the plant is in bloom.

**Soil**

Use a peaty mixture with some loam added.

# Jacobinea

THIS GENUS includes about 300 species, but only two are commonly grown indoors. Stems and branches are soft and woody; leaves are somewhat coarse in their appearance. Jacobineas' chief attraction is the appealing tubular flowers they produce.

*Jacobinea carnea*, a species which also masquerades under the splendid name of *Justicia magnifica*, is a shrubby, upright plant with soft gray-green leaves that are red on their undersides. Mature plants will produce a wealth of rose-colored bracts at the top of the several stems that develop as the plant ages.

*Jacobinea pauciflora* grows to approximately 18in (45cm) in height and bears scarlet flowers with yellow tips. This plant can be placed out of doors during the summer, but should be moved inside when weather starts to deteriorate.

Jacobineas need moist, humid, warm conditions. The temperature should be a minimum 65°F (18°C), and plants should be placed in the light shade. Water and feed freely in summer, and pot on into loam-based houseplant soil.

Plants need plenty of room in which to grow and will generally do best when growing in pots about 8in (20cm) in diameter. Jacobineas become very straggly-looking unless properly pruned, and are usually discarded after one or two years. The top sections of stronger stems may be used for propagating new plants in spring. Removing the growing tops will also encourage plants to bush out and become more compact.

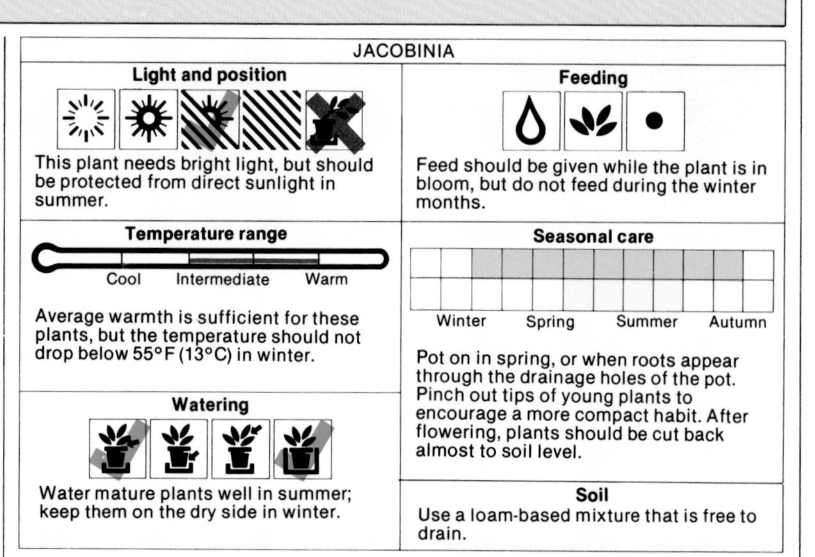

**Jacobineas** are shrubby plants with attractive tubular flowers. *J. carnea* (right) is one of two species commonly grown as houseplants. Like *J. pauciflora*, it is usually discarded when it becomes straggly.

# Maranta

Prayer Plant

MARANTAS ARE low-growing plants with the common name of Prayer Plant, because as daylight fades, leaves close together like hands in prayer. *M. leuconeura* is the only species grown indoors, but there are several varieties of it.

*M. leuconeura erythroneura* has a flat habit of growth, but can be encouraged to produce longer and more erect stems if the plant is provided with a supporting cane to which developing branches can be tied. Leaf coloring is a velvety olive-green with red veins; the underside is dull red. Flowers are small, insignificant and die off almost as soon as they appear, so their removal will tend to improve the appearance of the plant. Despite the exotic coloring of the foliage, this is one of the easier plants to care for, needing little more than average conditions and care.

*M. leuconeura kerchoevana* has pale-green leaves well-endowed with central spots, giving the plant the common name of Rabbit's Tracks. This is another easy plant to raise if protected from bright light.

**Marantas** are foliage plants with leaves beautifully marked with distinctive patterns and colors. *M. leuconeura 'Erythrophylla'* (above right) has red-veined dark-green leaves with lighter patches. The leaves of all varieties are rolled up when young.

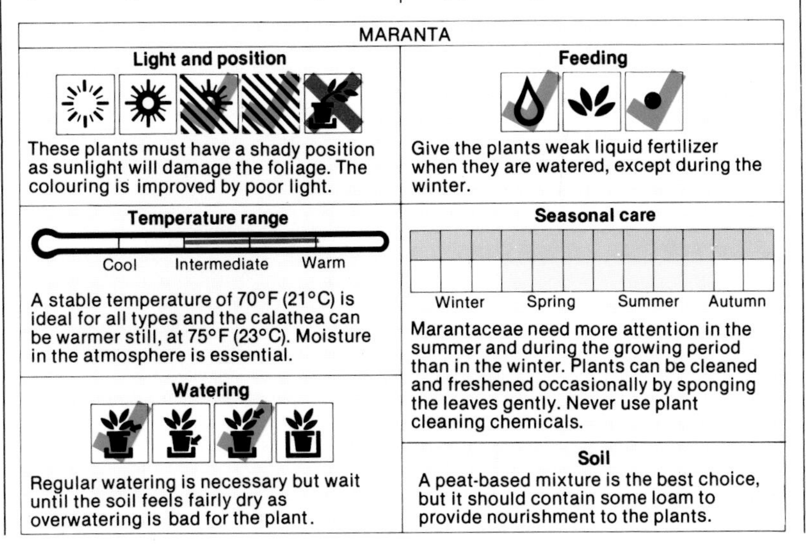

ARACEAE

# Monstera

Swiss Cheese Plant
Hurricane Plant
Mexican Breadfruit Plant

THIS GENUS includes *Monstera deliciosa*, one of the best known species of the purely foliage houseplants, having distinctive serrated green leaves on stout stems. It is an imposing plant once it has a few growing years behind it, and because it is easy to care for, it is found in all sorts of places.

The monstera is commonly called the Swiss Cheese Plant because of the holes that will in time develop in the leaves. An interesting feature of the plant is its ability to produce masses of aerial roots along its main stems. In natural jungle habitat, these roots serve a dual purpose. They wrap themselves around another tree for support and anchor the monstera, and they also provide nourishment for the plant, which may have its head up among the topmost trees. In ideal situations, these roots will find their way into a stream or water-hole, providing the plant with an ample supply of moisture. Obviously monsteras are not likely to find a water-hole in your living room, so tie roots neatly to the stem of the plant and direct them into the soil when they are of sufficient length. In this way they will provide the plant with additional moisture.

Monsteras that are well-grown change character and develop much larger leaves as they age. They also flower when they reach a reasonable age, and the flower may well be followed by the hard green monstera fruits. These are totally inedible until the fruit has ripened to the extent whereby it is pulpy and just beginning to disintegrate. Plants are generally six to eight years old before they ever develop fruits.

**Monsteras** have distinctive large leathery leaves which develop holes and deep indentations with age, so giving rise to the common name of Swiss Cheese Plant. *M. deliciosa* (above right) can grow to 8ft (2.5m).

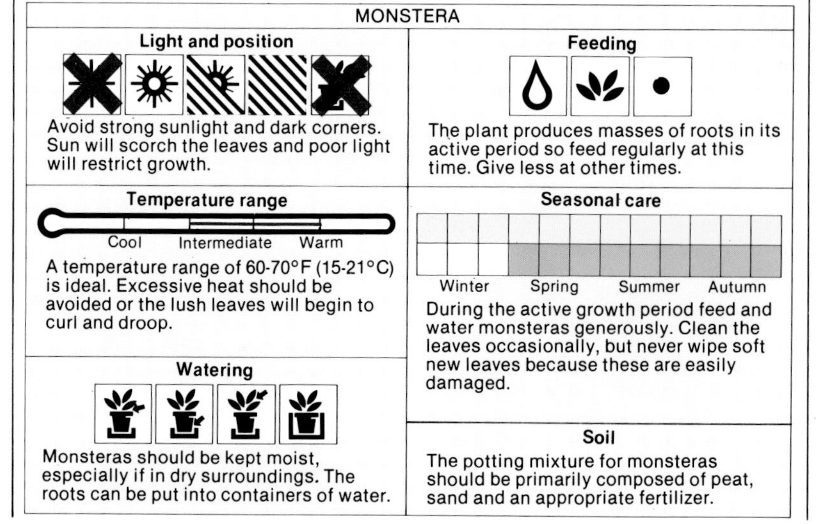

MONSTERA

**Light and position**

Avoid strong sunlight and dark corners. Sun will scorch the leaves and poor light will restrict growth.

**Temperature range**



A temperature range of 60-70°F (15-21°C) is ideal. Excessive heat should be avoided or the lush leaves will begin to curl and droop.

**Watering**

Monsteras should be kept moist, especially if in dry surroundings. The roots can be put into containers of water.

**Feeding**

The plant produces masses of roots in its active period so feed regularly at this time. Give less at other times.

**Seasonal care**



During the active growth period feed and water monsteras generously. Clean the leaves occasionally, but never wipe soft new leaves because these are easily damaged.

**Soil**

The potting mixture for monsteras should be primarily composed of peat, sand and an appropriate fertilizer.

Banana Plant

# Musa

IN THE GENUS *Musa* are 35 species of evergreen perennials, including several exotic banana plants. Of these, *Musa cavendishii* is the most suitable for indoor culture, being smaller and less vigorous. Plants are upright and attain a height of 5ft (1.5m) in time, developing stout trunks of have a brownish-yellow color. Leaves are bright-green, produced three and four at a time. Plants will naturally shed lower leaves as new top leaves are produced.

*Musa cavendishii* needs sufficient space for spreading leaves to develop and a light but not sunny position. The temperature should be a minimum of 60°F (16°C), and the soil should be kept moist at all times. While in active growth, plants will need regular feeding. Mist the leaves daily to produce adequate humidity.

Although it is optimistic to expect *Musa cavendishii* to produce fruit indoors, plants will occasionally do so in a heated greenhouse when high humidity can be maintained. The main stem will die down, but plants will almost invariably produce new shoots at the base. These will go on to form new plants.

It is possible to successsfully germinate seed from *Musa cavendishii* and other banana plants, but bear in mind that these are large plants; keep only one seedling if several should germinate. Red spider mites sometimes trouble these plants.

**Musa cavendishii** (above right) has only recently been grown as a houseplant. Yellowing leaves (above) at the base of the plant need nct cause concern, as these older leaves are shed naturally.

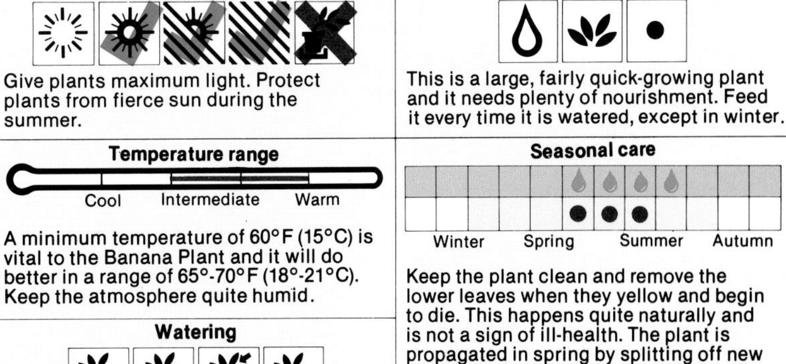

MUSA

**Light and position**

Give plants maximum light. Protect plants from fierce sun during the summer.

**Feeding**

This is a large, fairly quick-growing plant and it needs plenty of nourishment. Feed it every time it is watered, except in winter.

**Temperature range**



A minimum temperature of 60°F (15°C) is vital to the Banana Plant and it will do better in a range of 65°-70°F (18°-21°C). Keep the atmosphere quite humid.

**Seasonal care**



Keep the plant clean and remove the lower leaves when they yellow and begin to die. This happens quite naturally and is not a sign of ill-health. The plant is propagated in spring by splitting off new suckers and potting them on separately.

**Watering**

The Banana Plant needs plenty of water, but should not be left to stand in a full saucer.

**Soil**

Pot on a plant in loam-based mixture at any time during spring or summer if it seems necessary.

# Palms

PALMS ARE tropical plants with tall unbranched trunks topped by a crown of fan-shaped fronds. The palm family is very large, consisting of more than 200 genera and almost 3,000 species. Because of their strong growth and somewhat coarse foliage and stems, only a limited number, however, are suitable, for indoor use. But if growing space is adequate, palms are not difficult plants to raise.

Palms need good light but not bright sun. They should be kept moist at all times, but water more sparingly in winter. Do not allow palms to stand in water.

A note of warning: in spite of their tough appearance, many palms are sensitive to chemicals added to their foliage, and chemicals applied to plants that are exposed to bright sunlight can be especially harmful.

The Fishtail Palm, *Caryota urens*, is a plant that must have ample headroom. Strong spears of growth reach upwards before unfolding to expose coarse leaves that have a V-shape that resembles the tail of a fish — hence the common name. As plants mature, they develop a bulbous base to their main stems.

*Neanthe bella* (also called *Chaemodora elegans*), is one of the neatest and most compact of the palms used for indoor decoration. This plant is employed so

**Palms** are an extremely large family of plants, but only a few of them are suitable for growing indoors.Two of these are *Neanthe bella* (above) and *Cocos nucifera* (below). Probably the most popular palm of all is *Howea forsteriana* (left), an elegant plant with fans of arching leaflets.

often for this purpose, it has the common name of Parlour Palm. *Neanthe bella* has short, branching leaves and attains a maximum height of 3-4ft (91cm-1.2m) when grown indoors. Plants are usually either sold as seedlings a few inches tall for planting in bottle gardens, or as bolder plants some 3ft (91)cm tall with several plants grouped in the container.

*Chrysalidocarpus lutescens* is sometimes called *Areca lutescens*. This palm appears at its best when several young plants have been placed in the pot initially so that clustered orange-yellow stems are seen to good effect when plants mature. The foliage is generally soft, and since plants retain modest proportions they are fine for rooms that offer limited space for spreading leaves.

The Coconut Palm, *Cocos nucifera*, is a majestic, free-growing tree. Plants grown indoors have the actual coconut fruit buried in the pot. Roots develop, and growth then appears from the end of the large fibrous-covered coconut.

The most popular palm for indoor decoration the world over is undoubtedly the Paradise Palm, a plant which masquerades under a dual name — *Howea forsteriana* being more correct, but *Kentia forsteriana* being much more popular. This elegant palm has dark-green stems and upright dark-green fronds and attains a height of 15-20ft (4.5-6m) under optimum conditions.

Phoenix palms have stiff foliage that radiates from a central trunk. *P. canariensis* develops into a substantial plant that is only suited to more isolated positions where it can be out of the way of passersby; with finer foliage that is softer and more suited to domestic situations, *P. roebelenii* is a splendid plant if given proper care.

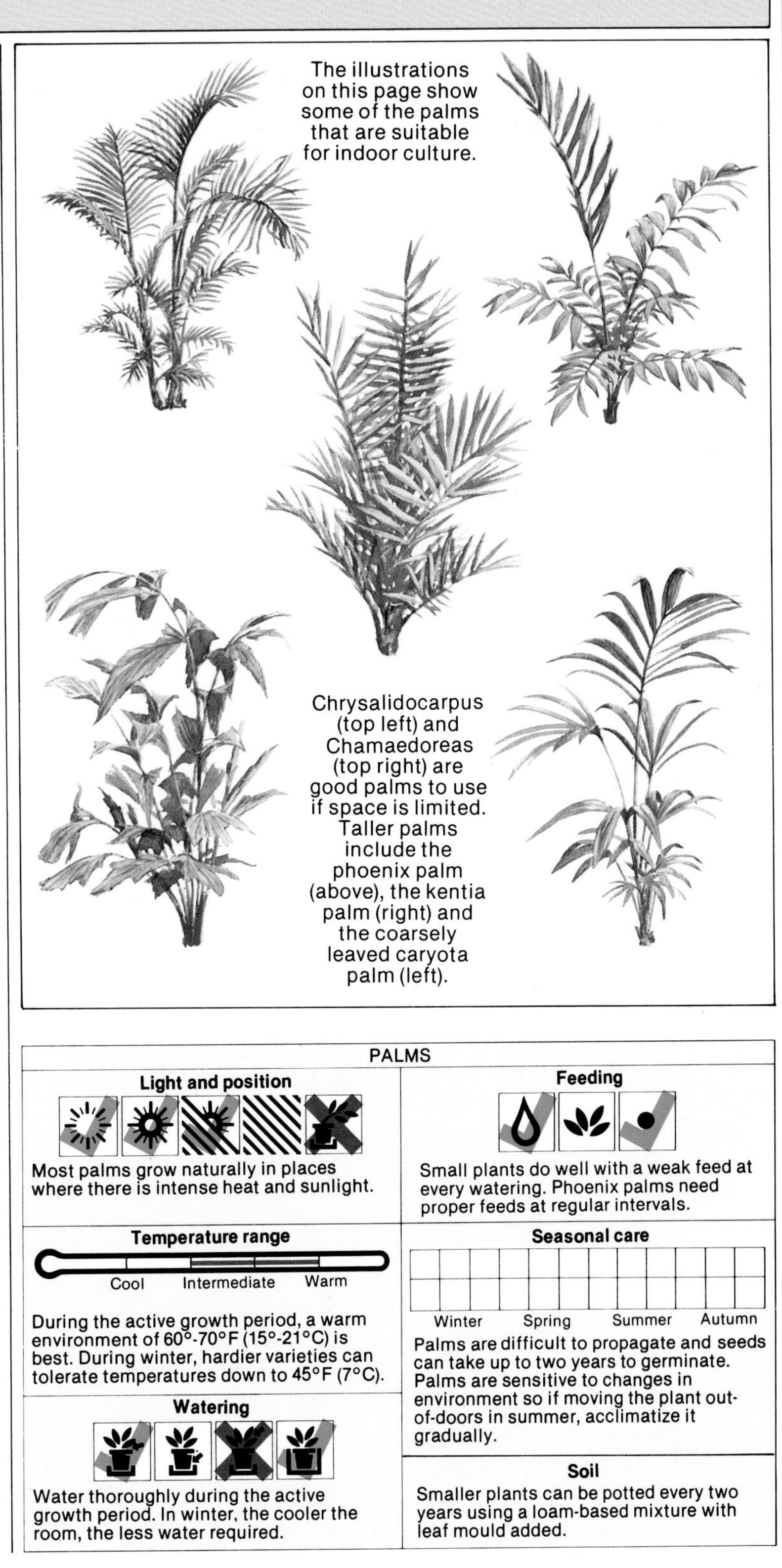


The illustrations on this page show some of the palms that are suitable for indoor culture.

Chrysalidocarpus (top left) and Chamaedoreas (top right) are good palms to use if space is limited. Taller palms include the phoenix palm (above), the kentia palm (right) and the coarsely leaved caryota palm (left).

PANDANACEAE

# Pandanus

Screw Pine

PANDANUS LEAVES are clearly designed to protect the plant from interference. They are spined along their margins, viciously so on the leaves' undersides. Because of their spiteful nature, all plants in the *Pandanus* genus should be treated with respect and placed well out of reach. Leaves have no petiole and radiate in splendid fashion from a short central trunk. These are tough plants that will tolerate almost everything except wet, cold conditions.

Two species of pandanus are sold as houseplants. Both are grown purely for their foliage; there is no possibility of them flowering in room conditions.

*Pandanus veitchii* is the more compact species, with leaves that are white and green in color. Plants grow 3-4ft (91cm-1.2m) tall with a similar spread when growing in 7in (18cm) and upwards pots.

*Pandanus baptise* is a more magnificent plant. Foliage is bright golden-yellow in color. The plant attains a height of 6ft (1.9m) with a similar spread. However, plants of such magnitude would be at least 10 years old and growing in ideal conditions.

Plants require the lightest possible location indoors, and it will help during the winter months if they can be placed under an artificial light during the evening. When potting, use a rich potting mixture and pot plants fairly firmly. Although plants must be kept on the moist side in spring and summer, it is important that they not get too wet during the winter months.

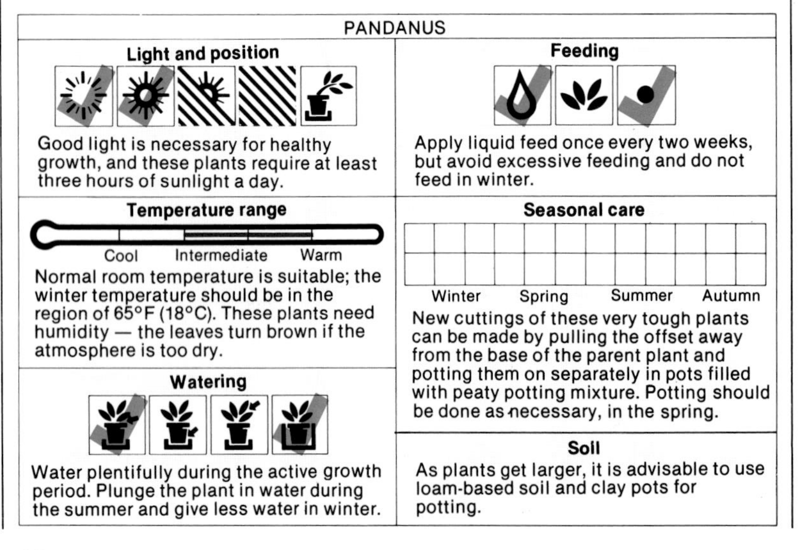


**Pandanus** plants have long arching leaves with sharp spines. *P. baptise* (above) is a large,spreading plant with golden-yellow leaves spiraling out from the central trunk. *P. veitchii* (below) is a smaller plant with striped leaves.

# Philodendron

THERE ARE numerous species of philodendrons grown as houseplants. Although some produce reasonably colorful spathe flowers, or inflorescences, philodendrons are principally prized for their bold and attractive foliage.

*Philodendron bipinatifidum* has large-fingered leaves attached to very strong petioles that radiate from a short trunk in the center of the plant. Not so spectacular when young, this is one of the most majestic of all foliage plants and in time may attain a height of 8ft (2.4m), but by then the diameter of the plant will be in the region of 12ft (3.6m) and it will not be easy to accommodate.

There are a number of philodendrons that are almost in the rarity class, something for the connoisseur, and among these is the species *P. wendlandii*, which produces pale-green leaves in the shape of a shuttlecock at soil-level. For this plant to do well, temperatures should be in the region of 70°F (21°C).

Some of the newer varieties of philodendron have *P. hastatum* in their breeding. *P. hastatum*, commonly called Elephant's Ears, has pale-green arrow-shaped leaves on strong upright stems and may attain a height of some 15ft (4.6m) if its roots are confined in a large pot and grown in the sheltered confines of the botanic garden greenhouse. However, plants are of more modest size if cared for indoors. The new varieties are very similar in habit, but they have attractive leaf coloring that ranges from almost wine red in *P.* 'Burgundy' to a blackish-red in *P.* 'Red Emerald' to a passable rusty yellow in *P.* 'Painted Lady'. Most varieties are reasonably easy to care for, with the exception of *P.* 'Painted Lady', which is a very indifferent grower, even in the heated greenhouse.

**Philodendrons** are popular foliage plants. Some, such as the easily cultivated *P. scandens* (left), are climbers. Others, such as *P. hastatum*, with its arrow-shaped leaves (detail below) and its numerous varieties including *'Red Emerald'* (above), are upright.

PHILODENDRON

**Light and position**

All philodendrons must be given locations that will provide them with protection from direct sunlight.

**Feeding**

The larger the plant the stronger and more frequent feeds it will require.

**Temperature range**

Cool Intermediate Warm

Philodendrons should not suffer a drop in temperature below 55°F (13°C). The maximum summer temperature at which they are comfortable is 75°F (21°C).

**Seasonal care**

Winter Spring Summer Autumn

These are plants for all seasons but they should be kept out of colder areas at all times. They have a short mid-winter rest period during which time they should have just enough water to prevent the soil from drying out. Water in moderation for the rest of the year.

**Watering**

Water sparingly. In winter, water just enough to keep the soil from drying out completely.

**Soil**

Use a peat-based mixture with some loam and pot on only when the roots completely fill the pot.

# Pleomele

ONE OF THE FINEST of all foliage plants is *Pleomele reflexa variegata*. Commonly called Song of India, it produces short leaves that are congested on slightly twisting stems. The leaves are medium-green when young but turn a rich golden-yellow as the plant ages. *Pleomele reflexa* is the green-leaved form. It is less branching in habit and generally less attractive.

Both *Pleomele reflexa* and *P. r. variegata* are very slow-growing and will take upwards of 10 years to develop into attractive branching specimens 5ft (1.5m) tall. In early stages of growth, plants will grow on a single stem but will branch naturally as they age.

*P. r. variegata* needs a light location in order to retain the bright coloring of the foliage. Plants require a minimum temperature of 65°F (18°C) and should be fed regularly during the summer. If soil is wet for long periods of time, plants will grow poorly and shed leaves. Pot on using a loam-based soil in early spring. Plants need free-draining soil, so place a few pieces of broken clay flowerpot in the base of the container prior to introducing the potting medium.

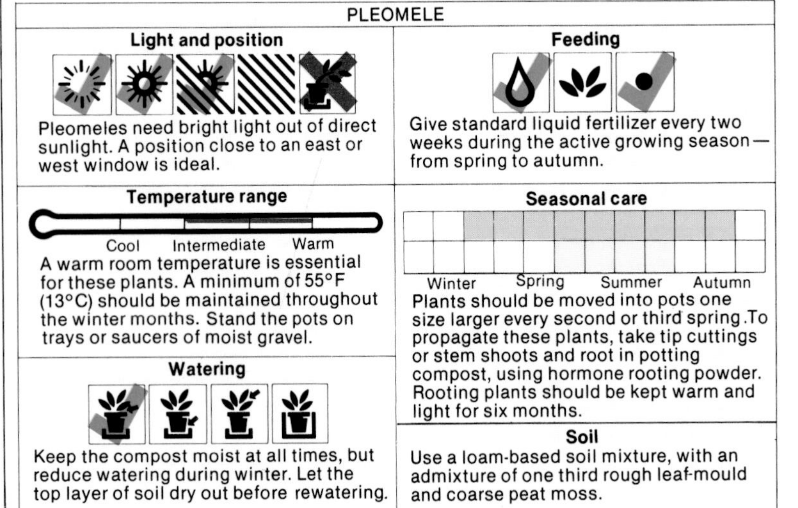

PLEOMELE

**Light and position**

Pleomeles need bright light out of direct sunlight. A position close to an east or west window is ideal.

**Feeding**

Give standard liquid fertilizer every two weeks during the active growing season—from spring to autumn.

**Temperature range**

Cool Intermediate Warm

A warm room temperature is essential for these plants. A minimum of 55°F (13°C) should be maintained throughout the winter months. Stand the pots on trays or saucers of moist gravel.

**Seasonal care**

Winter Spring Summer Autumn

Plants should be moved into pots one size larger every second or third spring. To propagate these plants, take tip cuttings or stem shoots and root in potting compost, using hormone rooting powder. Rooting plants should be kept warm and light for six months.

**Watering**

Keep the compost moist at all times, but reduce watering during winter. Let the top layer of soil dry out before rewatering.

**Soil**

Use a loam-based soil mixture, with an admixture of one third rough leaf-mould and coarse peat moss.

**Pleomeles** (above) are very closely related to the dracaenas. The variegated form of this plant is particularly fine when displayed as a mature specimen. Good light is essential for growth.

# Plumbago

THE ONLY species in the *Plumbago* genus that is grown indoors is *Plumbago capensis*. This plant produces lovely flowers throughout the summer and well into the autumn. Small leaves are attached to twiggy branches that grow rapidly if given suitable conditions and culture. Some support is needed, but the plant will rapidly cover a wall area, particularly if it has a free root run in the open border of the garden room.

The flowers of *Plumbago capensis* are a lovely powder-blue in color, and there is also a white form, *P. capensis Alba*. The latter is not quite so showy as the blue variety, but if both varieties are planted together the combination of blue and white flowers is most attractive.

Overactive growth of the plumbago can be trimmed to shape at any time. At the end of the flowering season, cut the plant well back, down to a foot or two from the base of the plant if very vigorous; it will quickly refurbish itself in the spring. Pot on at that season, using a soil-based potting mixture. Unless fresh pieces of growth are needed for use as propagating material, all prunings should be burned.

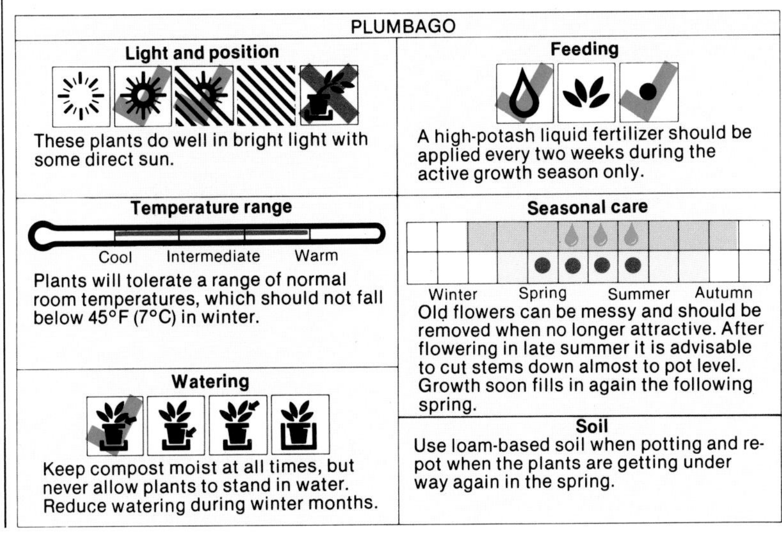


**Plumbago capensis** (above) is a shrubby climbing plant producing clusters of trumpet-shaped, powder-blue flowers (detail below). The delicate color of the flowers and the fact that it has a long flowering season make it a particularly pleasing houseplant.

# Polyscia

POLYSCIAS HAVE small, rounded leaves attached to rather coarse, upright stems, which in the wild attain a a height of 10ft (3m). However, plants rarely grow taller than 3ft (91cm) indoors, where they are prized for their decorative, variegated foliage.

There are several species of polyscias grown indoors, but the one most likely to be offered for sale is *P. balfouriana*, which has small, rather hard-looking leaves. These are attached to speckled, somewhat coarse stems. There are numerous varieties of *P. balfouriana*, differing mainly in the color of the leaves. *P. b.* 'Marginata' has leaflets bordered in creamy white. *P. b.* 'Pennockii' has pale yellow-green markings along the veins.

Polyscias are not easy plants to grow. They have a marked tendency to shed lower leaves if watering is not properly controlled — the soil should be neither very dry nor very wet. The growing temperature should be at least 60°F (16°C), but if red spider mites are present, keep temperature under 70°F (21°C) to control them. Fertilize regularly during the spring and summer.

**Polyscias** are prized for their variegated foliage. *P. balfouriana* is the most readily available of the species that can be grown indoors, and *P. balfouriana 'Marginata'* (above) is a variety with leaf borders of creamy white. Care must be taken when watering these plants or they will shed their lower leaves.

POLYSCIA

**Light and position**

Choose a position in bright light, but out of direct sunlight, for these plants.

**Feeding**

Standard liquid fertilizer should be applied every two weeks from early spring to late autumn.

**Temperature range**

Cool Intermediate Warm

These plants need warm temperatures above 65°F (18°C). You can maintain the right level of humidity by standing plants on trays or saucers of moistened pebbles.

**Seasonal care**

Winter Spring Summer Autumn

These slow-growing plants need little attention provided that their light and temperature needs are met. Repotting may be required every second or third spring, but plants should be examined for root development annually.

**Watering**

Regular, but moderate, watering is advisable throughout the year. Let the top layer dry out before re-watering.

**Soil**

A rich peaty mixture is suitable.

# Saintpaulia

African Violet

SAINTPAULIAS ARE almost certainly the most popular flowering plants produced in pots. Reasonably easy culture is one reason for their popularity, as is the very wide range of flower colors — from white to pink to red to deepest blue. Leaves are mostly rounded in shape and attached to short but firm petioles that radiate from a short central trunk that will increase in size as plants age. The leaves are heavily covered in hairs, so it is important not to clean them carelessly, and certainly not by any form of rubbing. It is also important not to get water onto the leaves when watering the plant, especially if the plant is exposed to direct sunlight.

The African violet needs good light, and natural daylight should be augmented by artificial light in the evening — the extra amount of light will encourage plants to flower more freely. Most houseplant fertilizers are high in nitrogen, but African violets will flower more if a fertilizer with high potash content is used instead. A weak solution of tomato fertilizer will generally work well. Besides good light, plants must be warm, and for conventional saintpaulias the temperature should not fall below 65°F (18°C). But new developments in the African violet field have created what is known as 'cold-tolerant' plants (marketed as the 'endurance strain'), which will not object to temperatures falling as low as 55°F (13°C). These plants come in many colors and bear the names of Arctic explorers.

How these plants are watered can be critical. Don't be heavy-handed, and use tepid water rather than cold water direct from the domestic tap. Pour enough water onto the surface of the soil so that surplus water drains through the holes at the bottom of the pot.

SAINTPAULIA

**Light and position**

The African violet requires good light and will tolerate direct sunlight so long as this is not magnified by glass.

**Feeding**

The leaves of this plant should be kept dry when feeding. Add a weak liquid fertilizer to the soil when watering.

**Temperature range**

Cool Intermediate Warm

African violets flourish in a temperature of 65°-70°F (18°-21°C). The warmth and humidity of bathrooms and kitchens provide ideal conditions for growth.

**Seasonal care**

Winter Spring Summer Autumn

The main difference in the care of the saintpaulia from season to season is in the amount of water required. The plant should never be overwatered, but in cold weather this is even more important. Remove dead flowers and leaves.

**Watering**

In summer, spray plants occasionally with a mist of rainwater. In cold weather, water sparingly.

**Soil**

In general, small pots are more suitable than large ones. African Violets flourish in peat-based potting composts.

**Saintpaulias**, or African violets, are extremely popular flowering houseplants. Their compact size and range of bright flower colors, displayed against a rosette of rich green hairy leaves, are the reason for this. Many hybrids of *S. ionantha* have been developed, including *S. ionantha Rococo* (above) with pink double flowers and *S. ionantha Endivance* (left) with single purple flowers. Great care is needed in watering these plants to avoid splashing the leaves.

ARALIACEAE

# Schefflera

SCHEFFLERAS MAKE bold and individual plants that are seen to best advantage when growing as individual specimen plants in large decorative containers. The leaves are glossy green with five to nine 'fingers' of leaves attached to stout petioles, which in turn radiate evenly from around rather slender stems.

*Schefflera actinophylla*, a plant which is also known as *Brassaia actinophylla*, is the species grown for indoor use. It has at least two common names as well: Umbrella Plant and Octopus Tree.

*Schefflera actinophylla* must have a large space in which to grow; it is neither suited to confined space nor very attractive when small. Plants require a temperature of 50-55°F (10-13°C) in winter and good sunlight. A lightly shaded location is ideal; avoid placing plants in very sunny or dark locations. Mature plants will require frequent feeding, and the soil should never dry out. Do not overwater, however. Pot on plants in early spring.

**Scheffleras** make handsome indoor plants. The genus is one of evergreen trees, but the species *S. actinophylla* (above) grows as a shrub when potted. A variable number of shiny leaflets radiate from the ends of slender leaf stems (detail right). This foliage plant is ideal for those who want a large specimen that is easy to care for.

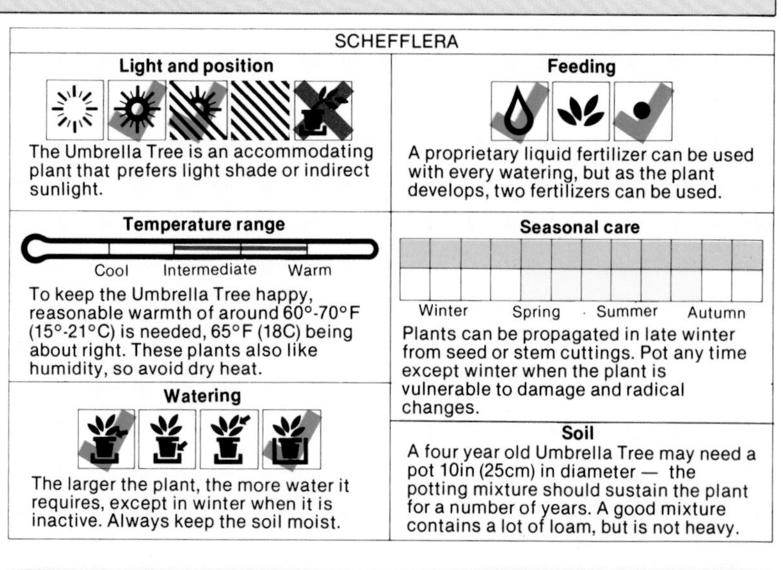

Devil's Ivy

# Scindapsus

SCINDAPSUS PLANTS grow 4-6ft (1.2-1.8m) tall indoors and have leathery, heart-shaped leaves. The most popular species, *S. aureus*, has wonderful mottled yellow-and-pale-green coloring that remains positive in all but the dakest locations. Without doubt one of our finest foliage plants, it can be used to climb or trail and will be little trouble indoors if kept warm, moist and lightly shaded.

Another form, *S. a.* 'Marble Queen', has white variegation that is very attractive in well-grown plants. But *S. a.* 'Marble Queen' is one of the problem plants as far as indoor culture goes. It is certainly not the plant for the beginner, and will test all the skills of the expert. Peaty soil is needed for both *S. aureus* and *S. a.* 'Marble Queen', and regular weak feeding while in active growth.

**Scindapsus** have heart-shaped leaves on trailing stems which usually wrap around any support within reach. *S. aureus* (below) with its mottled yellow and green leaves is the most popular species. A tough strain has been developed, making it a hardier houseplant. A variety of this species *S. aureus 'Marble Queen'* (right) has leaves marbled with white, but it is more exacting in its requirements.

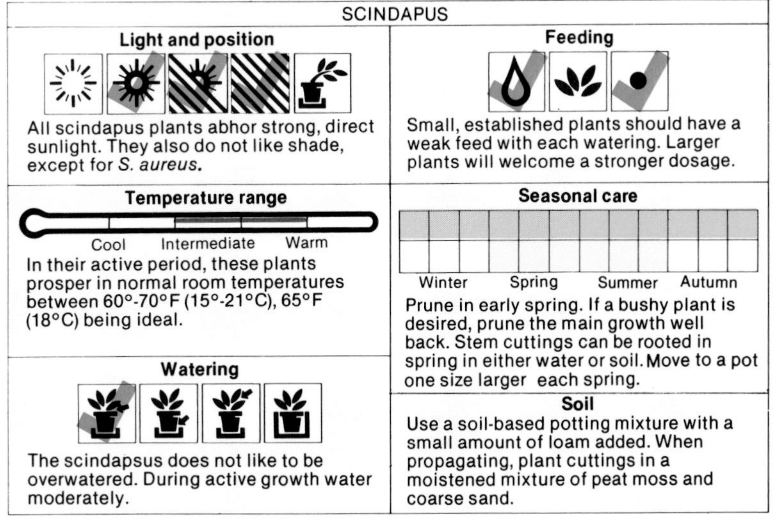

SCINDAPSUS

**Light and position**

All scindapus plants abhor strong, direct sunlight. They also do not like shade, except for *S. aureus.*

**Feeding**

Small, established plants should have a weak feed with each watering. Larger plants will welcome a stronger dosage.

**Temperature range**



In their active period, these plants prosper in normal room temperatures between 60°-70°F (15°-21°C), 65°F (18°C) being ideal.

**Seasonal care**



Prune in early spring. If a bushy plant is desired, prune the main growth well back. Stem cuttings can be rooted in spring in either water or soil. Move to a pot one size larger each spring.

**Watering**

The scindapsus does not like to be overwatered. During active growth water moderately.

**Soil**

Use a soil-based potting mixture with a small amount of loam added. When propagating, plant cuttings in a moistened mixture of peat moss and coarse sand.

GESNERIACEAE

# Sinningia

Gloxinia
Florist's Gloxinia

THERE ARE a number of sinningia species, most with brightly colored flowers and foliage to match. The most common is the florists' gloxinia, *S. speciosa*, which is available for many months during the summer. Plants are low-growing and produce large, soft green leaves that are topped by brightly colored trumpet flowers in many shades. Plants growing in 7in (18cm) diameter pots develop many more flowers than plants in smaller pots.

*Sinningia cardinalis* grows from a tuber and has most attractive foliage, emerald-green in color and velvety in appearance. Flowers appear in clusters and are bright scarlet with a purple throat. A group of these plants in a large bowl can be a very impressive sight, and will be ample reward for the care required to grow them. In early autumn plants naturally shed their flowers and foliage, and this is a sign that watering should be reduced until such time as the soil is bone dry, in which condition the corm rests warm and dry over winter. In the spring, the corm should be planted into fresh soil to renew the growing process for another year.

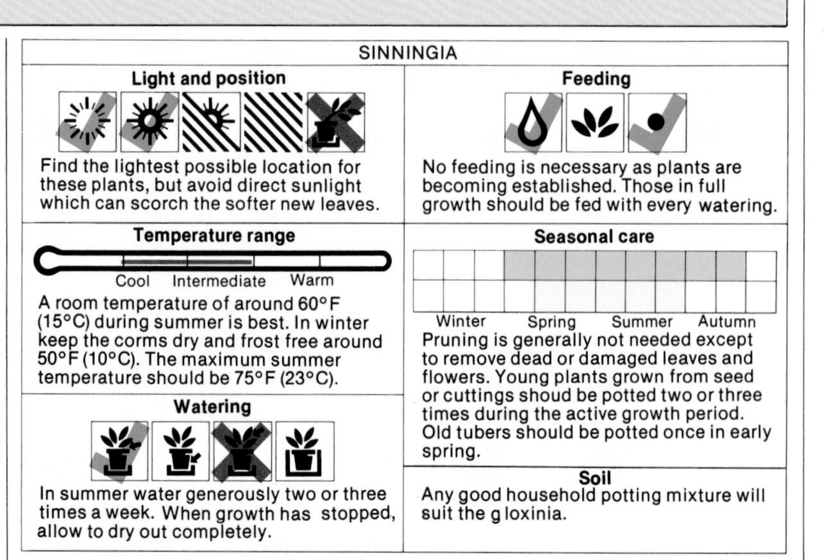

SINNINGIA

**Light and position**

Find the lightest possible location for these plants, but avoid direct sunlight which can scorch the softer new leaves.

**Temperature range**



A room temperature of around 60°F (15°C) during summer is best. In winter keep the corms dry and frost free around 50°F (10°C). The maximum summer temperature should be 75°F (23°C).

**Watering**

In summer water generously two or three times a week. When growth has stopped, allow to dry out completely.

**Feeding**

No feeding is necessary as plants are becoming established. Those in full growth should be fed with every watering.

**Seasonal care**



Pruning is generally not needed except to remove dead or damaged leaves and flowers. Young plants grown from seed or cuttings shoud be potted two or three times during the active growth period. Old tubers should be potted once in early spring.

**Soil**

Any good household potting mixture will suit the gloxinia.

**Sinningias** have spectacular trumpet-shaped flowers and large velvety leaves. The scarlet red-flowers of this gloxinia, *S. speciosa* (right), are just one of the many colours available. The mixed display of *S. speciosa* (above) shows the variety of flower shades that have been developed. All sinningias naturally die down in the winter, but if repotted in the spring, they will grow again.

# Spathiphyllum

SPATHIPHYLLUMS ARE prized both for their foliage and for their arum-shaped flower heads. Plants produce glossy green leaves on short petioles that sprout direct from soil level, forming into bold clumps of growth in time.

The most popular species is *S. wallisii*, which produces insignificant clumps of thin green leaves and white spathe flowers on short petioles. It is a neat plant for the windowsill and offers the prospect of flowers at almost any time of the year.

Much more spectacular and generally bolder in appearance is the hybrid *S.* 'Mauna Loa', which produces its large white spathe flowers on stems that exceed 24in (61cm) in length.

Both *S. wallisii* and *S.* 'Mauna Loa' need damp, shaded conditions. The temperature should be reasonably warm, around 60 to 70°F (16 to 21°C). Once established in their pots, these plants should be fed at every watering during the spring and summer months of the year. To make new plants, split clumps of growth into small sections, making sure that each piece has two or three leaves attached, and pot individually. Grow plants in loam-based soil.

**Spathiphyllums** are arum lily plants whose attraction lies in the contrast of their glossy green leaves and long-stemmed white spathe flowers with protruding central spadix. *S. wallisii* (above) has leaves growing in thick clusters and is a good plant for keeping on a windowsill, as it is slightly smaller than other species. Spathiphyllums need regular, generous feeding in the spring and summer; otherwise the edges of leaves will become yellow and ragged.

SPATHIPHYLLUM

**Light and position**

Spathiphyllums like a sunny position but direct sunlight shoud be avoided.

**Temperature range**

Cool Intermediate Warm

Spathiphyllums should be kept at temperatures between 60°-70°F (15°-21°C). They do not like draughts and need a humid atmosphere.

**Watering**

The spathiphyllum should be watered with moderate amounts — the potting mixture should never dry out completely.

**Feeding**

Use a standard liquid fertilizer and adminster every two weeks while the plant is growing.

**Seasonal care**

Winter Spring Summer Autumn

The plant grows fastest in summer and should receive greater quantities of water then. Avoid water-logging — worms in the soil may block up the drainage holes with their casts so check for these. Decrease food in winter.

**Soil**

The plants should be repotted every spring in a loam-based mixture. Ensure that they are properly drained.

ASCLEPIADACEAE

# Stephanotis

ONLY ONE species in the *Stephanotis* genus is grown as a houseplant. *Stephanotis floribunda* has oval-shaped leaves that are set opposite one another and are dark-green in color. The flowers are tubular, creamy-white and borne in clusters of five or more. They will appear at intervals throughout the spring and summer months. Flower clusters that are removed and inverted in a dish of water will last for several days, during which time the house or flat will be filed with their fragrance.

Stephanotis is a twining plant and can be trained along a trellis, wall or ceiling in the same way as hoyas. Growth can be quite vigorous; suitably trained stephanotis can grow more than 12ft (3.6m) tall.

Stephanotis need a minimum temperature of 55°F (13°C), and temperature should be kept as constant as possible. Keep plants on the dry side during winter, but water plentifully during the growing season. Mealy bugs can be a problem.

**Stephanotis floribunda** (above) is a vigorous climbing plant which twines around any available support. Its outstanding feature is the overpowering fragrance of the clusters of star-shaped waxy white flowers (detail right).

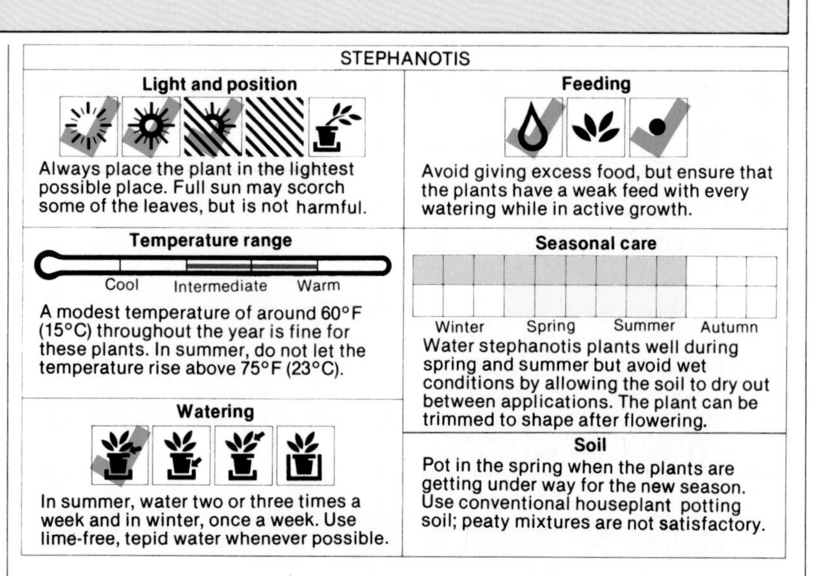

# Strelitzia

THIS GENUS contains one of the most striking of all flowers, *Strelitzia reginae*, commonly called the Bird of Paradise. Spear-shaped metallic-green leaves are carried on rigid petioles and may attain a length of 3-4ft (91cm-1.2m). Flowers are mainly orange and blue in color. They bloom from an almost horizontal bract; the three-petalled flowers have a crested appearance and emerge over the course of several weeks. Plants may be anywhere from five to seven years old before they produce flowers, by which time plants should be in pots 10in (25cm) in diameter.

Strelitzias need bright light, with at least a few hours of direct sunlight every day. High temperature is not necessary, and plants may remain out of doors except when freezing conditions are expected.

**Strelitzia reginae** (above and right) is a striking plant that may be grown with reasonable ease from seed. However, it may take many years for plants to produce their flamboyant flowers.

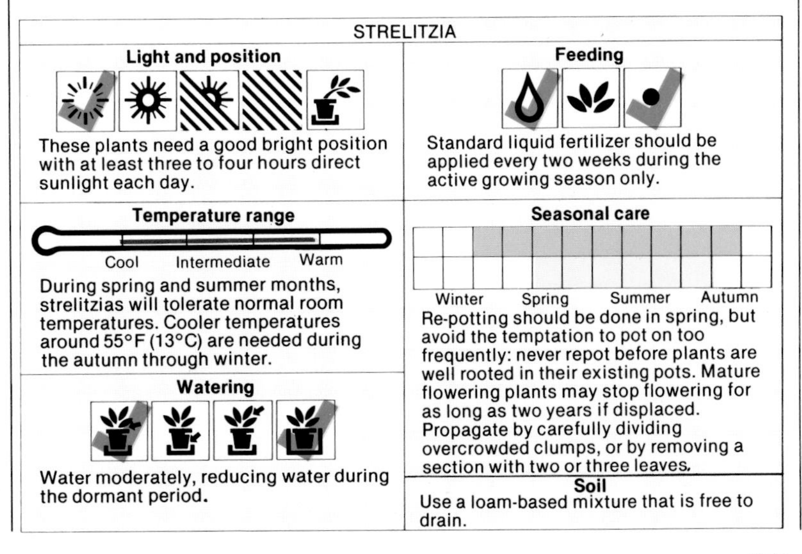

STRELITZIA

**Light and position**

These plants need a good bright position with at least three to four hours direct sunlight each day.

**Feeding**

Standard liquid fertilizer should be applied every two weeks during the active growing season only.

**Temperature range**

Cool Intermediate Warm

During spring and summer months, strelitzias will tolerate normal room temperatures. Cooler temperatures around 55°F (13°C) are needed during the autumn through winter.

**Seasonal care**

Winter Spring Summer Autumn

Re-potting should be done in spring, but avoid the temptation to pot on too frequently: never repot before plants are well rooted in their existing pots. Mature flowering plants may stop flowering for as long as two years if displaced. Propagate by carefully dividing overcrowded clumps, or by removing a section with two or three leaves.

**Watering**

Water moderately, reducing water during the dormant period.

**Soil**

Use a loam-based mixture that is free to drain.

# Cacti and Succulents

Succulent plants have many rare and unusual features, developed during a long and slow evolutionary process. One of their principal characteristics is the ability to adapt to harsh conditions, conditions which would cause most other plant groups to perish. The various peculiarities associated with succulents, cacti in particular, probably result from this. Thus we find the intriguing shapes, some bordering on the grotesque but beautiful nevertheless, evidenced in over 50 different plant families — these include over 350 genera, of which about 250 belong to the Cactaceae.

The shapes and sizes of succulent plants are well-nigh endless. Their common feature is a fleshy inbuilt structure that is apparent in either their stems, leaves or roots. This structure enables them to store moisture and helps to protect them against environmental conditions and changes.

Succulent plants are to be found growing almost everywhere in the world — even in the much more unpredictable weather and temperature conditions that prevail in many northern parts of Europe, Asia and America. Cactaceae, which are distinguished from other succulents in having a growing point called an areole, have their habitat almost entirely in the Americas. The larger succulent plant families — Euphorbiaceae, Mesembryanthemaceae, Asclepiadaceae — are to a great extent natives of the Old World, particularly Africa and Arabia. Australasia also has its indigenous succulents.

There is a saying that 'cactus thrive on neglect'. However, this aphorism is utterly false. Succulents *may* survive, but certainly not thrive. After all, nature never intended plants to grow in pots in houses or greenhouses; plants have been introduced to and forced to accept whatever provisons are made available for their care and protection. So give due attention to detail. Monitor your plants' response to treatment given, and use personal initiative and enterprise.

The number of succulents suitable for indoor culture is enormous. Comparatively few are mentioned in these pages, but those described are representative of hosts of others that will add brightness and interest to the home. Obviously, some are not as easy to grow as others. Those from equatorial regions often demand more warmth than those from tropical and sub-tropical areas, so should not be lumped together with incompatible plants.

### Caring for cacti

Not all succulents are from arid or semi-arid regions. A great number are jungle or rain-forest plants, some growing in trees just as many orchid species do. These forest plants require a somewhat different culture from desert succulents. Probably the most well-known cactus houseplant is *Schlumbergera bridgesii* — the popular Christmas Cactus. There are a few of its close relations referred to later, and those things necessary for the care of the Christmas Cactus — sun, water and fertilizer — also apply to these.

### Light and Temperature

Place plants in a bright location, not in full sun, or scorch could affect them at certain times of the year.

Give plants the appropriate temperature. You can't water, fertilize or even wisely repot if the air temperature is very much below 55-60°F (13°C) During growing and flowering times in particular, plants demand higher temperatures. Failure to supply such conditions may cause either leaves to wither or buds to drop.

### Compost and Potting

Provide plants with a really rich compost that consists of thoroughly decomposed leafmold, peat and sharp sand in equal parts. In some instances, additional humus may be advisable. It is vital that the compost be porous. If extra humus prevents this, add more sand.

Potting is important. Never use a container that is too small

**Cacti and Succulents** (above) come in many different shapes and sizes. While all succulent plants have a swollen, fleshy structure in either their roots, stems or leaves that enables them to store moisture, cacti, the largest group of succulent plants, also have an areole. This round or elongated cushion of hairs is the growing point from which develop any offsets, branches or spines. Flower buds are produced from the upper area of the areole.

By definition a succulent is a plant which stores moisture in its leaves, stems or roots. The echeveria (left), with its fleshy leaves, typifies a leaf succulent.

Cacti are suuculent plants belonging to the cactaceae family. All cacti have a growing point called an areole — a cushion-like area from which grow the spines and flowers.

or too large — both are equally unsuitable. Repotting should be done soon after plants have flowered, certainly not just before, or a year's flowering could be lost.

**Watering**

With jungle plants, it is not necessary, and probably not advisable, to allow the soil to dry out completely at any time. During the growing season, water freely but never permit the soil to remain drenched, which will cause root rot. Good crocking of the pot should prevent excess water accumulating.

**Fertilizing**

Once new growth is observed, or flower buds appear, fertilizing is essential. If throughout these periods, plants are fertilized when watered — always in a weak, liquid form — plants will often prosper. An old-fashioned method of guaranteeing a good flowering plant is to introduce thoroughly decomposed cow manure into the compost. This is still a first-class method and does away with the need to use artificial fertilizers.

One further point on fertilizers and fertilizing: There are numerous brands offered in stores, but very few have been specifically prepared for succulent-plant culture. The majority contain nitrogen and potash. These are essential ingredients, but too much nitrogen will encourage growth as opposed to flowering. There are fertilizers that contain these two elements plus trace elements — iron, manganese, magnesium, copper, boron, molybdenum. Use these fertilizers, and you are well on the way to success. Never fertilize when plants are not in growth or when they look sickly, dehydrated or generally off-form.

**Disease**

Excessive watering, particularly to the root structure, causes many diseases. If your plant shows signs of disease, examine the roots, cut away any damaged parts, dust the plant with sulfur powder, and repot in fresh soil. Black-rot may attack certain plants, such as stapelias and some epiphytes, usually at soil level. Black rot is caused by bacteria getting into the plant's system and turning the tissues black and soft. The affected parts should be cut out very thoroughly. Dust the cut with sulfur powder, and keep the plant on the dry side until the cut is healed. A copper-based fungicide applied occasionally will help to restrain the problem. Damping-off primarily affects young seedlings. A good fungicide will remedy this; use one containing captan or zineb.

**Propagation**

Charts of the following species of succulents discuss propagation by seeds. A little guidance is necessary here. It is obvious that all plants can be propagated from seeds. Unfortunately, some seeds are difficult to obtain. The majority are available, but must be obtained from reputable sources. The process of sowing is simple.

**Propagation** Many succulents can be propagated from cuttings, which may also improve plants' shape and encourage basal growth. The red lines on the opuntia (below left) and echeveria (below right) show where the cuts can be made. Let the cuts heal before rooting offsets in a mixture of equal parts peat and sharp sand.

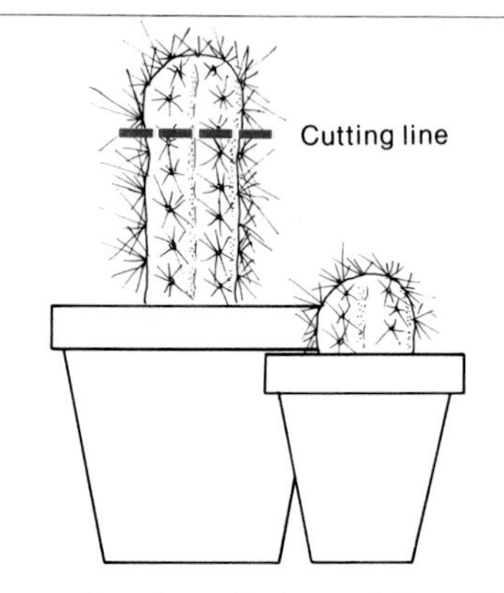


Because they have their own internal water supply, succulents are not so disturbed by a temporary stoppage in water flow and lend themselves readily to vegetative propagation by division, offsets, suckers, cuttings or grafting.

This globular cactus can be increased two ways. The top section may be cut off (above left) and the cutting left in an airy, light shelf until a protective callus has been formed over the wound. (Some growers recommend dipping the cut in a rooting powder). After callusing has taken place, insert the top section in a new pot. To prevent rot, do not bury the base too deeply.

The plant that has been divided will grow new offshoots (above right) from the top of the stump. These may also be cut off and rooted in smaller pots. Use a rooting compost of equal parts sifted sharp sand and peat.

With few exceptions, the soil can be the same as that recommended for plants in the individual charts, but extra-sharp sand should be added. Succulent seeds germinate readily, but if soil is not porous they may rapidly rot. It is common practice to cover the seeds with just a sprinkling of fine-sifted sand to a depth equivalent to the size of the seeds. If seeds are dust-like seeds, carefully sprinkle them onto the sandy surface of the container and, even more carefully, water them in. Soak the containers thoroughly Drain them completely and keep in a shaded but warm area until germination. Then provide more light gradually. After about three months, place containers in a very bright position, but not in full sunshine until the seedlings have assumed their characteristic forms.

### Caring for desert succulents

With plants from more arid surroundings, there can be slight variations to the guidelines listed above. With few exceptions, these plants are sun-lovers; place them in the sunniest spot available. Much the same type of soil will suit many — in a few instances it may be wise to add a little lime or substitute loam for peat. It is possible to purchase ready-prepared composts. Many brand-name soil-based composts can give excellent results, but it is often necessary to add additional grit to ensure they are porous. Soil-less composts have gained in popularity in recent years, and there is much to commend them, but 30 percent or more sharp sand should be added to the bulk. Nutrients have already been added to these pre-prepared composts. These nutrients may only last for a limited period of time — succulent plants usually prove to be very hungry plants — so remember to fertilize.

## SUCCULENT FAMILIES

Succulent plants come from all parts of the world and range in size from tiny weeds to enormous trees. The family Cactaceae is the largest succulent family, with other 250 genera and approximately 3,000 species and varieties. There are 50 other plant families that have species possessing some degree of succulence. In many cases, however, only a very few species in a family are succulent. All the plants in the section that follows belong to one of these families. Plants are classified according to genera, each of which can be found in this chart.

**Apocynaceae**
Most species of this family of about 180 genera are non-succulent shrubs or climbing plants found in tropical or sub-tropical countries. Though few in number, succulent genera such as *Pachpodium* and *Plumiera* contain some of the most exotic plants in the world. Flowers are beautiful and fragrant — seed-pods appear in the form of horn-shaped fruit.

**Asclepiadaceae**
There are over 200 genera in this large plant family, including *Ceropegia, Hoya, Huernia, Luckhoffia, Stapelia* and *Stultitia*. Succulent species originate from Africa, Arabia, the Far East and Australasia. Flowers are usually beautiful and colorful, and are often sweetly scented.

**Cactaceae**
Plants in the best-known and biggest family of succulents are largely native to the Americas. The many thousands of species vary tremendously, but all bear an areole, a distinguishing feature not known in any other plant family. The areole is the round of elongated cushion of 'felt' or hairs that is the growing point from which develop any offsets, branches or spines.

**Convolvulaceae**
Species in this gigantic 'bindweed' family are found in many parts of the world. Their habit varies tremendously; plants may be shrubs, trees, climbers, trailers, even parasites. Succulent species generally have large colorful flowers. They are represented in the genera of *Ipomoea, Turbina* and *Merremia*.

**Eurphorbiaceae**
There are over 400 genera in this plant family, but only a few contain succulent plants. *Euphorbia, Jatropha, Synadenium* and *Monadenium* are the principal succulent genera. The structure of the inflorescence distinguishes plants in this family: Flowers are either all-male or all-female. Hence, pollination is best guaranteed where there are colonies of the same species.

**Crassulaceae**
This is a family of succulent genera and includes *Crassula, Echeveria, Graptopetalum, Sedum, Tacitus* and *Cotyledon*. Species are mainly native to temperate Europe, Asia, Australia and America.

**Geraniaceae**
This well-known plant family contains about 800 species, which are distributed among a small number of genera. The two genera that contain succulents are *Pelargonium* and *Sarcocaulon*; plants are native to South Africa.

**Liliaceae**
This large family of plants has over 3,000 species. Succulent genera include *Aloe, Haworthia* and *Gasteria*; most plants are native to Africa and Madagascar.

**Mesembryanthemaceae**
This is the largest family of succulent plants after the Cactaceae, numbering about 125 different genera (among them *Conophytum* and *Lampranthus*) and several thousand species. Most species are native to South Africa, though a few originate in Australasia, Arabia and the Atlantic islands.

**Pedaliaceae**
This Old World family of plants contains only 12 genera and probably no more than 50 species. They are all from tropical or sub-tropical regions, primarily Africa. Plants in only two genera, *Pterodiscus* and *Sesamothamnus*, are considered perennial succulents.

# Astrophytum/Cryptocereus/Disocactus

## Astrophytum

This is an important genus and the comparatively few species in it are among the most sought-after of plants. The generic title derives from Latin and means 'star-plant' — the starry aspect is evidenced by the numerous star-like scales completely covering the epidermis.

*Astrophytum myriostigma var. nudum* is spherical in shape, sometimes becoming slightly cylindrical when fully matured. The body is more or less spineless and has five to six symmetrical ribs running from crown to base, furrowed in between. The miter-like shape created amply justifies the plant's common name — the Bishop's Cap.

This plant has a characteristic not shared by other varieties within the species — namely, the distinctive green coloring of the body. Other varieties are mainly gray. It comes from north-central Mexico, and usually grows within the limited shade provided by native scrub, at altitudes of around 2,300ft (700m).

Flowers are bright yellow and have a silk-like luster. They appear near to or in the crown of the plant. Blooms appear when specimens are a few years old.

### ASTROPHYTUM

**Light and position**

Astrophytums require good light at all times and an airy position. Full sun can scorch, and draughts are dangerous.

**Feeding**

In growing season, feed plants with weak fertilizer at each watering.

**Temperature range**

Cool Intermediate Warm

In winter, keep temperatures at 50°-55°F (10°-13°C). In summer, plants will accept high temperatures.

**Seasonal care**

Winter Spring Summer Autumn

Keep plants completely dry and free from draughts in winter. Repot in spring if necessary. Never over-pot or under-pot.

**Watering**

Water above or below, but only when the soil has dried out. Then soak and allow soil to drain thoroughly.

**Soil**

A porous, sandy soil is essential. Use a mixture of equal parts peat, leaf-mould and sandy gravel, plus a little lime.

**Astrophytum myriostigma var. nudum** (above) has symmetrical ribs running from crown to base and furrowed in between.
**Cryptocereus anthonyanus** (right) has some of the most colorful flowers of all epiphytic cacti and an attractive rick-rack stem.

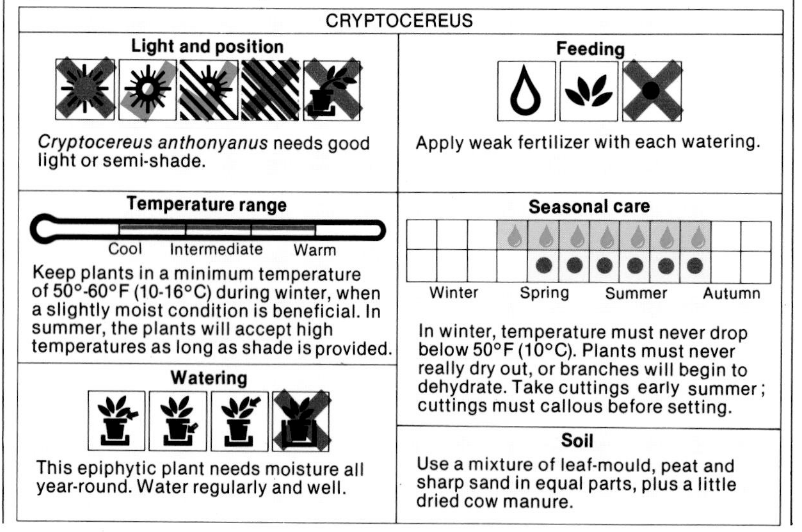

### CRYPTOCEREUS

**Light and position**

*Cryptocereus anthonyanus* needs good light or semi-shade.

**Feeding**

Apply weak fertilizer with each watering.

**Temperature range**

Cool Intermediate Warm

Keep plants in a minimum temperature of 50°-60°F (10-16°C) during winter, when a slightly moist condition is beneficial. In summer, the plants will accept high temperatures as long as shade is provided.

**Seasonal care**

Winter Spring Summer Autumn

In winter, temperature must never drop below 50°F (10°C). Plants must never really dry out, or branches will begin to dehydrate. Take cuttings early summer; cuttings must callous before setting.

**Watering**

This epiphytic plant needs moisture all year-round. Water regularly and well.

**Soil**

Use a mixture of leaf-mould, peat and sharp sand in equal parts, plus a little dried cow manure.

## Cryptocereus

This is a small genus of epiphytic plants. The generic title means 'hidden cereus', for the flower bud is hidden in the notched and lobed, flattened stems of the plant. It has what is often termed a 'rick-rack' stem, which in itself is a pleasing feature. The branches can attain 6ft (2m) or more in length.

*Cryptocereus anthonyanthus* is a comparatively recent discovery. In fact, it was first located growing on a native's hut, and some time elapsed before its actual habitat was confirmed. It is a true epiphyte and grows in trees. The aerial roots produced on the stems enable the plant to anchor safely in the tree branches, from which it hangs pendent. This Mexican plant from the forest regions of Chiapas is easy to cultivate. Grown in a well-placed hanging basket, this plant will flourish either in a shaded area of the home or in a greenhouse.

The flower is one of outstanding beauty — a true exotic. The brick-red sepals and the yellow throat combine to make this an exceptional flower within the Cactaceae family. Flowers open in late afternoon and remain so throughout the night. They have a light, pleasant scent.

**Disocactus**

Only a few species can be said to truly belong to this genus. All are somewhat similar in habit and appearance, but differ in quite obvious features. Stems are long, often 12in (30cm) in length and 1-2in (3-5cm) wide. They are notched or serrated, have a tendency to twist slightly, and are rather pointed at the tips. Flowers can be quite numerous. They are produced in the upper portion of the stems, are about 2in (5cm) long, carmine-red and trumpet-shaped. The protruding style is an important feature.

*Disocactus eichlamii* is a very interesting and unusual epiphytic species that comes from the forest areas of Guatemala. It has flattened stems and branches, similar to but more dwarfed than those plants in the genus *Epiphyllum* to which it is related. Plants are somewhat bushy, branching out from the base of the plant, but eventually develop the pendent habit characteristic of all epiphytes.

There is little problem in growing *Disocactus eichlamii* satisfactorily. Plants require much the same treatment as the well-known Christmas Cactus. Flowers occur rather late in the year, hence the need to maintaining a temperature of around 53°F (12°C) for good results. Plants are suitable for home or greenhouse culture and can grow either in pots or hanging baskets. It is wise to keep plants slightly moist all the time.

**Disocactus eichlamii** (above) is an epiphytic species native to the forest areas of Guatemala. An array of vivid-colored flowers is produced quite late in the year, the blooms persisting over a period of several weeks. Stems are long, notched or serrated, and have a tendency to twist.

DISOCACTUS

**Light and position**

Disocactus needs good indirect light or semi-shade. Fresh air is essential, but keep plants away from draughts.

**Feeding**

Weak fertilizers should be included with each watering in late spring, summer and autumn. Do not water in winter.

**Temperature range**

Cool Intermediate Warm

Flowers need a minimum temperature of 55°F (13°C) at all times. Plants will take a high temperature in summer and early autumn as long as they are shaded.

**Seasonal care**

Winter Spring Summer Autumn

Take cuttings in spring, which is also the time any pruning should be done. Repot in spring. Watch for pests at all times.

**Watering**

Keep plants just moist at all times. In hot weather, occasionally spray plants with water.

**Soil**

An acid compost - decomposed leaf-mould and sharp sand in equal parts, plus a little peat - will give good flowering results.

# Echinocereus/Echinopsis

## Echinocereus

Plants in this genus are diverse in their characteristics — they may be cylindrical, globular, erect or prostrate — but all bear medium to large colorful flowers. The generic title is from the Greek 'echinus' and means 'hedgehog' – a reference to the many-spined bodies of the plants. Certain species do indeed merit the term 'Hedgehog Cactus'. Echinocereus species are found in southwestern areas of the USA and in northern and central Mexico.

One of the better-known species in the genus is *Echinocerus pentalophus*. Many varieties of this plant develop offsets — some elongated, others short, but all eventually becoming prostrate and forming large 'cushions' or 'mats'. *E. pentalophus procumbens*, a plant from northern Mexico, is one of the best examples of the group. Stems are somewhat slender, less than 1in wide (about 2cm), frequently 5in (12cm) or more long. The few ribs develop a spiral effect, with the white areoles bearing a few brown spines. The prostrate or 'procumbens' aspect is vividly displayed, and when in full bloom with its large, glistening flowers, this plant presents a feature of attraction almost unequaled in this genus of beautiful flowers.

The popularity of this variety has been in evidence for many years. The stems do not necessarily captivate the imagination of the collector seeking species with particularly intricate body and spine formations, and the plant's prostrate, almost creeping habit can quickly demand a large space. The flowers, however, are adequate compensation — rich in color, 4in (10cm) or so long, 3in (8cm) in diameter.

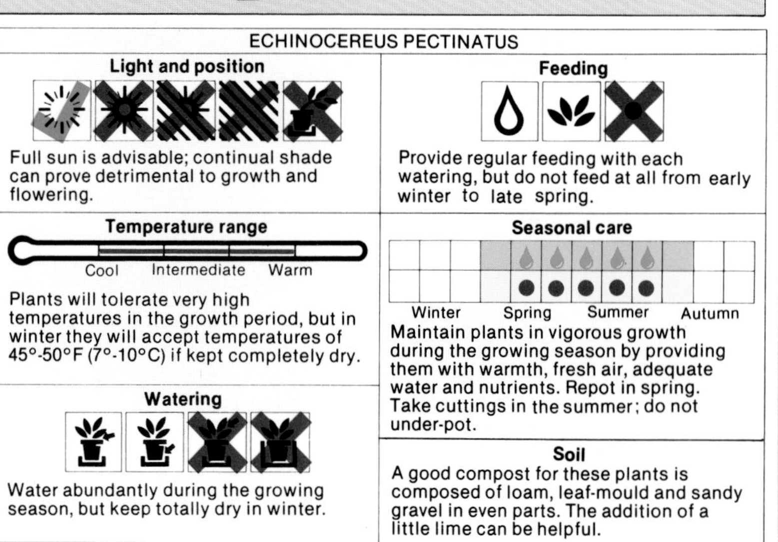

**Echinocereus pentalophus var procumbens** (above) is native to northern Mexico and produces large cushion-type offsets.

In common with the majority of echinocereus species, this plant is free-growing and tolerant of cold weather, though it resents extreme cold. A sunny location is best, and throughout the growing and flowering season it tends to be a thirsty plant.

## Echinopsis

This is a large genus of South American cacti. The title refers to the spination of the plants — 'echinus' means hedgehog, and 'opsis' appearance.

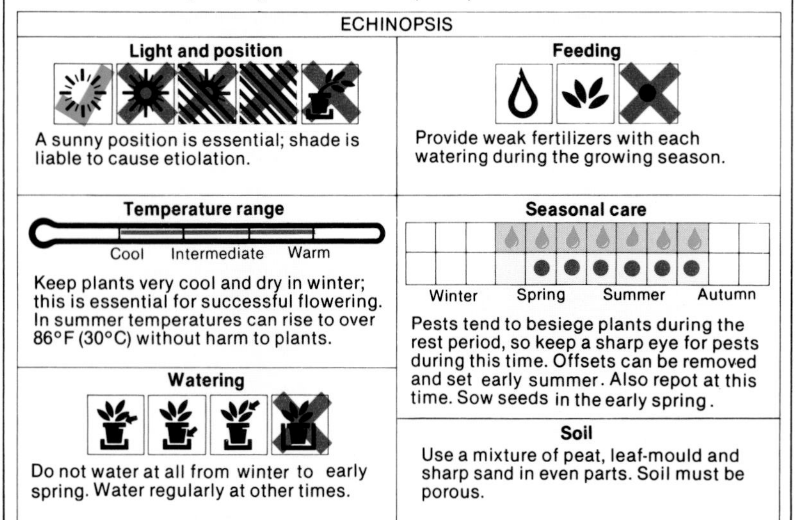

# Encephalocarpus

*Echinopsis aurea var. aurantiaca* is a colorful species that remains somewhat uncommon in collections. It was originally described by the German authority Curt Backeberg as a member of the *Lobivia* genus, but after subsequent research it has usually been included under *Echinopsis*. Whatever its title, it is nevertheless a plant deservedly coveted because of its unusually colored flowers.

Its actual origin remains uncertain, but records suggest that its habitat is in Argentina. In growth, the species is very variable, sometimes remaining solitary, but frequently offsetting quite freely. The body of the plant is a dull brownish-green, and has many ribs and somewhat twisted and untidy spination — some of the spines are as much as 2-3in (5-8cm) long. The handsome brownish-orange flowers appear from late June to August.

**Echinopsis aurea var aurantiaca** (above) has unpredictable spination and flowers an uncommon shade of brownish-orange.

**Encephalocarpus**

This is a monotypic genus, and one that has excited the imagination of collectors for many years. A very distinguished species of peculiar charm and attraction, *E. strobiliformis* differs from any other cacti on account of the flattened tubercles or scales tightly enclosing the plant body. Its native habitat is Mexico, near the Nuevo León.

The plant has a very pronounced taproot, which indicates it may be related to the genus *Ariocarpus*. The grayish-green tubercles keel outwardly and are pointed at the tips, each having an areole bearing minute spines and wool. Many flowers are usually produced; their vivid coloring provides a sharp contrast to the greyish tubercles. Each flower is about 1in (3cm) long, borne from the tips of the young tubercles, and usually opens in late morning and lasts for one day.

This is a real connoisseur's plant, but for all its unique features, *Encephalocarpus strobiliformis* is not necessarily a difficult subject in cultivation. Really good light is necessary, or the tubercles tend to 'bronze' and loose their attractiveness.

**Encephalocarpus strobiliformis** (above) is a distinctive species native to Mexico. Scale-like tubercles, compressed together in the form of a cone, distinguish this species from any other cacti. The large, delicately colored flowers frequently open several at a time, and the flowering period can extend over several weeks.

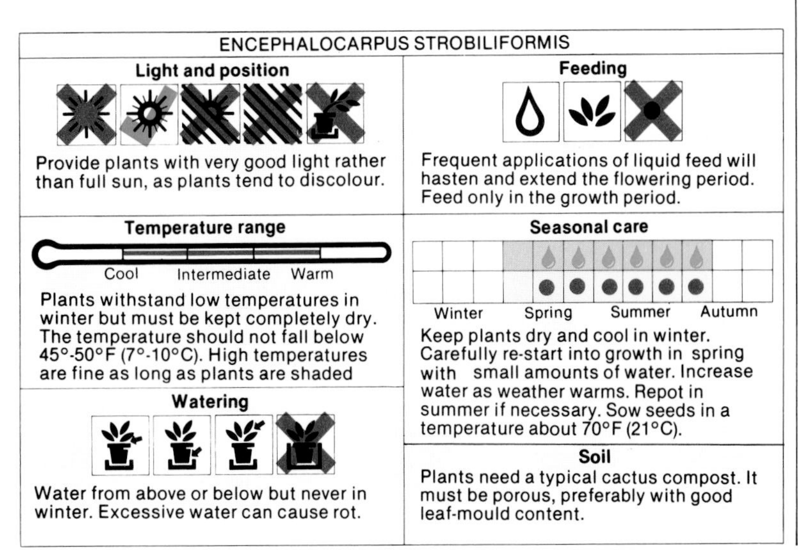

ENCEPHALOCARPUS STROBILIFORMIS

**Light and position**

Provide plants with very good light rather than full sun, as plants tend to discolour.

**Temperature range**



Plants withstand low temperatures in winter but must be kept completely dry. The temperature should not fall below 45°-50°F (7°-10°C). High temperatures are fine as long as plants are shaded

**Watering**

Water from above or below but never in winter. Excessive water can cause rot.

**Feeding**

Frequent applications of liquid feed will hasten and extend the flowering period. Feed only in the growth period.

**Seasonal care**



Keep plants dry and cool in winter. Carefully re-start into growth in spring with small amounts of water. Increase water as weather warms. Repot in summer if necessary. Sow seeds in a temperature about 70°F (21°C).

**Soil**

Plants need a typical cactus compost. It must be porous, preferably with good leaf-mould content.

# Epicactus

**Epicactus**

The title 'Epicactus' refers to the numerous hybrids of *Epiphyllum* crossed with other closely related genera. For many years *'Phyllocactus'* was a name associated with such plants, but it was never botanically acceptable – it means 'leaf-like cactus', and a great number of the plants dubbed this were certainly not leaf-like.

Epicactus plants have been popular for over 100 years. Even in Victorian times many a cottage window was adorned with *'Epiphyllum' ackermannii*, hybrids which produced a succession of scarlet flowers during the early months of the year, and the plant still retains a place of consequence today. Hybridizers around the world, particularly those in Europe and America, have sought repeatedly to produce new and more exotic strains, resulting in numerous cultivars of almost every color imaginable — from purest white through cream, yellow, orange, pink, scarlet to deepest purple, plus innumerable tones in between —as well as plants with multicolored blooms. Really, only green or blue have to date eluded the hybridizers. In earlier times the red cultivar held pride of place, but with the introduction of new color forms it now competes for popularity.

All epicactus are essentially houseplants. With isolated exceptions, all succeed in the home environment. Flowers last for up to five days, and they are forthcoming successively from March to late June or July.

All cultivars accept the same conditions in cultivation. Very good light, but not full sun, supports continuing good growth. Water regularly throughout the growing season, keeping the soil moist but never wet.

*Epicactus cv. Regency* is an improved form of *cv. Cooperi*, a direct product of *Epiphyllum crenatum*, a beautiful white flowering species, and *Selenicereus grandiflora*, which is better known as Queen of the Night and has creamy-white, almost yellow flowers. Both parents are truly epiphytic and are responsible for the plant's beautiful scent. In flowering, *Epicactus cv. Regency* is very similar in habit to *Epiphyllum crenatum*, being day-flowering. In shape, it is also similar, with its trumpet-shaped bloom, 5in (13cm) in diameter. The coloring is obviously derived from both parents, the pale yellowish-cream being very much in evidence. Stems are flat, thick and smooth, often 16in (40 cm) or so in length.

*Epicactus cv. Queen Anne* has a more complicated parentage, the result of a hybrid being crossed with a hybrid in an attempt to create a yellow form. This dwarf yellow cultivar is one of the finest epicactus. Stems rarely exceed 12in (30 cm) in length, are mainly flat but somewhat twisting, and give a wonderful succesion of flowers, medium in size, from late March to June.

*Epicactus cv. Giant Empress* is an improved form of *cv. Deutsche Kaiserin*, one of the earliest of hybrids. Here again the stems are slender and flattened, with a pendent habit.

**Epicactus cv. Giant Empress** (top) is a plant that makes an excellent subject for a hanging basket.
**Epicactus cv. Regency** (above left) is a sturdy, late-blooming plant.
**Epicactus cv. Queen Anne** (above right) is valued for its compact growth.

This plants makes an excellent subject for a hanging basket, and as such will thrive in normal house conditions.

*Epicactus cv. Court Pink* is a spreading plant. The stems and branches rarely stand erect, but are certainly not pendent. The medium-sized blooms are produced freely along the branches, and while predominantly pink, there is just a suggestion of an orange suffusion in the coloring. This plant is of British origin, but little is known of the parentage, except that it is apparently not a direct hybrid between definite species. One interesting characteristic of the plant is that the buds are deep yellow before opening.

*Epicactus cv. Impello* is one of the author's hybrids, developed over a period of seven to eight years in Sussex. Some hybrids are planned; others 'just arrive'. Indeed there was planning in this particular instance — an attempt to produce a yellow epicactus. However, when this plant's unusual coloring made itself manifest, it was decided to cultivate the hybrid for its own sake. It is highly scented, and with its delicate shadings of pink, lilac and pale violet and the erect yet not over-tall growth, it has proved itself to be one of the best of the paler, multicolored cultivars

*Epicactus cv. Pegasus* is of American origin and is undoubtedly outstanding. Flowers are extra-large, with reddish-orange petals. Sepals are edged brownish-violet and often have a ruffled appearance. The plants are generally rather tall, as high as 24in (61 cm); the branches are flat and wide and very firm. This is one of the best of the darker-colored varieties with multi-colored flowers. Flowers are readily and regularly produced, and for those who have space for larger plants, this cultivar will be a rewarding showpiece.

**Epicactus cv. Court Pink** (top) is a spreading plant with pink flowers. **Epicactus cv. Impello** (left) has fragrant flowers in pastel shades. **Epicactus cv. Pegasus** (above) is a tall plant that demands space but flowers for several weeks.

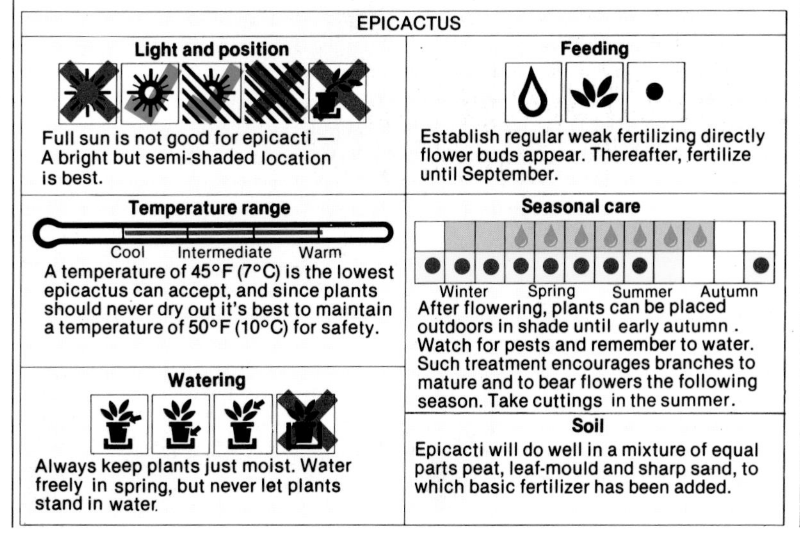

# Epithelantha/Ferocactus/Gymnocactus

## Epithelantha

*Epithelantha micromeris* is the sole member of the *Epithelantha* genus, for although there are supposedly a few varieties of the species, they are more likely to be just local forms.

The habitat of *Epithelantha micromeris*, sometimes called the Button Cactus, covers quite a widespread area, from West Texas in the USA to Coahuila in northern Mexico.

The body of the plant is basically spherical, although sometimes it elongates or even develops small groups. Numerous minute white spines cover the whole plant, and these are longer toward the crown. It is from the often woolly area of the crown that the flowers develop.

Flowers are mainly pink, rather small in size, but with several opening at once they make a most pleasing effect. The seed capsules that develop later are scarlet, somewhat club-shaped, and contain a few black seeds. If sown the following year, these should germinate successfully.

Care should be taken in cultivation. A sunny position is important, together with a very open soil to which lime is added. Excellent drainage will avoid the possibility of root-rot — plants with taproots such as *Epithelantha micromeris* are susceptible to overwatering. Keep completely dry from late October to March. Flower buds appear soon after.

**Epithelantha micromeris** (above) has pink flowers and is one of the neatest of miniature cacti. Use rich calcareous soil to maintain the distinctive color of the tubercles.

## Ferocactus

The generic title refers to the rather fierce spination that is apparent on all species of this popular genus.

*Ferocactus fordii* is one of the lesser-known cacti, found in a rather limited area of Baja California in Mexico. It is also one of the most beautiful cacti, particularly when in flower. The fact that it rarely grows too large makes it welcome in the greenhouse.

The dark grayish-green body is globular in shape, rarely exceeding 5in (13cm) in diameter. The horizontal ribs, usually 21 of them, carry areoles situated about 1in (3cm) apart, and with these are associated about 15

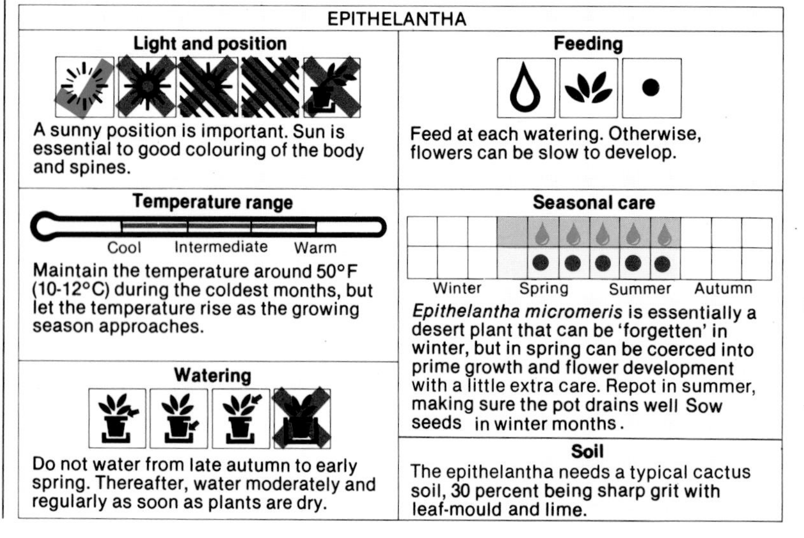

**Ferocactus fordii** (above) is smaller than most ferocactus species. It enjoys full sun in its native habitat and needs excellent light to flourish indoors.

stiff spines, white in color and radiating around four larger central spines, one of which is hooked and thick, about 2in (5cm) long.

This is a plant that grows in full sun. In nature it is seldom found in scrub country, so place it in the sunniest spot available in your house or greenhouse. Without excellent light, the spines are liable to lose their luster and flowering will be affected. Only with good light do blooms come readily and maintain their attractive coloring. The majority of ferocactus have yellow flowers, but *Ferocactus fordii* boasts of deep rose-red or pale-violet blooms, all carried within the crown of the plant. Guard against overwatering — plants require no water at all from early November to late March — but when watering commences, be sure to add fertilizers regularly.

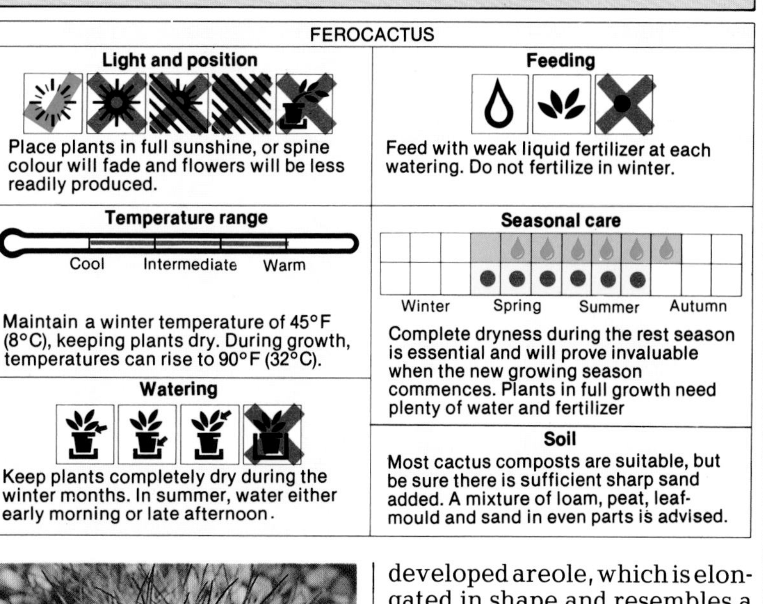


## Gymnocactus

A small genus of plants created in quite recent years, *Gymnocactus* contains a number of plants originally included under *Thelocactus*. There is certainly a close affinity, but species of gymnocactus tend to have much smaller flowers. These arise from the well developed areole, which is elongated in shape and resembles a short furrow.

**Gymnocactus viereckii** (above) is a lesser-known Mexican cactus. The dense spination almost obscures the bluish-green body and is an outstanding feature of the plant.

*Gymnocactus vierecki* is one of the more uncommon species, but is gradually becoming more available as nurseries develop plants from seeds. Native to eastern Mexico, it has a globular stem densely covered with longish spines of silvery white, almost obliterating the ribs. The stem only grows to about 3in (8cm) in diameter, is deep bluish-green in color and crowned with twisted white wool. Through this wool emerge the flowers, and their unusual coloring emphasizes the beauty of the species.

With care, *Gymnocactus viereckii* will produce its seed capsules quite readily — these are entirely spineless, as is the ovary. This is a particular feature of the genus and probably accounts for its generic title — 'gymno' means 'spineless'.

In cultivation, plants need good light. They succeed quite well on a window ledge, but not if the window faces north. Keep plants completely dry during winter, but water regularly while in active growth. Fertilize during the growing season to ensure flowering.

GYMNOCACTUS

**Light and position**
Plants will take full sunshine, but a position in good direct light is preferable.

**Feeding**
Use weak liquid fertilizer with each watering, but withhold fertilizer in winter.

**Temperature range**
Cool — Intermediate — Warm
Try to maintain a temperature of 50°F (10°C) in winter. Thereafter, plants can receive higher temperatures without injury.

**Seasonal care**
Winter — Spring — Summer — Autumn
Repot immediately after the rest period. Be sure not to overpot; plants like to feel they 'belong'. Sow seeds in the early spring. Watch for pests at all times.

**Watering**
Keep plants quite dry during dormancy. Water from April onwards. Never allow plants to stand in water.

**Soil**
Use equal parts loam, peat and sharp sand, and add a basic fertilizer.

# Heliocereus/Mammillaria

## Heliocereus

This genus represents some of the most glamorous flowers within the Cactaceae. Without exception, each species carry blooms of outstanding beauty, but *Heliocereus speciosus var. superbus* is supreme in size, color and elegance. This variety, together with other species of heliocereus, has been instrumental in introducing some of the original spectacular colorings apparent in early-day epicactus cultivars.

An erect growing plant, the Sun Cactus is up to 24in (60cm) tall. The stem has six to seven angles or ribs and very prominent areoles, with many short brownish-yellow spines. Its habitat is in central Mexico, near to Mexico City, where in shady areas its habit can be that of a clambering plant. Occasionally it is an epiphyte, rooting in the shade and bearing flowers toward the tips of the stems in the sun.

The flowers are the plant's important feature. Their brilliant, dark, crimson-red blooms, frequently 6in (15cm) long, give this variety a place of consequence; in flowers of this coloring, it has no equal in the world of cactus. Plants will take a shady place so long as their flowers can open in the sun. They are generally easy to cultivate and do not demand a high temperature. A compost including leaf-mold, peat and sand in even proportions is recommended.

**Heliocereus speciosus var. superbus** (above), commonly called the Sun Plant, is native to Mexico. The superb crimson-red blooms this plant produces makes it a popular parent for epicactus cultivars. Despite its exotic appearance, this plant is not difficult to cutivate indoors.

### HELIOCEREUS

**Light and position**

Place pots in semi-shade. The tips of the stems will grow in the direction of the light and help flower production.

**Temperature range**

Cool Intermediate Warm

The Sun Cactus should be kept quite cool during overwintering, around 45°F (7°C). Beginning in spring, gradually raise the temperature a few degrees at a time.

**Watering**

Keep plants dry while temperatures are low. Then water freely once growth is underway.

**Feeding**

Fertilize while watering. It's the easy way of obtaining flowers.

**Seasonal care**

Winter Spring Summer Autumn

After winter dormancy, trim or prune the plant if necessary. Cuttings can be taken in summer before flower buds appear; they will root readily once they have callused. Overwatering in very hot weather can prove dangerous, causing stem-rot.

**Soil**

Equal parts leaf-mould, peat and sharp, gritty sand suit this plant well.

## Mammillaria

*Mammillaria* is one of the most important and justifiably popular genera of the large cactus family. To provide even a representative selection of these 400 or more species and varieties would prove a mammoth task. Cushion Cactus, the common name, is certainly applicable in many instances, but not in all. While a numerous species offset freely and develop 'cushions' — flat mounds of growth — others remain solitary plants, attaining quite sizable dimensions. The majority are of North American origin, native to Mexico and to varying places in the USA. A very few, particularly choice species have their natural home in the West Indies. It is perhaps significant that a specialist society exists just to encompass this and a few kindred genera — such is its importance to cactus enthusiasts.

In cultivation, mammillarias generally are among the least difficult plants to manage. Cushion-type plants seem to benefit from good light rather than full sun. In nature, the majority of species are found near, or even under, scrub. However, plants with a solitary habit

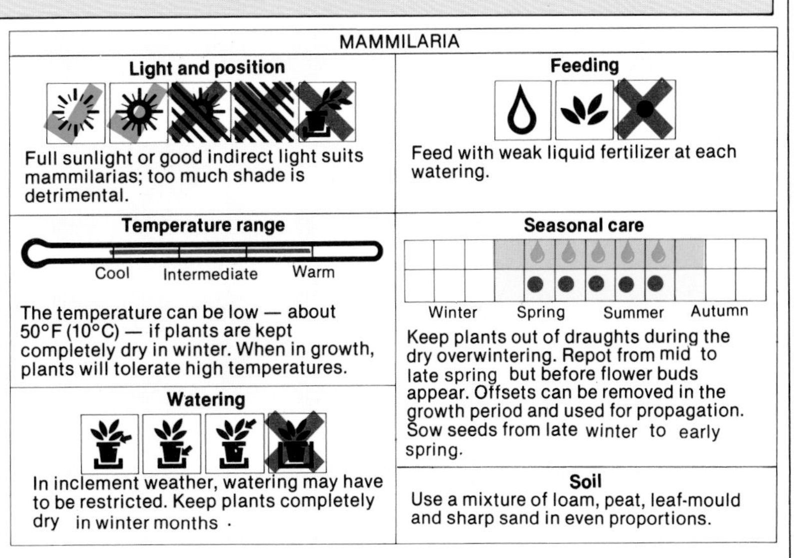

MAMMILARIA

**Light and position**

Full sunlight or good indirect light suits mammilarias; too much shade is detrimental.

**Feeding**

Feed with weak liquid fertilizer at each watering.

**Temperature range**

Cool Intermediate Warm

The temperature can be low — about 50°F (10°C) — if plants are kept completely dry in winter. When in growth, plants will tolerate high temperatures.

**Seasonal care**

Winter Spring Summer Autumn

Keep plants out of draughts during the dry overwintering. Repot from mid to late spring but before flower buds appear. Offsets can be removed in the growth period and used for propagation. Sow seeds from late winter to early spring.

**Watering**

In inclement weather, watering may have to be restricted. Keep plants completely dry in winter months.

**Soil**

Use a mixture of loam, peat, leaf-mould and sharp sand in even proportions.

prefer full sun. Careful watering is essential with all species, perhaps to a greater degree with the cushion type, for if water remains too long around the plant in inclement weather, when natural evaporation is less likely, rot can set in. All species require a really porous soil; good drainage must be a major concern.

*Mammillaria oliviae* is one of the species with the inclination to group, the offsets appearing toward the base of the plant. In current botanical opinion, this plant is represented as a variety of *Mammillaria microcarpa*, with which it obviously has a close affinity. It is native to Sonora in northern Mexico and also appears in southern Arizona in the USA.

**Mammillaria mystax** (above) is one of over 400 mammillaria species found in Mexico and the USA. The symmetrical arrangement of the spiny tubercles in conspicuous spirals is an outstanding feature. In *Mammillaria mystax*, reddish flowers form rings around the crown.

**Mammillaria oliviae** (right) has a clustering habit and produces large flowers that are variable in color. The species is native to Mexico and the southwestern USA, where in habitat it enjoys the rather sparse protection of surrounding scrub.

A heavily spined plant, *Mammillaria oliviae* has 25-35 whitish spines to an areole, including up to three longer central spines. The flowers are the crowning feature, their pale to medium-pink blooms are in evidence for a number of weeks in late spring and early summer. With individual flowers close to 1in (3cm) in diameter and occurring successively over a long period, it is a very desirable plant. Flowers can be variable in color. White and violet tones are frequently apparent.

*Mammillaria mystax* is one of the most well-known species originating in high ground in southern Mexico, at altitudes of around 6,000 feet (1800m). The stem is usually solitary, as much as 12in (30cm) tall, darkish-green, sometimes reddish-green, often woolly on the crown. The tubercles are symmetrically arranged, the areoles white and wooly, especially on young growth. Spines can be variable in number, size and color, but are usually white. One of the most pleasing aspects of the plant is the arrangement of the flowers; these occur in a ring around the crown and are numerous. Each of these flowers is around 1in (3cm) or a little less in diameter and is reddish-pink, sometimes carmine-red in color. Flowering is during the early months of summer.

*Mammillaria mystax* needs more sun than *Mammillaria oliviae*. If this is provided, it makes an excellent houseplant, thriving quite as well on a window ledge as in a greenhouse.

# Melocactus/Neogomesia/Notocactus

## Melocactus

Turk's Cap Cactus were among the very earliest cactus species introduced into cultivation, and due to their exceptionally unusual body shape, they have fascinated collectors for years.

All known species are native to South America, and are also found in Central America, Mexico and several of the West Indian islands. Many specific titles are debatable, as it's very difficult to determine what species young plants are until they reach reasonable maturity.

Great understanding must be exercised in cultivation — melocacti are not easy plants to grow in either greenhouse or home. They need a considerably higher temperature than other kinds of cactus; a miniumum of 59°F (15°C) is required to maintain the majority of melocacti successfully. Placing plants in good light with as much sun as possible is advantageous, for in their native habitat they are constantly exposed to the sun and receive little or no shade.

The plants depicted are *Melocactus bahiensis*, a Brazilian species. Note the cephalium, or crown, which develops as plants mature, and from which the pinkish-red flowers emerge.

## Neogomesia

This is a controversial genus created for just one species. Its title commemorates a certain Marte Gomez, a governor of Tamaulipas, where *Neogomesia agavoides* was discovered.

*Neogomesia agavoides* is a mountain plant from limestone slopes near Tula (Tamaulipas) in eastern Mexico. The species name refers to the shape and formation of the elongated tubercles, which resemble a miniature agave's leaf structure. Plants are quite small, only 3in (8cm) or so above ground level, grayish-green in color, and rise from a large rootstock in the form of a somewhat round taproot. Flowers are somewhat bell-shaped, about 2in (5cm) long and pale to deep reddish-pink. They are produced from the newest, large wooly areoles found near the tips of the upper surfaces of the tubercles.

This is yet another plant for the 'specialist' collector. Although its existence has been known for a great number of years, it still remains uncommon.

**Notocactus claviceps** ( right) has whitish-yellow spines and soft-textured flowers that bloom in summer.

**Melocactus bahiensis** (below) is a Brazilian species whose pinkish-red flowers emerge from the cephalium of the plant.

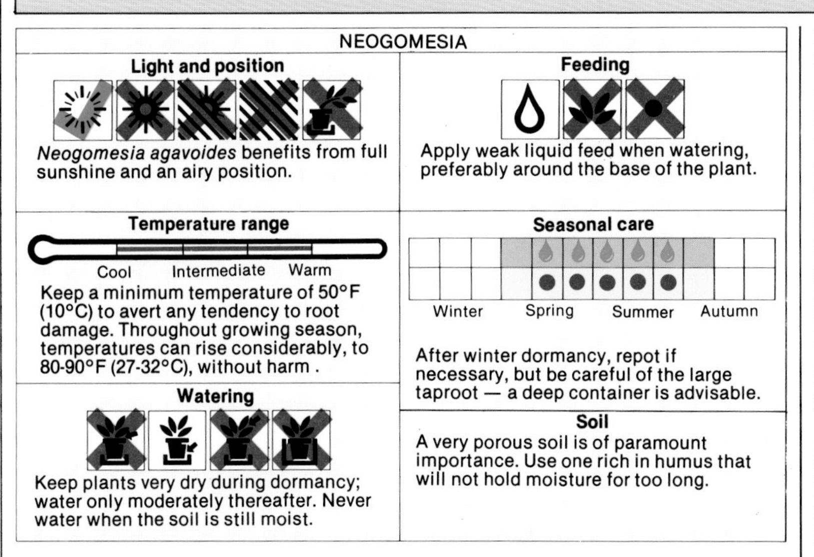

**Neogomesia agavoides** (left) has elongated tubercles and bell-shaped flowers. Native to eastern Mexico, the plant now faces extinction.

## Notocactus

*Notocactus* is a very important, popular and colorful genus.

While the flower color range is limited — primarily varying shades of yellow and reddish-purple — the different shapes these plants assume are an eye-catching feature. All known species are of South American origin. Plants are mainly solitary, but with maturity several of the species sprout offsets at the base, thus developing attractive clusters.

Notocactus generally are considered excellent subjects for cultivation in the home and greenhouse. The main requirement is a good sunny position with a winter temperature of around 50°F (10°C). During the growing and flowering season — spring and summer — plants must be watered freely and fertilized regularly. This encourages the plant to develop and flower. Flowers may last for several days. A rich compost is necessary — the introduction of leaf-mold will work wonders. This, with peat and gritty sand in even proportions, makes an ideal growing medium.

*Notocactus claviceps* would appear to be closely related to the popular *Notocactus leninghausii* species, but has certain distinctive differences. The spines of *N. leninghausii* are golden-yellow. Those of *N. claviceps* are whitish-yellow, longer, and untidily arranged along the 26-30 ribs, which have deep furrows between them. Flowers have been described as whitish-gold — they undoubtedly have a silvery sheen on their pale-golden petals. This species has its habitat in Brazil, where it is found at altitudes of around 6,500ft (2,000m).

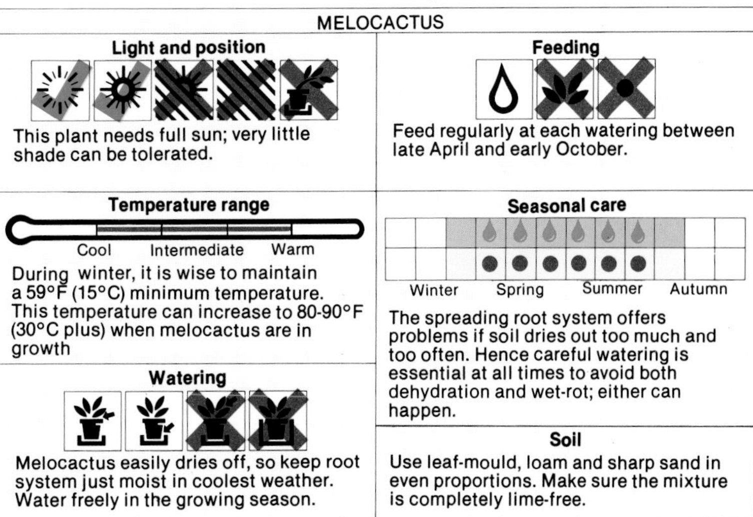

# Notocactus/Selenicereus/Weingartia

*Notocactus uebelmannianus* is a rather flattened, globular plant of glossy dark-green, some 7in (18cm) in diameter and 5in (13cm) high. The 14 or more ribs are bedecked with grayish spines of unequal length — some directed upwards, other downwards, without any set pattern. The rich violet-red flowers caused a sensation when this species was discovered just a few years ago and became available to amateur collectors. Such coloring is not common in the genus.

The 2in (5cm) diameter flowers, produced several at a time in the crown of the plant, with the whitish style and yellow filaments adorning their centers, make this an outstanding species. It is found only in a very limited area near Cacapava in Rio Grande do Sul, Brazil.

**Notocactus uebelmannianus** (top left) is remarkable for its violet-red flowers. **Selenicereus innesii** (left) is an epiphytic species native to the West Indies that bears fragrant flowers.

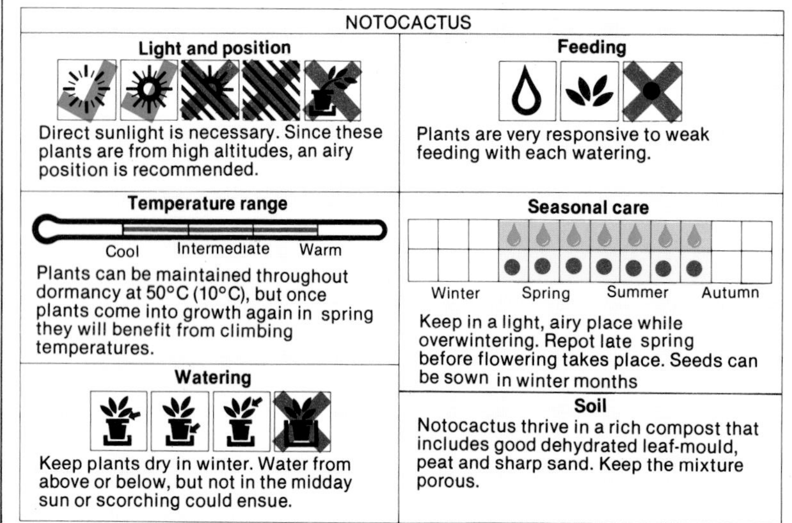

NOTOCACTUS

**Light and position**

Direct sunlight is necessary. Since these plants are from high altitudes, an airy position is recommended.

**Temperature range**

Cool Intermediate Warm

Plants can be maintained throughout dormancy at 50°C (10°C), but once plants come into growth again in spring they will benefit from climbing temperatures.

**Watering**

Keep plants dry in winter. Water from above or below, but not in the midday sun or scorching could ensue.

**Feeding**

Plants are very responsive to weak feeding with each watering.

**Seasonal care**

Winter Spring Summer Autumn

Keep in a light, airy place while overwintering. Repot late spring before flowering takes place. Seeds can be sown in winter months

**Soil**

Notocactus thrive in a rich compost that includes good dehydrated leaf-mould, peat and sharp sand. Keep the mixture porous.

## Selenicereus

All species of selenicereus are ephiphytic or partially so. They are climbing or clambering plants, occasionally pendent in habit.

*Selenicereus innesii*, which this author discovered growing on a shoreline rock-face in the West Indian island of St Vincent,has proved to be unique in the world of cacti. While most cacti bear flowers with both male and female organs, some *Selenicereus innesii* plants produce flowers that have either only male organs or only female organs. The species may have been completely destroyed in habitat because of the volcanic disturbances in the 1970s that played havoc with the northerly parts of that beautiful island.

There are no special difficulties in growing *Selencereus innesii* in cultivation. The plant with its flowers is here depicted — each trumpet-shaped bloom is slightly scented and provides a display for several weeks on end, particularly in late summer. It is an ideal subject for a hanging basket; most of the branches hang down, but some are occasionally semi-erect.

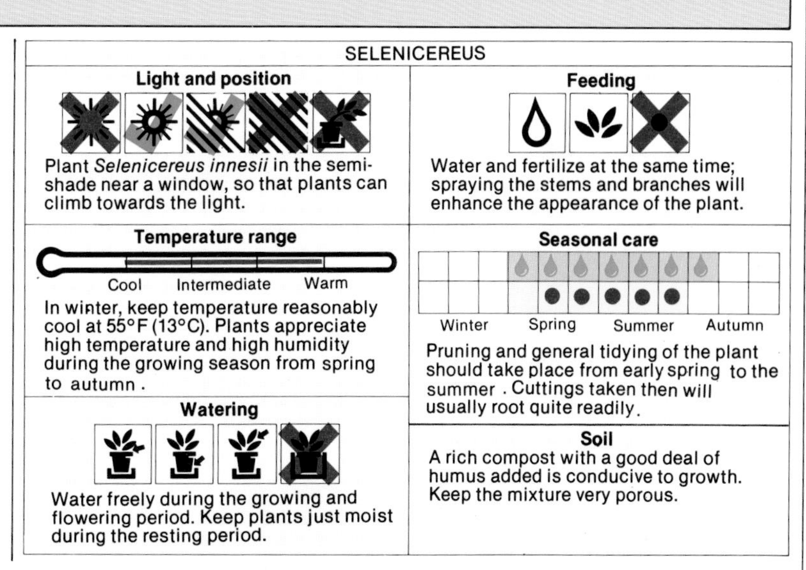

**Weingartia multispina** (left) is one of the most densely spined cactus.

## Weingartia

The genus *Weingartia* comprises a few very desirable species. One of the most unusual is *Weingartia multispina*, which is found in Bolivia near Aiquile, Cochabamba. The stem or body can attain 6in (15cm) or more in diameter and is bright-green in color. At first it is almost globular, but it often becomes somewhat cylindrical in maturity. Areoles are densely and evenly distributed, each bearing 25-30 thin, spreading spines, pale to deep brown in color, about ½in (1cm) long, and 20 or more longer central spines of similar color.

The symmetrical flowers are numerous. They are carried around the crown of the plant, and are yellow in color with a greenish sheen , accentuated by the greenish-yellow style.

By no means a common plant in cultivation, *Weingartia multispina* needs a position in good sunlight. Water and fertilize regularly during summer months, but keep very dry throughout the winter. Heavily spined plants are subject to wet-rot if incorrectly watered.

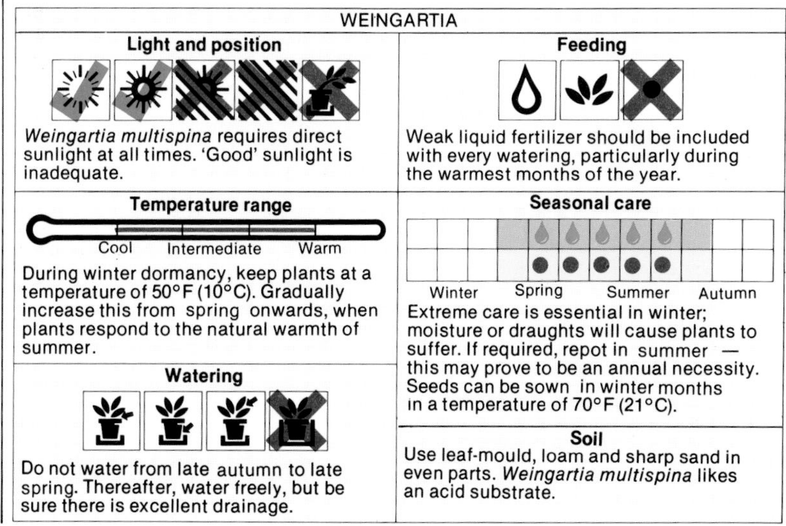

# Aloe/Ceropegia

## Aloe

One of the foremost genera of succulent plants, the *Aloe* genus comprises Old World plants originating from various parts of Africa, Arabia and Madagascar. These are indeed succulent lilies, possessing many of the same characteristics as the more familiar varieties of the lily family. With only a few exceptions, the foliage is thick and fleshy, exuding moisture if broken. Their succulence lie in their leaves; plants are able to store nourishment to withstand periods of drought in a countryside where little rainfall is registered for months at a time.

*Aloe niebuhriana* is quite a unique species, and, though discovered over two decades ago, it still remains uncommon in private collections. It is one of the comparatively few plants of the genus so far located in Arabia. It was found in South Yemen at altitudes up to 1,640 feet (500m), growing on hot, dry hillsides and low-lying valleys in semi-arid country. The first plants discovered had scarlet flowers. Later, when plants that had a yellowish-green color were found, it was thought that they constituted another new species. It is now an accepted fact that the flowers are variable, but regardless of color they have the peculiarity of being pubescent, which is not often characteristic of African species.

Leaves are thick and grayish-green. The rosette is comprised of 15-25 leaves, their margins armed with dark-brown teeth. Flowering occurs during the early weeks of the year, the stem developing from the side of the rosette, not the apex.

**Aloe niebuhriana** (left) is one of the few Arabian species grown indoors. Plants are fluffily pubescent and covered with short, fine hairs.
**Aloe cv. Sabra** is a floriferous hybrid that bears pink blooms in the autumn.(above)

*Aloe cv. Sabra* is a hybrid, developed by the author several years ago. It derives from *Aloe bellatula*, a pinkish-flowered species, and *Aloe albiflora*, one of the few white-flowering plants of the genus. The latter is distinctive in having a wide bell-shaped bloom about ½in (1cm) in diameter. That of *Aloe bellatula* is more rounded and cylindrical. Both species are Madagascan plants in origin. The leaves indicate their very close affinity; in shape, length and color there is little to distinguish one from the other. The resultant cultivar retains leaves similar to both parents; the flowers have the shape of *Aloe albiflora* but have the coloring of *Aloe bellatula.*

There are no untoward problems with cultivation. The flowers of *Aloe cv. Sabra* begin to show in mid-September and continue over a period of several weeks. They are borne on stems about 12in (30cm) tall; there are usually two or three inflorescences on each plant. Given a bright position, *Aloe cv. Sabra* makes an excellent flowering houseplant. *Aloe niebuhriana* flowers later and is considerably taller than *Aloe cv. Sabra*, reaching a height of 35in (90cm) when in full spike.

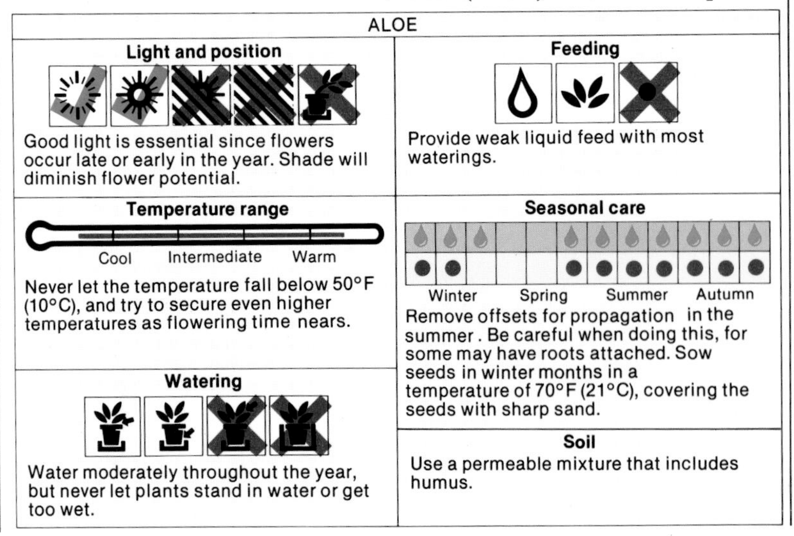

ALOE

**Light and position**

Good light is essential since flowers occur late or early in the year. Shade will diminish flower potential.

**Feeding**

Provide weak liquid feed with most waterings.

**Temperature range**

Cool Intermediate Warm

Never let the temperature fall below 50°F (10°C), and try to secure even higher temperatures as flowering time nears.

**Seasonal care**

Winter Spring Summer Autumn

Remove offsets for propagation in the summer. Be careful when doing this, for some may have roots attached. Sow seeds in winter months in a temperature of 70°F (21°C), covering the seeds with sharp sand.

**Watering**

Water moderately throughout the year, but never let plants stand in water or get too wet.

**Soil**

Use a permeable mixture that includes humus.

## Ceropegia

There are few groups of succulents that are as captivating to the eye as ceropegias. The rootstock of these consists of a globular or elongated fleshy tuber, producing long twining or trailing stems. Flowers are the most intriguing feature of cereopegias, more than compensating for the somewhat uninteresting stem and leaf growth. Flowers take the form of old-fashioned lanterns, and bloom in a combination of colors rarely encountered in the plant world. The plants are native to many parts of Africa, India and the Canary Islands, and almost all are adaptable to growing indoors. Many of these plants trail; narrow stakes, wires or slim trellis can afford stems a good anchorage and will help display the flowers to advantage.

*Ceropegia adelaidae* is quite possibly a variety of *Ceropegia de-vecchii*, a Somali plant that is itself a remarkable species. With its intricate markings and artistic shape, almost artificial in its contours, the flower is the outstanding feature. It is produced from attractive mottled stems, which are divided into long internodes. From the nodes small leaves sometimes appear but quickly fade. The flower is also produced from the nodes. The plant is native to northern areas of Kenya and the neighboring Somalia border.

*Ceropegia haygarthii* is a fine trailing and twining species with elongated, slender green stems. Greenish, ivy-shaped leaves develop in pairs at intervals along the stems and are always set opposite one another. The flower is startling in shape and coloring — a purple-spotted trumpet-shaped bloom, with pinkish ground color is crowned by the incurved lobes that unite to produce the slender, pistil-like column. This species is from South Africa.

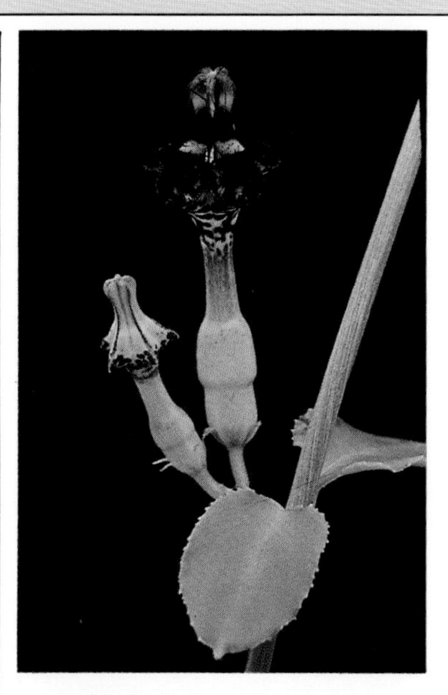

**Ceropegia nilotica** (above), **Ceropegia haygarthii** (above right) and **Ceropegia adelaidae** (right) produce lantern-shaped blooms in which pollinating insects are often trapped. Insects are released only after pollination is effected.

*Ceropegia nilotica* is a tropical East African plant. The four-angled fleshy stems arise from a tuberous rootstock. Leaves, set opposite one another, are very succulent. They are oval in shape, tapering to a point at the tip, and persist until after the flowers have faded. Flowers form from the axils of the upper leaves, usually blooming two together. They have an intricate shape and are dark-brown, with unusual yellow markings.

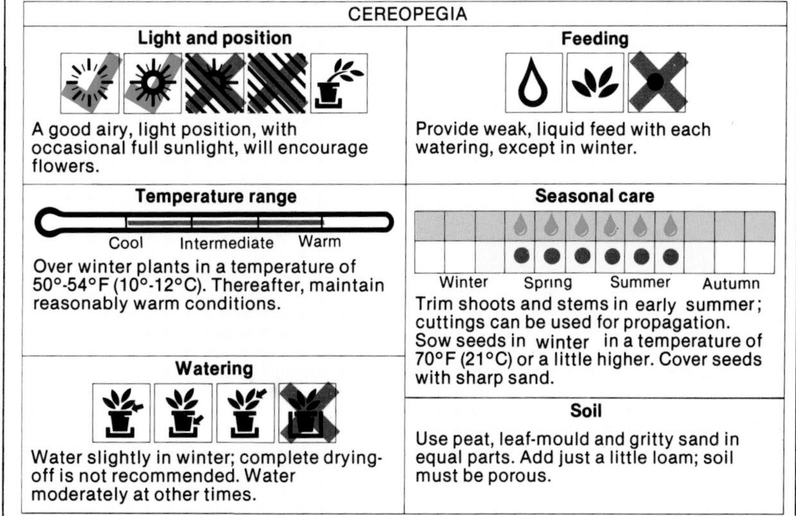

# Crassula/Euphorbia/Hoya

**Crassula**

This is the largest genus of plants within the Crassulaceae family and has over 300 species. They are extremely varied. Some are large and shrub-like; others have densely compacted leaves in the form of a miniature column only 2in (5cm) or so high. In all instances, leaves are set opposite one another, and flowers are usually borne in panicles.

*Crassula falcata* is native to southeastern parts of Cape Province in South Africa, and can grow to a height of 3¼ft (1m) when in flower. While the flowers are very beautiful, the plant can be a little unwieldy for normal households.

A number of hybrids have resulted from *Crassula falcata*, and are probably the product of cross-pollination with *Crassula perfoliata*. A rather miniaturized replica of the former, *Crassula falcata hyb.*, has become a most useful plant. It has the species' leaf shape and flower color, but rarely grows taller than 12in (30cm) tall. Being of hybrid origin, it can only be reproduced by vegetative means. Two methods are possible — sectional stem cuttings, or leaf cuttings. The latter method is slower, but more satisfactory.

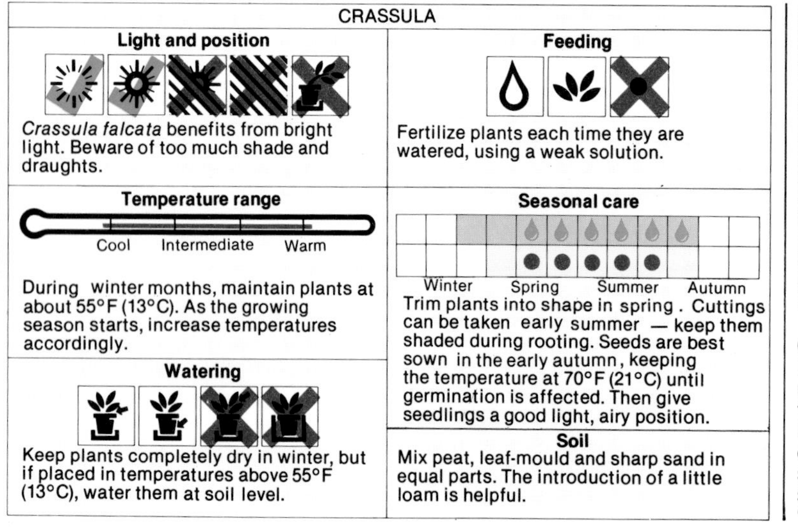

CRASSULA

**Light and position**

*Crassula falcata* benefits from bright light. Beware of too much shade and draughts.

**Temperature range**

Cool Intermediate Warm

During winter months, maintain plants at about 55°F (13°C). As the growing season starts, increase temperatures accordingly.

**Watering**

Keep plants completely dry in winter, but if placed in temperatures above 55°F (13°C), water them at soil level.

**Feeding**

Fertilize plants each time they are watered, using a weak solution.

**Seasonal care**

Winter Spring Summer Autumn

Trim plants into shape in spring. Cuttings can be taken early summer — keep them shaded during rooting. Seeds are best sown in the early autumn, keeping the temperature at 70°F (21°C) until germination is affected. Then give seedlings a good light, airy position.

**Soil**

Mix peat, leaf-mould and sharp sand in equal parts. The introduction of a little loam is helpful.

**Crassula falcata hyb.** (top) bears long-lasting blooms. It is smaller and more suitable for indoor cultivation than its parent.
**Euphorbia flanaganii** (above) has a caudex whose head is crowned with spreading branches. Because of its shape, this species is said to have a 'Medusa' head.

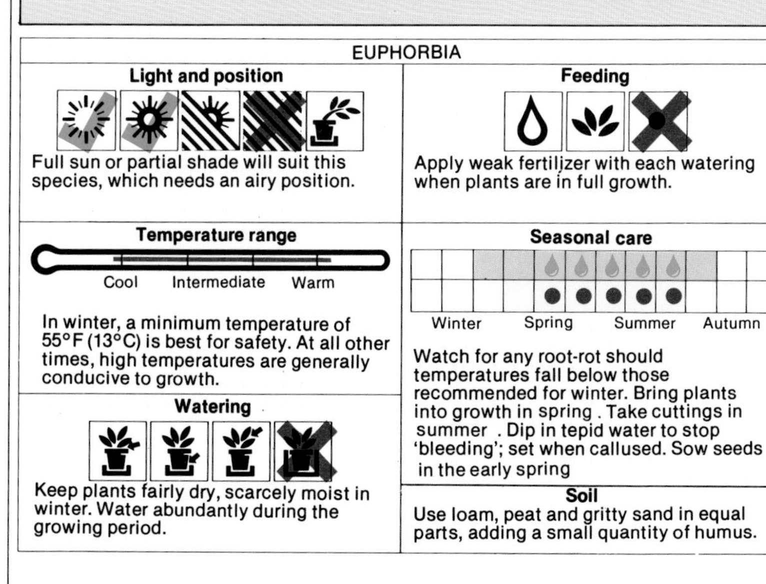

**Hoya multiflora** (above) has only recently been grown as a houseplant. It is one of many succulent species in the *Hoya* genus.

## Euphorbia

*Euphorbia* is one of the largest genera of plants and is said to include over 2,000 different species. A number of species are succulent, principally those found in Africa, Madagascar, Arabia, the Indian subcontinent and parts of Central and Southern America. Their weird, often almost grotesque shapes attract the attention of the plant enthusiast, but no less so than the many species with growth of perfect symmetry.

*Euphorbia flanaganii* grows in South Africa. It has a low, subcylindrical caudex at just above ground level, crowned with two to three rows of more or less erect 'branches' set around the tuberculate head of the caudex. The older branches tend to spread and help to create the attractive form depicted. The inflorescence, or cyathia, is a characteristic of the whole genus — some have male or female 'flowers' on the same plant, others are unisexual.

All euphorbia plants have a dangerous white sap or latex that will exude upon any injury to the plant. Care should be taken that this sap does not reach cuts or any sensitive part of the body.

## Hoya

Fleshy, wax-like flowers are a generic characteristic of hoyas. A few species, like *Hoya carnosa* and *Hoya bella*, have held pride of place as houseplants for many years. *Hoya multiflora* is yet another species now adorning many homes. Its habitat is the Malacca Straits region — Sumatra, Borneo and Java.

There appears to be two forms of *Hoya multiflora*. One is of climbing habit; the other remains bushy, but leaf and flower are identical. The leaves are large, leathery, dark-green, often with whitish blotches. Flowers are borne in terminal clusters, 25-30 individual flowers in each. The bloom is straw-colored, has a brown center, is sweetly scented and proves to be long lasting.

Like *Hoya carnosa, Hoya multiflora* requires training. Otherwise the plant becomes untidy and loses its appeal. Prune carefully in late spring. Make certain that any flow of the white sap is staunched by inserting the cuts in water.

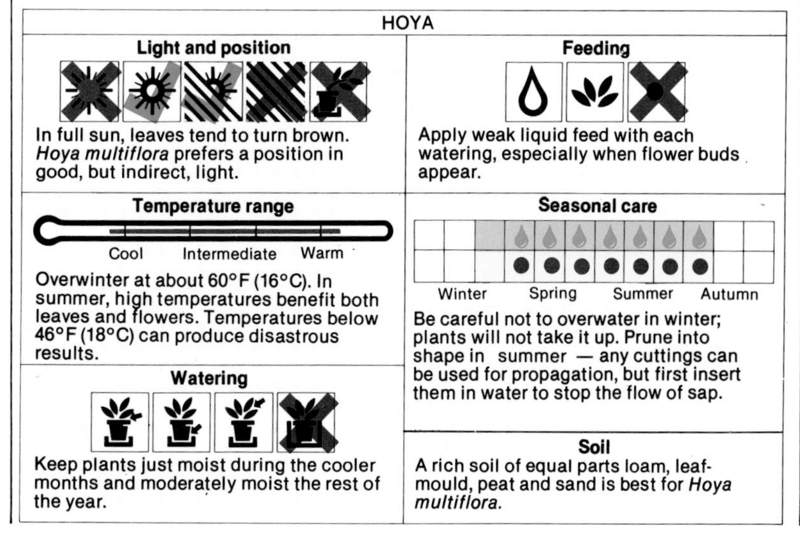

# Huernia/Ipomoea/Lampranthus

### Huernia

This is an important genus in the Asclepiadaceae family. There are a large number of species in this genus, and they are all found in an area stretching from South Africa to Ethiopia. They belong to the milkweed family, and in the main develop into cushion-like plants, the stems and side branches continually spreading and rooting, rarely growing more than 2in (5cm) high. While the stems of various species are usually quite similar, flowers vary and present an elaborate array of colors and shapes.

*Huernia schneiderana* was discovered many years ago by a Dutch missionary. His name was Justus Huernius, and the genus was subsequently named in his honor. The species was found on the northern side of Lake Malawi, and its habitat extends from Malawi through to Mozambique.

The stem growth of *Huernia schneiderana* is remarkably rapid. The slender green cylindrical stems quickly form a compacted grouping. Each stem is about 2in (6cm) long, though in cultivation stems may become considerably longer. Stems are five-to-seven-angled, with inconspicuous acute teeth.

The shallow bell-shaped flowers, about 1½in (3cm) in diameter, appear toward the base of the stem and bloom in late summer. Externally, the flowers are dull brown in color; internally, they are velvety blackish-purple with reddish margins, the lobes recurving so as to display the rich coloring. Plants are equally suitable for home or greenhouse. They need good light and frequent watering during the growing season.

*Huernia verekeri* is from southern Zimbabwe, near the Mozambique border. Stems are always diminutive, only about 1½in (4cm) high, and have five

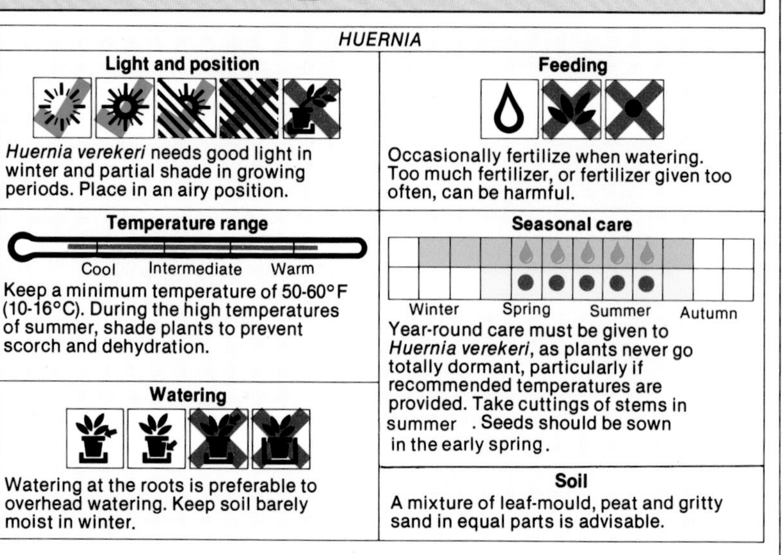

**Huernia verekeri** (above) has tapering flower lobes that are covered by minute purplish hairs.
**Huernia schneiderana** (above right) has fleshy stems and basally produced flowers. It exemplifies the general growth patterns of the huernia species.

to seven angles bearing triangular, pointed teeth. Flowering is from the base of the stem; there are usually one to three flowers to a stem. The rather small size of the flower is more than compensated for by the exotic patterning of the bloom.

Flowers develop and open during middle to late summer, occasionally a little earlier. It is essential to maintain good moisture around the root system during this period of general growth when the absorbtion of water and nutrients is at its peak.

### Ipomoea

This is a very large genus of about 400 species, many of them native to sub-tropical and tropical regions. Not all are succulents, and those that are must be termed 'root succulents' due to the often large tuberous root-systems.

*Ipomoea holubii* is a South African root succulent that was, until recently, included under *Merremia*, a genus of exotic plants within the Convolvulaceae family. In the wild it grows in coarse gravel in open grass-

lands. The round caudex body is usually about 4in (10cm) underground. Only the slender grass-like leaves, often lying flat on the ground, are visible. Due to the close resemblance to grass, plants avoid detection until they produce their bright blooms. Flowers may vary in color from deep purple to much paler pastel shades.

This is not a difficult plant to cultivate. However, the caudex should not be buried but left exposed at ground level. This prevents any rot that might otherwise set in. With just the very base set in the ground, roots readily develop, followed by leaves and then flowers. By no means a common plant, it is something of an indoor floral 'novelty' — vivid flowers are followed by the rounded, leathery seed pods.

**Ipomoea holubii** (above left) bears large, showy flowers freely produced. **Lampranthus conspicuus** (above) is a thickly branching species remarkable for its vivid violet-red flowers.

## Lampranthus

This large genus of over 200 species has remarkably bright, shining flowers. The generic title registers this outstanding fact: 'lampros' means 'shining'; 'anthos' means 'flowers.' With scarely an exception, all species of *Lampranthus* are native of Cape Province in South Africa, where at certain times of the year the veldt is literally carpeted with these wonderful flowers.

*Lampranthus conspicuus* is thought to have originated in the area of Albany, but this is not certain. It is a densely branching species with thick stems and branches reaching 12in (30cm) or more in length. Leaves are thick and fleshy, somewhat cylindrical in shape and narrowing toward the tips. They appear in dense formation at the tips of the branches. Flowers are the central feature. The rich violet-red bloom, of an almost iridescent brightness, appears in early to quite late summer. As a rule, the plant blossoms singly, but sometimes two or three blooms appear together.

Given a position in full sun, plants will do well in either home or greenhouse. They may even be used as garden bedding plants when summer conditions are good.

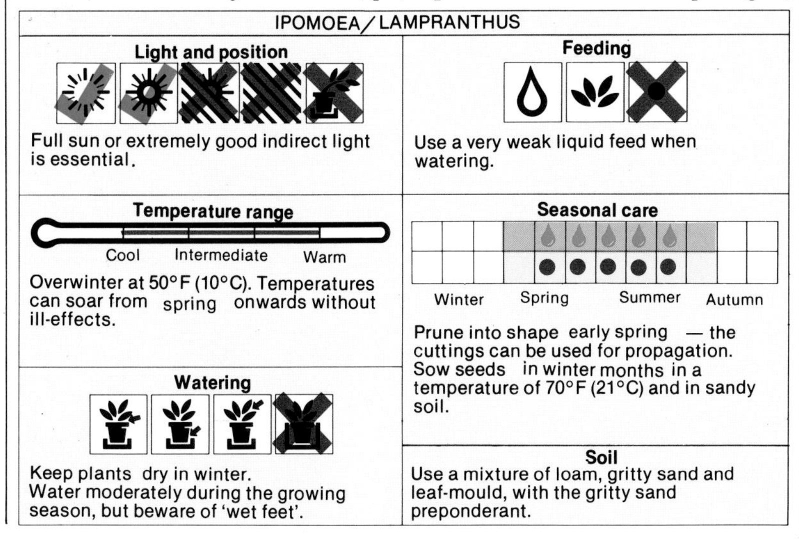

# Luckhoffia/Pachypodium

## Luckhoffia

The species *Luckhoffia beukmanii* is an uncommon plant and the only member of this monotypic genus. It is interesting to note that both the discoverer of the plant, C. Beukman, and the author of the genus, Dr. J. Luckhoff, are commemorated in the plant's title. It was first located in the Pakhuis Mountains, in South Africa and considered to be a new species of stapelia, a title under which it was first described. While it is said to have an exceptionally long flowering season in habitat, in cultivation flowering occurs during a comparatively short period.

It is quite a tall plant; the stems are up to 30in (76cm) high and 1in (3cm) in diameter. The compressed tubercles, grayish-green in colour, give added prominence to the eight-angled formation of the stems. Flowers are variable, usually pale brown and densely yellow-spotted but sometimes deep reddish-brown, on 1in (3cm) long pedicels.

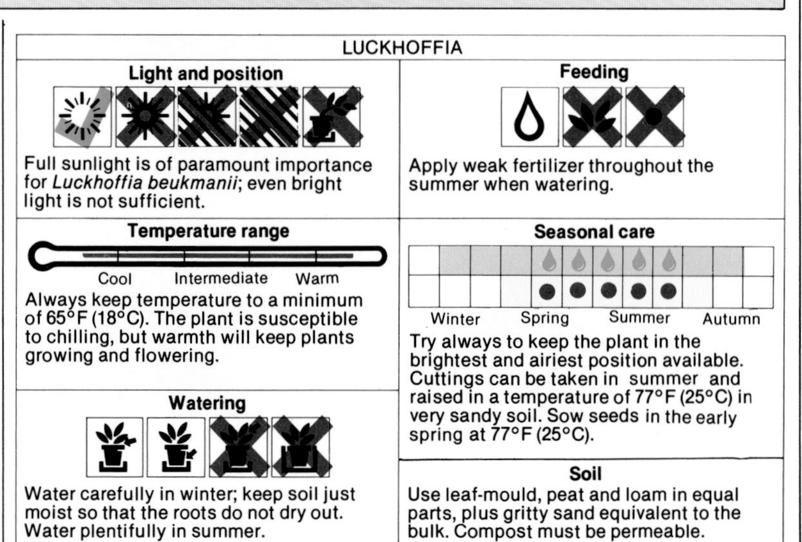
LUCKHOFFIA

**Light and position**

Full sunlight is of paramount importance for *Luckhoffia beukmanii*; even bright light is not sufficient.

**Feeding**

Apply weak fertilizer throughout the summer when watering.

**Temperature range**

Cool Intermediate Warm

Always keep temperature to a minimum of 65°F (18°C). The plant is susceptible to chilling, but warmth will keep plants growing and flowering.

**Seasonal care**

Winter Spring Summer Autumn

Try always to keep the plant in the brightest and airiest position available. Cuttings can be taken in summer and raised in a temperature of 77°F (25°C) in very sandy soil. Sow seeds in the early spring at 77°F (25°C).

**Watering**

Water carefully in winter; keep soil just moist so that the roots do not dry out. Water plentifully in summer.

**Soil**

Use leaf-mould, peat and loam in equal parts, plus gritty sand equivalent to the bulk. Compost must be permeable.

This is closely akin to species of the genus *Hoodia*, another genus of cylindrical-shaped plants. Like hoodia , Luckhoffi beukmanii is not considered easy to grow but will nevertheless thrive in a dry atmosphere indoors. Excessive watering causes stem-rot; do not overwater.

## Pachypodium

*Pachypodium bispinosum* is but one species of a genus renowned for plants of outstanding character, their habitat extending through the dry regions of South Africa, Namibia, Angola and Madagascar. They are erect plants that have spirally arranged leaves and resemble shrubby

**Luckhoffia beukmanii** (above) is an unusual species demanding careful attention. It needs full sun and *plenty* of water during the growing season. **Pachypodium bispinosum** (right) is a plant easily grown indoors. Pink, bell-shaped flowers appear in summer.

# Pelargonium

trees. All species have fleshy stems and some are caudiciforms — that is to say, plants with a caudex root system.

*Pachypodium bispinosum* from Namaqualand in southern African is one of the species with a caudex. The caudex is mainly subterranean, often completely below ground level. A tangle of dark-green branches, well armed with prickles, develops at the crown of the plant, which produces leaves from between the spines and, later, small, bell-shaped pink flowers. There is a similar plant from the same locality, *Pachypodium saundersii*, which has white flowers and is inclined to be variable in its growth.

*Pachypodium bispinosum* responds exceedingly well to cultivation conditions. Given satisfactory care, it can become a most floriferous houseplant. Knowing when to water and, just as important, when not to water is important to whether this plant succeeds in doors.

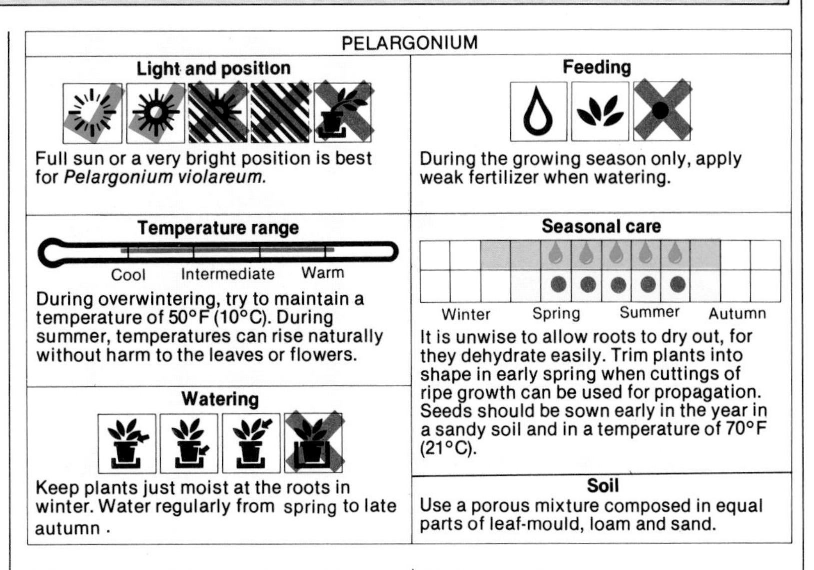


**Pelargonium violareum** (below) is very much a feature plant, whether grown in a sunny spot indoors or bedded out in the garden during the warmer months. This South African plant bears flowers of exceptional beauty, which bloom during the summer months.

## Pelargonium

It may be surprising to some that pelargonium species are considered succulents. A large number of plants in this genus are extremely succulent, others not at all and some fall within a 'border-line' category. *Pelargonium violareum*, the viola geranium, is such a plant. It is included principally on account of its pleasing flowers and because it is seldom mentioned in botanical books.

*Pelargonium violareum* is native to the southern part of Cape Province in South Africa, where it grows about 14in (35cm) high on stony, sandy hillsides. The plant is small and bushy in appearance; the stems and branches are quite densely covered with fine, hairy gray-green leaves with indented margins. Without question, flowers are the distinguishing feature — the pedicels bear two to four blooms of decidedly unusual coloring. The lower three petals are almost pure white, sometimes slightly suffused pink, while the upper two are ruby-red.

In habitat, plants bloom in autumn, but in cultivation plants provide their flowers for several weeks in the summer.

# Pelargonium/Plumiera/Pterodiscus

*Pelargonium oblongatum*, which may soon be renamed *Pelargonium ensatum*, is found in Namaqualand in South Africa, where it grows at altitudes from 1,000 to 3,000ft (300 to 900m) on the slopes of the Langehoof Mountains.

This is an excellent representative of 'stem succulents'. It possesses a roundish, tuberous base, just above ground level, which is covered with thin layers of brownish skin. The few leaves, somewhat oval-oblong in shape and tapering toward the tips, are borne on hairy stalks and precede the flowers.

Flowers appear in umbels on stems about 12in (30cm) long. The broad, rounded pale-yellow petals — the two upper ones bearing pale-red stripes — present an unusual flower. In cultivation it is likely that the leaves will fall before the flowers show themselves.

This plant is recommended for pot culture, but do not overpot — it seems to prefer a compacted rooting area to being able to spread roots around. Follow this suggestion for other species of pelargoniums that have comparable stem growth. Flowering is from late summer to autumn.

**Pelargonium oblongatum** (left) is a 'stem succulent'. The leaves invariably wither before the flower buds appear.
**Plumiera acutifolia** (above) produces flowers with exquisite perfume.

## Plumiera

The genus *Plumiera* comprises only a few species, all of which are shrubby or tree-like in their growth. The main stem or trunk is very succulent, thick and fleshy and frequently branches, and can attain a height of 8ft (2.4m) or more. However, careful pruning will restrain this growth to a size more convenient for indoor decor.

*Plumiera acutifolia* is a well-known plant familiar to anyone who has traveled in subtropical and tropical countries. While it is native to Mexico and some of the West Indian islands, frangipani, also called West Indian jasmine, has become an important cultivated plant in many parts of the Far East. In India it is referred to as the 'Temple Tree of India'. It was first described as *Plumiera acuminata*, and even now some doubt remains as to which title is valid.

Flowers develop readily on comparatively young, sparsely leaved plants three to four years old. The fragrant, funnel-shaped flowers are waxy white

PELARGONIUM

**Light and position**

Good light is necessary for *Pelargonium oblongatum*; shade will affect the habit of the plant.

**Temperature range**

Cool Intermediate Warm

During overwintering, maintain a temperature of 55°F (13°C). Beginning in late spring gradually increase temperature. Give light shading *only* if temperature rises too high–over 85°F (30°C).

**Watering**

Water freely above or below during the growing season. Keep roots slightly moist in winter.

**Feeding**

Apply weak liquid feed with each watering between spring and autumn.

**Seasonal care**

Winter Spring Summer Autumn

Make sure there is not dehydration or rotting of roots in winter due to failure to follow the treatment prescribed above. Seeds may be sown in the early spring or immediately after ripening. The temperature should be 72-77°F (22-25°C).

**Soil**

Use equal parts of leaf-mould and loam to equal the bulk in sharp sand.

suffused with yellow. In many parts of the world these beautiful flowers are traditionally used at marriage feasts.

Frangipani is becoming increasingly available. There are other species of the genus bearing red, cream and totally yellow blooms, all requiring much the same attention.

### Pterodiscus

This is a very small genus of African plants, none of which tends to grow more than about 12in (30cm) high. The more succulent species usually have a fleshy rootstock, and this feature is true of *Pterodiscus speciosus*. This is one of only two or three species native to South Africa — the others are mainly East African, found as far north as Ethiopia.

*Pterodiscus speciosus* has quite a widespread habitat, extending from Griqualand West in Cape Province through to Transvaal. The rather rounded, often mis-shapen stem, is a development from the subterranean taproot and will grow about 6in (15cm) high, developing many leaves. These leaves are usually rather narrow and elongated, dentate on the margins and are from 1-2in (3-5cm) long. Flowers appear in early summer, and the flowering period can last for a number of weeks. The purplish-red blooms are produced from near the tips of the stems.

This is very much a deciduous plant. The leaves dry off in late summer, and the plant becomes almost totally dormant in October. There are two closely related species with almost identical characteristics — *Pterodiscus luridus*, with reddish-yellowish flowers, and *Pterodiscus aurantiacus*, with blooms of intense yellow.

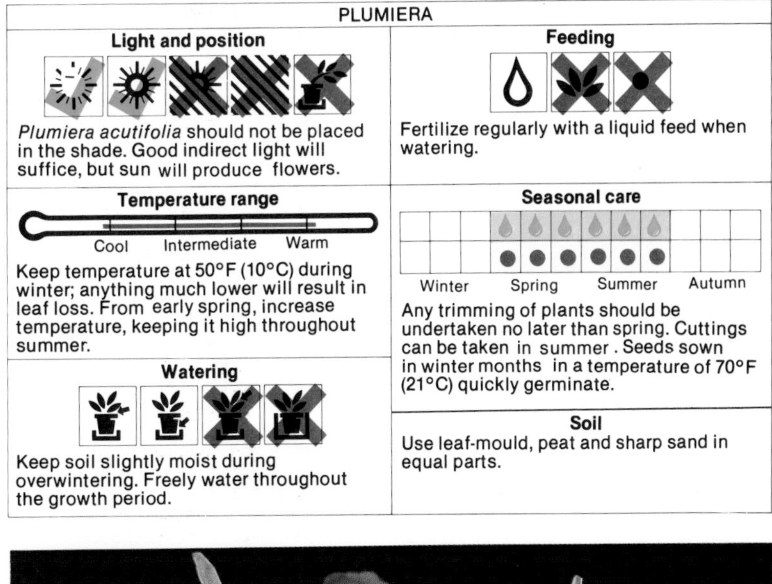

**Pterodiscus speciosus** (above) is one of the more uncommon species in cultivation. This South African plant produces purplish-red flowers.

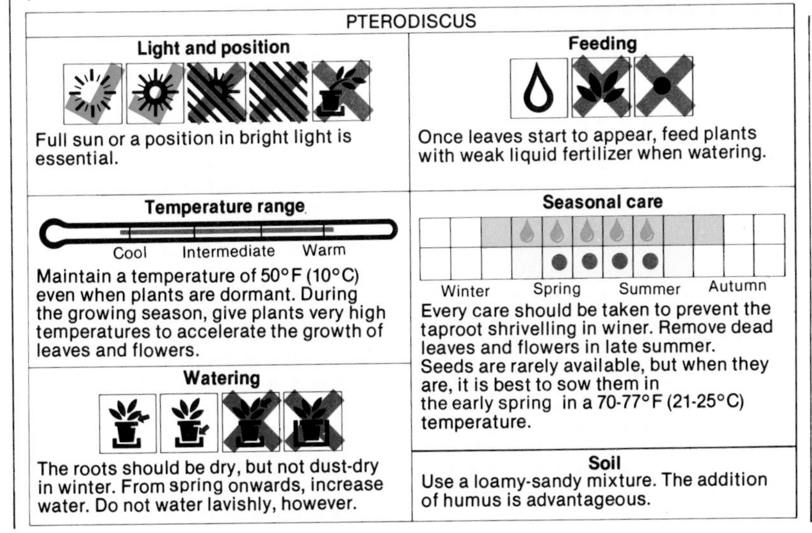

# Stapelia/Stultitia/Tacitus

## Stapelia

There are a great number of species in *Stapelia*, one of the larger genera in the Asclepiadaceae family of plants. Many species are similar both in stem appearance and in flower.

Though it is slow-growing, *Stapelia erectiflora* has outstanding merits. Stems often reach 6in (15cm) in length and ⅓in (1cm) in diameter. Flowers are borne on a pedicel or stalk 2-4in (5-10cm) in length. The corolla lobes of the flower are tightly recurved, creating a cap-like effect. The lobes are mainly purple and the densely set white hairs completely covering them give the plant a glamor all of its own. However, the flower is not large — in its recurved state, only about ½in (1cm) in diameter.

This plant, like the majority of stapelia species, is native to South Africa. Cultivation requirements are much the same as those for huernias. a warm situation is better than a cool one, and it thrives better in an airy position. Complete dormancy is not advisable, as roots can quickly dehydrate and the plant may take a long time to recover from damage and shriveling of the stems. Nevertheless, it can be recommended as a houseplant since it does better in the dry conditions that prevail indoors than in the greenhouse.

## Stultitia

This is a very small genus of South African plants that is closely related to the *Stapelia* genus. The main difference bet-

**Tacitus bellus** (left) is a recently discovered species native to Mexico. Compacted leaves and brilliant flowers combine to make this dwarf succulent exceptionally appealing to the eye. Clusters of flowers appear in spring and late summer; there may be as many as 10 blooms to a stem.
**Stultitia cooperi** (above) is a miniature species that bears purplish star-shaped blooms and is ideal for indoor cultivation.

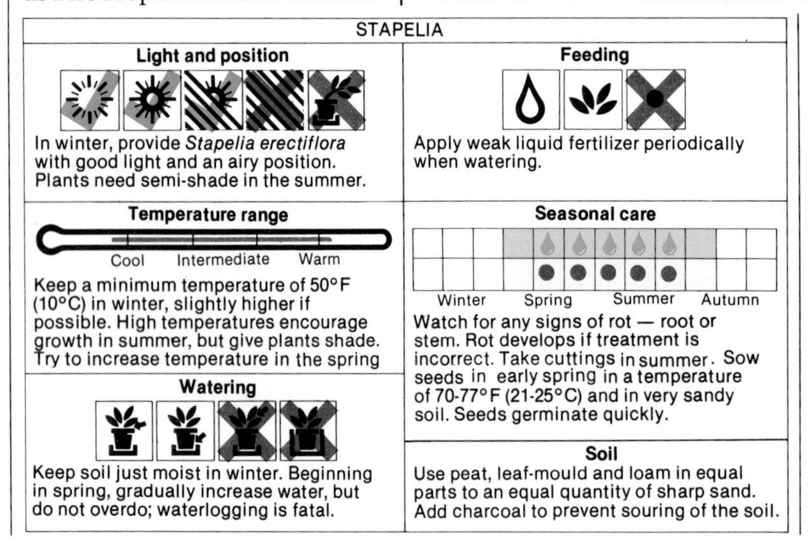

ween stultitias and stapelias is that the former have a pronounced ring around the mouth of the flower tube.

*Stultitia cooperi* is one of the more dwarf plants in the genus. Stems are erect and only 1in (3cm) high. The four-angled stems are most pronounced, and they are emphasized by the stems' round and pointed protuberances. Flowers arise from low on the stem. Several buds may appear almost together, but usually buds open only one or two at a time. The complex bloom is borne on a pedicel, and when fully open presents a starlike flower 1½ inch (3-4cm) in diameter. The flower is basically purplish but has lines and dots of other coloring; the margins of the lobes are decidedly hairy.

*Stultitia cooperi* bears a seed pod, shaped like a horn . Within this horn are numerous flat seeds, each with a little 'parachute' attached. The parachutes contribute to the dispersal of seeds from the ripe horn. Plants are native to South Africa.

## Tacitus

*Tacitus bellus* has become a very sought-after plant. It is the only species in the *Tacitus* genus and is currently considered so close to those in *Graptopetalum*, another genus of succulent rosette plants, as to be inseparable. *Tacitus*, however, is still the most common generic name.

The plant was discovered at altitudes of around 5,400ft (1,600m) on the slopes of Sierra Obscura in Mexico. The plant develops a rosette of darkish gray-green leaves, exceptionally compact and with an almost flattened surface. Flowers are produced in small clusters on stems only 1-2in (3-5cm) long. As many as 10 or more may adorn each stem. They appear in spring and early summer; flowers bloom successively. The vivid reddish-pink petals, widely spreading, surmounted by white, equally spreading stamens makes this one of the most beautiful of dwarf succulents.

The popularity of *Tacitus bellus* has been phenomenal. No other new species has created such enthusiasm on the part of the collector. There is no difficulty in its cultivation. Being from high altitudes, it is able to withstand cold, dry winters.

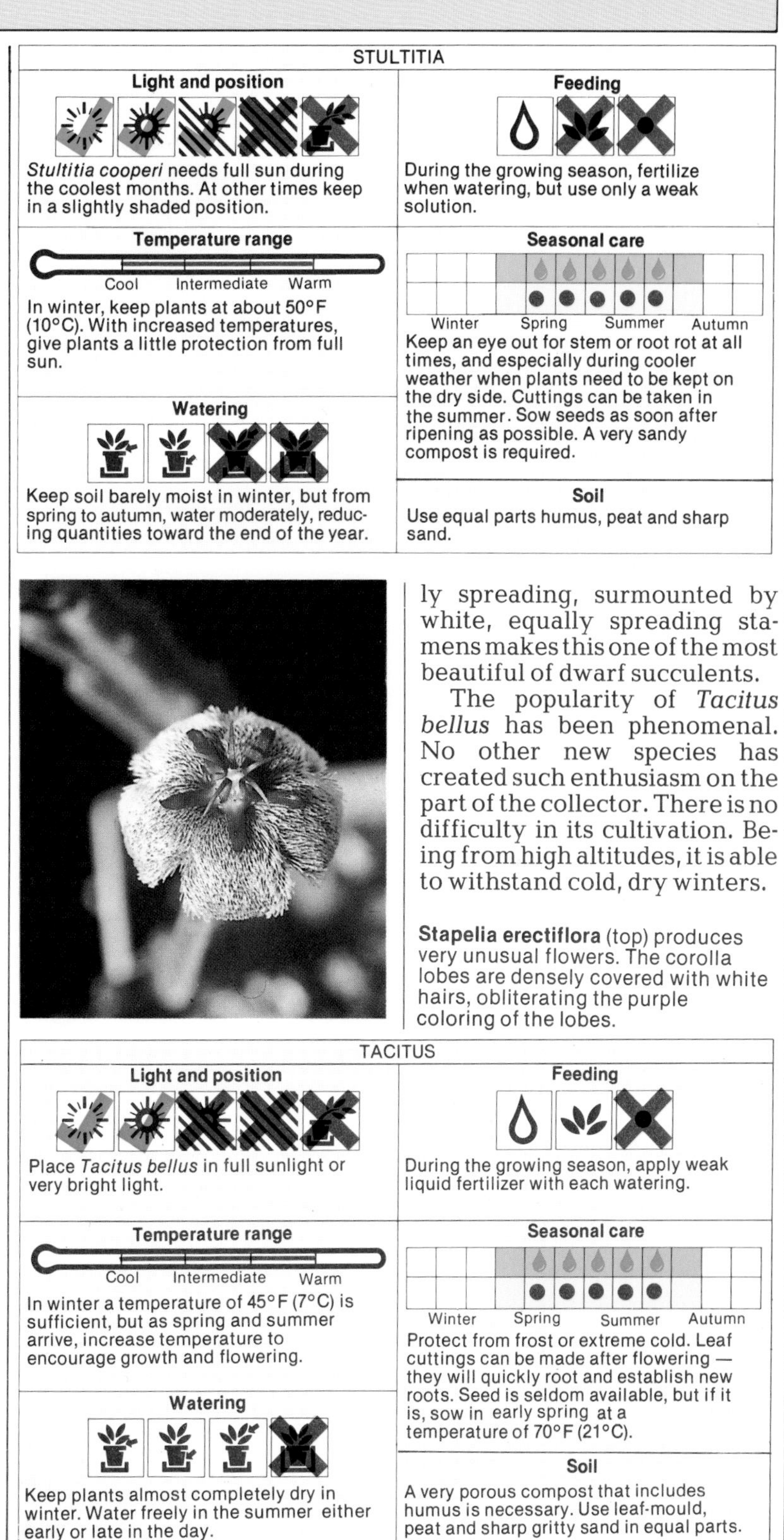


**Stapelia erectiflora** (top) produces very unusual flowers. The corolla lobes are densely covered with white hairs, obliterating the purple coloring of the lobes.

# Orchids

MAGNIFICENT, MYSTERIOUS, fascinating, beautiful: Many superlatives have been rightly used to describe the greatest family of flowering plants — the Orchidaceae. Yet, along with the mystique of orchids go the myths and fallacies that surround them — that they are expensive, that they are parasites, that they need expensive osmunda fiber imported from Japan, that they all require high temperatures.

The truth is that today's modern hybrids are available at reasonable prices and are not too difficult to cultivate. Orchids thrive in a wide range of conditions, and, by the way, no orchid is parasitic!

Though unknown in Europe until the mid-seventeenth century, orchids have a long history. Certainly the ancient Greeks were aware of them. The Greek philosopher Theophrastus (372-287 B.C.) referred to a group of plants called 'orchis' in his manuscript, 'An Enquiry into Plants', and the name orchid derives from the Greek word 'orchis', which means 'testicle' — a term that describes the roots of orchids, testiculate tubers occurring in pairs. This part of the plant was considered of great medicinal value for many centuries. Scientists now believe that orchids originated as early as 100-120 million years ago, probably in Malaysia.

Orchids grow in one of two ways, either in a monopodial growth pattern or a sympodial growth pattern. Most orchids are sympodial, including the cymbidiums, paphiopedilums and odontoglossums. These orchids produce a succession of growths connected by a short rhizome. They often produce a pseudo-bulb as well. This is not a true bulb, but a swelling at the base of growth. It enables the plant to store water and nutrients used in adverse conditions.

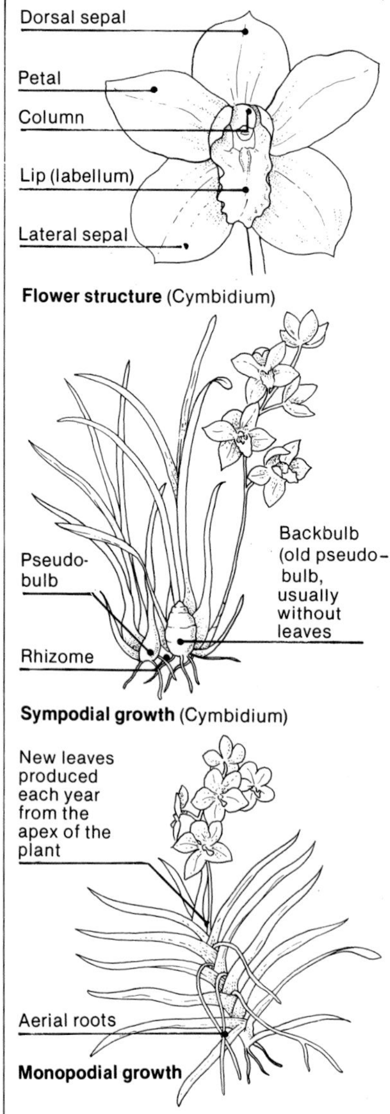


All orchids have the same flower structure (top). Shown here are two examples of growth patterns — sympodial (center) and monopodial (bottom).

Phalaenopsis and vandas are examples of monopodial orchids. They have a single stem that each year produces new leaves from the apex of the plant, and they often have aerial roots. Most of the monopodial orchids are epiphytic, originate from the tropics and do not produce pseudobulbs.

All orchids are alike insofar as they have three outer floral segments (the sepals), and three inner segments (the petals), one of which is modified into a lip or labellum. The stamens and the stigma — the sexual parts of the plant — form what is known as the column. This structure is common to all orchids, but the great variety in orchids is probably more striking than their similarity. Approximately 100,000 orchid species and hybrids exist today. Flowers range from massive blooms to those that almost require a magnifying glass to be seen. Some orchids are flamboyant and colorful; others are dull and insignificant. Some have delightful perfumes, others give off noxious odors. Flower structure also varies.

Much of this variety is due to the work of modern hybridizers. In nature, only a very small percentage of seeds ever develop into plants. New scientific advances, however, have enabled hybridists to grow larger populations of seedlings. The production of plants by tissue culture, a technology developed in the 1960s, was an immense breakthrough for orchid breeders, making it possible to propagate, or 'clone', several thousand plants from a single piece of orchid tissue.

Partly because of their increased availability, partly because orchids are such good value for money — many orchids will last up to three months in flower and, provided instructions are followed, will flower the next year — orchids are now increasingly common as houseplants. Some of these magnificent flowering plants, classified according to genus, are described in the section which follows. Though there are many genera of orchids, the four represented here encompass those orchids most suitable for indoor cultivation.

Hybrid varieties of orchids like these (above) have been produced in large quantities by the tissue-culture method developed in the 1960s. The materials used in this method are shown below.

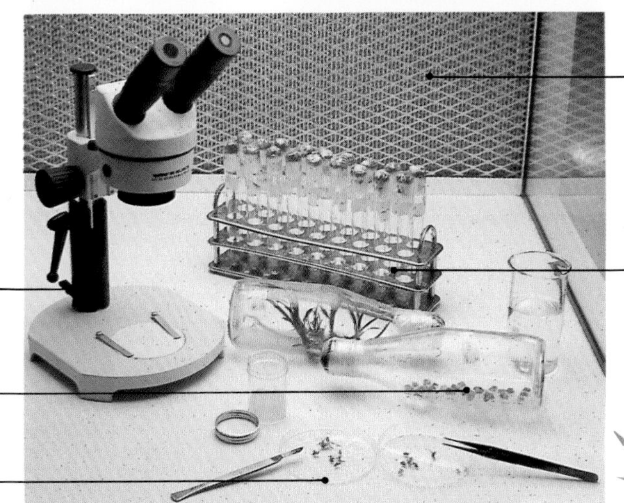

Dissecting microscope, used during the removal of tiny slivers of tissue from the shoot tip of the plant.

Flasks containing nutrient jelly. Sterilized, they are planted with divided tissue from the test tubes.

Sterile petri dishes containing orchid tissue ready for sectioning.

Instruments and materials within a sterile work cabinet.

Test tubes containing nutrients, sugar and glucose, vitamins and growth hormones in liquid form. Slivers of tissue are grown in this solution to many times their original size.

Flasks containing growing orchid tissue (left). The flask in the foreground shows tissue ready for removal and further sectioning. The flask behind contains tissue which has been allowed to go on to produce roots and shoots. The cloned plants — thousands from a pinhead-sized piece of tissue — are grown on in special trays (right).

### Temperature

Orchids are grown in three temperature ranges. The cool-house varieties need a minimum winter night temperature of 50°F (10°C). In summer, night temperature should not rise above 65°F (18°C). Intermediate varieties need a minimum temperature of 55°F (13°C) and summer night temperature is best at 60°F (16°C). Warm-house varieties should be raised in a night temperature not less than 60°F (16°C) in winter. In summer, night temperature should be a minimum of 65°F (18°C).

In all cases, daytime temperature should be at least 9°F (5°C) higher than night temperature. Most orchids do poorly if daytime temperature rises above 90°F (32°C), although they can tolerate higher temperature levels for a short time if humidity is also high.

### Watering

With today's peat-and-perlite mixes, it is best to wait several days after the surface of the plant becomes dry before watering. When you do water, give a thorough soaking from the top, using a watering can. Rainwater is preferable to tap water.

### Feeding

The orchid growers of the past thought that giving orchids fertilizers was the road to certain disaster. Now, however, orchid growers realize that the orchid plant, like other members of the plant kingdom, needs some form of nourishment. The main nutrients required by most plants are nitrogen, phosphate and potassium — a threesome often referred to as n.p.k. During the spring and early summer months a fertilizer containing n.p.k. in the ratio of 20:10:10 is most suitable. During the late summer, early autumn and winter months, a fertilizer containing equal concentrations of nitrogen, phosphate and potassium (20:20:20) is ideal; during the early autumn period a high-potash fertilizer is beneficial. Most fertilizers should be used at half the prescribed strength and given at regular intervals. It is of great importance to flush out the compost with pure water periodically; the best practice, therefore, is to feed your plant with each watering (giving water with the levels of fertilizer indicated), changing to pure water every fourth time. Make sure that you give the compost a really thorough soaking, so that any build-up of salts will be flushed away.

### Light

Orchids need good light, but also some protection from direct sunlight. Therefore, place plants on an east- or west-facing window in spring, summer and autumn, moving plants to a south-facing window during winter. Protect plants in the greenhouse from sun with either lath blinds or a greenhouse shading material.

### Humidity and ventilation

Orchids need a humid atmosphere in order to thrive. Plants grown indoors should be placed on a tray of gravel that is kept moist at all times. Growing several plants together is also a good practice, for plants will then create their own microclimate.

Orchids also need ventilation. The normal opening and closing of windows that goes on during the course of the day should provide indoor plants with adequate refreshment of air. However, if orchids are grown in greenhouses, ventilators are required.

### Compost

In different parts of the world, orchids are grown on various types of compost, including bark, rice husks, peach stones, peat, perlite, pumice, charcoal, sand and gravel. The most popular compost in the U.S. is one based on sphagnum moss, peat and perlite, used at a ratio of 2 parts peat to 1 part perlite. The pH of the mix should be ad-

## TIPS ON ORCHID CARE

Observing the following points will keep your orchids in top condition.

**1.** Select plants that have properly trained flower spikes to show the flower to best advantage.

**2.** Plants in flower will bloom for a longer period if the temperature is slightly lower than optimum.

**3.** Never stand a plant on or close to radiators.

**4.** If possible, grow plants together in groups.

**5.** Try to provide plants with some sort of gravel tray or bowl and keep the base material on the tray or bowl moist. This will help create humidity around the plant.

**6.** Plants will lose the odd leaf now and again. Do not worry. This is quite normal.

**7.** When the plant finishes flowering, cut the stem within 1in (3cm) of the base.

**8.** Do not water until the compost has become partially dry. Then give a thorough soaking.

**9.** Give the plant fertilizers as recommended. Do not increase the concentrations; plants cannot utilize the nutrients, and excessive fertilization can cause other problems.

**10.** When repotting, choose a pot that provides enough space for one year's growth (the plant may look crowded in the pot) rather than overpot.

**11.** After repotting, soak the compost three times. The compost should then dry out — this may take as long as two to three weeks — before it is watered again.

**1 Propagating an orchid** This plant is ready for division. First, remove dead bracts. Each new division should have two bulbs with leaves and, if possible, new growth.

2 Use a sterile knife to sever the short rhizome which connects the bulbs, but ease the bulbs apart before severing the rhizome.

3 The plant can now be removed from its pot and the divisions pulled apart. If necessary, cut the roots in order to ease the divisions apart.

4 At this stage, trim back any decayed or broken roots to healthy tissue or unbroken roots. Broken roots are likely to decay and poison the new compost.

5 Remove the leafless bulbs (called back bulbs) from the main divisions. Sever the short rhizome which connects them and trim the roots right back.

6 Here two divisions have been made and three back bulbs obtained. The roots of the divisions have been trimmed and the back bulbs cleaned up.

7 For the division select a pot that allows for one year's growth and place a good layer of drainage material at the base (see repotting procedure on page 138 ).

8 For the back bulbs, which will probably be without roots, select a pot just large enough to accomodate it with plenty of drainage at the base.

9 Place the back bulb in the center of the pot. Repotted divisions and back bulbs should be given a thorough soaking, allowing the compost to dry before the next watering. Seal the back bulbs in a plastic bag and hang in a warm position until they begin to shoot.

**Repotting an orchid** The first step is to clean up the base of the plant by removing dead bracts and weeds. Remove plant from pot.

Select a pot which allows for one year's growth. Place a layer of drainage material — polystyrene or perlag will do — at the bottom of the pot.

Place plant on top of the drainage material and start filling in round the root ball with compost. Continue to pour compost around the root, tapping the pot a few times on the bench to ensure good packing. Apply firm finger pressure down the sides and top up with compost to within 1in (2.5cm) of the top.

justed to pH 6.0 by the addition of limestone and Dolomite of lime; a fertilizer which contains an even balance of nutrients and trace elements should also be added. Some growers find perlite mixes difficult, especially with regard to watering, and they often add bark to open up the compost.

**Propagation**

Propagate sympodial orchids during the early spring or directly after the plant has finished flowering. Clean and trim the plant before dividing it. Do not make divisions of less than two or more than three bulbs. Sever the short rhizome that connects the bulbs, using a sterilized knife. Once all the cuts have been made, knock the plant from its pot, pull the plant apart and sort out your new divisions.

It is also possible to increase your stock of sympodial orchids by removing leafless back bulbs and potting into small pots. The bulbs should be placed in warm shaded positions or, alternatively, enclosed in a polythene bag and hung up. After a few weeks, most will have made a new growth, and can be removed from the bag and grown normally.

Monopodial orchids propagate with difficulty. However, 'keiki' (small plantlets produced as offsets) sometimes sprout from the base of the plant or the node of the flower stem. Once these keiki have produced roots, sever plantlets and pot in the normal way.

**Pests and diseases**

Orchids are not particularly susceptible to pests. Slugs and snails may attack young plants, flower spikes and flower buds, but a pellet of metaldehyde and bran, placed between spike and bulb before the buds emerge, should prevent damage. (If growing small plants, it is good practice to scatter pellets among the plants to prevent slug damage.) Red spider mite, aphids and scale insects sometimes appear but can usually be controlled with insecticides.

Prevent disease by purchasing good, clean stock. Should a plant show signs of virus, destroy it immediately. If it remains in your collection, it will endanger your other plants.

**Repotting**

Orchids should be repotted at different intervals depending on the particular species or hybrid. When repotting, always be sure to trim and tidy the plant first. (In the case of sympodial orchids, remove the dead leaf bracts around the pseudobulbs.) Then, knock the plant out of its pot and check the compost to see if it is still in good condition. At the same time, look at the root system for evidence of decay.

If roots and compost are in excellent condition, select a pot that will allow for one year's growth. At the base of the pot, place chunks of polystyrene or coarse perlag to give free drainage. Place the plant in position, pouring the new compost around the root ball. Tap the pot a few times to ensure that the compost is evenly packed around the root ball. Then apply firm finger pressure down the sides of the pot, filling it to within ¾in (2cm) from the top.

If the roots and compost are decayed, remove all the compost and trim the roots so that only healthy ones remain. If orchids are sympodial, remove any leafless pseudo-bulbs by cutting with a sterilized knife the short rhizome that connects the bulbs. Plants with decayed roots should be divided into pieces that contain two pseudobulbs and a new growth. Repot, and place drainage material at the bottom of the pot.

# Cymbidiums

CYMBIDIUMS ARE by far the most popular orchid the world over. The reason for their popularity is obvious to anyone who has seen a well-grown and flowered collection of them. These sympodial plants have very graceful foliage. They produce flowers in a wide range of colors and have lip-markings that may contrast or harmonize with the rest of the flower. The word cymbidium derives from the Greek 'kymbe', meaning 'boat', and refers, in fact, to the boat-like appearance of the lip. Cymbidiums are the easiest of all orchids to cultivate. In nature, they grow in a variety of climates, from tropical rain forest to desert.

Two types of cymbidium are available. Growers refer to

**Miniature Cymbidiums**
Flowering time — late autumn.

Miniature cymbidiums have the species *Cymbidium pumilum* in their background. This fine selection (above) shows the range of colors available during the pre-Christmas period.

**Cymbidium Strathbraan**
(*C.* Putana x *C.* New Dimension)
Flowering time — late autumn.

This outstanding new hybrid (left) flowers very early in the season. It is extremely free-growing and easy-flowering. Clones range in color from very fine white to ice green to blush pink. Lips are beautifully marked, often heavily splashed with deep crimson.

them as 'standard' (large-flowered) or 'miniature' cymbidiums. The latter is more suitable for houseplants, as the large-flowered types tend to be too big for most modern rooms. If you do have the space, however, then nothing is so spectacular as a well-grown standard cymbidium in full flower.

Most miniature cymbidiums today have been bred from the Japanese species *Cymbidium pumilum*. This species figures two generations back in the pedigree of most cymbidiums available today, which are thus termed the second-generation types. These miniature cymbidium hybrids are compact in stature and grow and flower easily. They have attractive blooms in a wide range of colors and last up to 12 weeks in flower.

Hybrids of the miniature species *Cymbidium devonianum* have arching and sometimes pendulous spikes of flowers. These can be green, yellow, bronze, or shades in between, and most flowers have well-marked lips.

Hybrids of *Cymbidium ensifolium* have attractive flowers and a lovely fragrance.

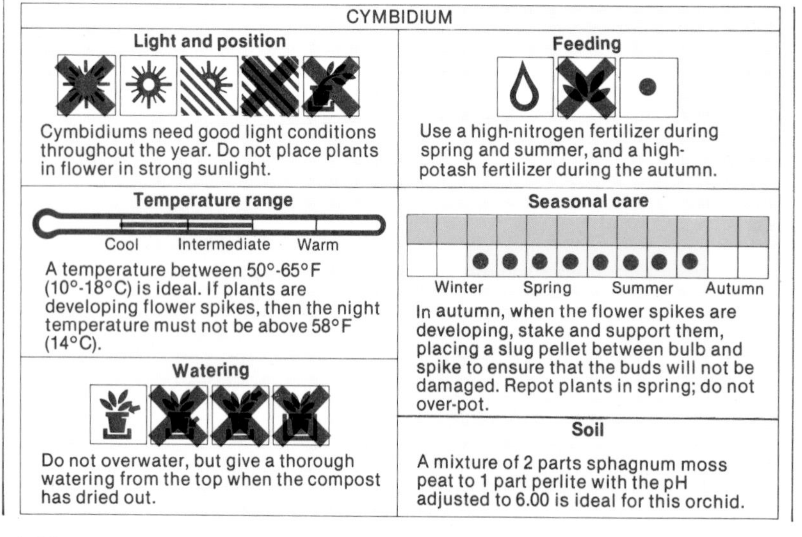


**Cymbidium Mary Pinchess 'Del Rey'**
(*C. pumilum* x *C.* Pajaro)
Flowering time — mid-winter.

Although the variety illustrated (above) was produced many years ago in the United States, it still remains one of the finest early-flowering yellows. While it is not as easy to grow as *C. Strathbraan*, it does flower easily when mature.

**Cymbidium Annan 'Cooksbridge'**
(*C.* Camelot x *C.* Berwick)
Flowering time — late winter.

This plant (right) is by far the finest clone in its color range, with one of the most spectacular lips in the whole of the *Cymbidium* genus. The plant grows and flowers very easily; blooms are carried on fine upright spikes. The first flowering on a young plant will often be during December and January, but in subsequent years the plant will bloom during April and May.

**Cymbidium Western Highlands 'Cooksbridge Ice Green'**
(*C.* Western Rose x *C.* Miretta)
Flowering time — early spring.

The crossing of the fine green breeding plant *C.* Miretta with the white-flowered *C.* Western Rose has produced many outstanding varieties. The illustrated clone (above) is by far the most impressive in the ice-green coloration, having up to 18 large flowers carried on long semi-arching spikes.

**Cymbidium Sutherland**
(*C.* Vieux Rose x *C.* Miretta)
Flowering time — spring.

The pink coloration is unusual for this hybrid (right), which can bear as many as 16 blooms.

**Cymbidium Bullbarrow 'Our Midge'**
(*C.* Western Rose x *C. devonianum*)
Flowering time — spring.

The hybrid *C.* Bullbarrow (right) is the most exciting yet produced from the species *C. devonianum* and the hybrid *C.* Western Rose has been highly awarded both in England and overseas. It produces plants with medium-sized spikes. The flowers are nicely shaped and come in green, bronze and pink shades. Most have beautifully marked crimson lips.

**Cymbidium Highland Wood 'Cooksbridge Poly'**
(*C.* Wood Nymph x *C.* Western Rose)
Flowering time — late winter.

Late-flowering miniature cymbidiums have proved very difficult to produce. The miniature species *Cymbidium tigrinum* has been used to attain this objective. In the case of *C.* Highland Wood,(left) the species features two generations back in the pedigree.

**Cymbidium Castle of Mey**
(*C.* Putana x *C.* Western Rose)
Flowering time — late winter.

The large-flowered *C.* Western Rose has been an outstanding parent and in combination with the miniature *C.* Putana has produced the superb *C.* Castle of Mey. This hybrid (above) produces upright spikes with flowers mostly in white and pastel pink with attractive crimson-marked lips.

**Cymbidium Strathmore**
(*C.* Nip x *C.* Rincon) Flowering time — late autumn.

The large-flowered *Cymbidium* Rincon is the parent of many fine early-flowering cymbidiums. The hybrid has been combined with the exceptional miniature *Cymbidium* Nip to produce delightful plants with attractive pink flowers (left).

**Cymbidium Angelicas Loch**
(*C.* Angelica x *C.* Loch Lomond) Flowering time — early winter.

*Cymbidium* Angelica has proved to be an exceptional parent for early-flowering hybrids. The combination of it and the beautiful, green *C.* Loch Lomond produces a range of varieties in the yellow and green shades, most having quite outstanding crimson-banded lips. The illustrated clone (below) has fine large flowers carried on upright flower spikes.

**Cymbidium Strathdon 'Cooksbridge Noel'**
(*C.* Nip x *C.* Kurun) Flowering time — late autumn.

The hybrid *C.* Strathdon (bottom) produces pink-colored blooms. The variety 'Cooksbridge Noel' is one of the finest yet produced.

**Cymbidium Christmas Song 'Cooksbridge Flamboyance'**
(*C.* Kurense x *C.* Rincon) Flowering time — early winter.

Bright attractive bicolored cymbidiums are a rarity, and this fine early-flowering clone (above) is one of the most exceptional in its class. It produces up to 15 flowers, and is easy-growing and free-flowering.

**Cymbidium Sylvia Miller**
(*C.* Mary Pinchess x *C.* Sussex) Flowering time — winter.

This hybrid (left) produces flowers in shades of yellow, orange and green. Most plants have strong, upright flower spikes and tend to be large. Hybridists are working to improve the plant growth habit. One or two clones are late-flowering.

However, flowers often last only a few days, and the foliage may develop unsightly black marks. Breeders are working to correct these problems.

The third most important miniature species is *Cymbidium tigrinum*, used chiefly as a stud plant because of its late-flowering habit and the fact that it produces dwarf plants that are compact, with short, broad leaves on small pseudo-bulbs. Until recently the color ranges of hybrids derived from the species has been limited to yellow, green, and bronze, but there are now hybrids available in some very attractive pastel shades as well.

Most of the large-flowered cymbidiums have been bred from Burmese, Thai, Vietnamese and north-eastern Indian species — *C. eburneum, C. grandiflorum, C. insigne, C. iansonii, C. lowianum* and *C. parishii*. The early-flowering types have the genes of *C. traceyanum* and *C. erythrostylum*. Due to the hybridists' work, it is now possible to obtain larger-flowered cymbidiums in almost every color except blue. These plants flower from autumn until late spring.

The cymbidiums are cool-growing orchids. They can tolerate night temperatures near to freezing and day temperatures up to 110°F (43°C), though these extremes are not desirable. The best daytime temperature for mature plants is 55-75°F (13-24°C). Temperature in spring, summer and autumn will vary, but try to keep the daytime temperature below 85°F (29°C) and the night temperature about 60°F (16°C). In winter, the night temperature should be 50°F (10°C). Daytime temperature should be 10°F (6°C) higher. Repot cymbidiums in spring, and place them out of doors in a sheltered position during the summer months.

**Collection of miniature cymbidiums**
Flowering time — mid-winter.
The fine miniature breeding plant *C.* Nip has produced many high-quality hybrids in the pink, red and orange shades. The plants illustrated (left) are typical. During early winter they produce flower spikes easily.

**Cymbidium Aviemore 'December Pinkie'** (*C.*Putana x *C.*Kurun)
Flowering time — early winter.
The crossing of *C.* Putana and *C.* Kurun produces superb-quality flowers in pastel shades through to deep pink and orange. The variety illustrated (below) is free-growing and easily flowers. It blooms early.

**Cymbidum Highland Surprise 'Cooksbridge Alba'**
(*C.* Loch Lomond x *C.* Sussex Dawn)
Flowering time — late winter.
The cymbidium hybridist has been hard at work in recent years, attempting to produce high-quality albino orchids. The variety illustrated (above) is free-flowering, with upright spikes of up to 10 flowers.

**Cymbidium Caithness Ice**
(*C.* Caithness x *C.* Miretta)
Flowering time — late winter.
This fine hybrid is the product of two illustrious parents, *C.* Caithness and *C.* York Meredith. The progeny of this union have green flowers with attractive round, red-marked lips. The illustrated clone (above) is an easily grown, free-flowering plant.

ORCHIDACEAE

# Phalaenopsis

Moth Orchid

THE DUTCH BOTANIST Karel Lodewijk Blume established this genus in 1852 when he discovered *Phalaenopsis amabilis* and thought the flowers looked like tropical moths. The generic name is Greek, 'phalaina' meaning 'moth', 'opsis' meaning 'appearance'.

These exotic, tropical orchids from the Far East are still popularly referred to as the Moth Orchid. They are monopodial in growth and have a single stem that continues to grow upwards, producing new leaves at regular intervals. These plants are mostly epiphytic. They grow on trees and frequently produce numerous aerial roots.

Hybridists have produced plants that are striped and spotted and come in a range of colors. The flowers can be 1in (3cm) to 5in (13cm) wide, and are often borne on long arching sprays.

Many species have gone into the breeding of these hybrids. *P. lueddemanniana* produces flowers that open successively on the spike so that a plant may be in flower for several months of the year. Hybrids are attractively barred or spotted in color.

*P. stuartiana* has flowers that are white with a brownish-purple lip, and the lower sepals are similarly marked. These characteristics are passed on to its progeny.

*P. schilleriana* is a magnificent species with beautiful foliage and attractive pink flowers, and it is in the background of today's fine pink phalaenopsis.

Native to the Philippines, *P. amabilis* is responsible for the large, white phalaenopsis orchid seen today, and figures in the pedigree of some other phalaenopsis as well.

Other species that today's modern hybrids have been bred from include *P. fasciata, P. fuscata, P. mariea, P. amboinensis* (mostly used to produce fine yellow types) and *P. equestris*. This is probably the commonest phalaenopsis in the Philippines, and has been used to breed the candy-striped and red-lipped types.

Phalaenopsis orchids need high humidity and high temperature. The ideal night temperature is around 65°F (18°C); the best day temperature is 70-75°F (21-24°C). Some orchid growers use a compost mix of 2 parts bark, 2 parts sphagnum moss peat, 1 part perlite with a pH of 6.0 for phalaenopsis. Excellent results can also be obtained with a bark compost — the size of the bark should be approximately ½in (1cm). When watering this orchid, try to keep the center of the plant dry, as water here can cause rotting. If by chance you do fill the center of the growth with water, then make sure this is emptied out before nightfall. Place plants in a light location.

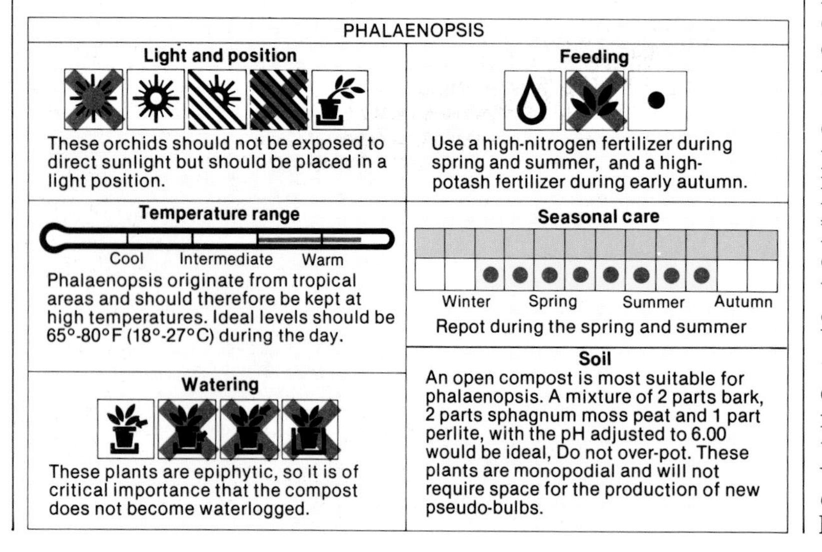

**Phalaenopsis Temple Cloud 'Mount Hood'** (*P.* Opaline x *P.* Keith Shaffer) Flowering time - various.

This fine example (other page) of a modern white phalaenopsis has been line-bred from the species *P. amabilis*. This hybrid is capable of producing a spike of up to 18 large flowers on a graceful arching spray.

**Phalaenopsis Space Queen 'White Gold'** (*P.* Temple Cloud x *P.* Barbara Moler) Flowering time - various.

On strong plants, this hybrid (above) gives good-size flowers and often produces branched spikes of up to 20 blooms.

**Phalaenopsis Solvang 'Portland Star'** (*P.* Lena Martel x *P.* Barbara Moler) Flowering time - various.

Phalaenopsis Barbara Moler has proven to be an exceptional parent for the production of spotted, candy-striped and yellow flowers as well as the type illustrated (right). This hybrid can produce up to 15 blooms.

# Odontoglossums

THE GENUS *Odontoglossum* was founded by W.H. Alexander von Humboldt in 1815 and includes approximately 300 species. Its name combines two words from the Greek — 'odous' meaning 'tooth' and 'glossa' meaning 'tongue' — and refers to the tooth-like projections on the lip of plants in this genus. The odontoglossum is sometimes called the 'Princess of the high Andes'; most species come from Central and South America and grow at high altitudes. In the last part of the nineteenth century and early part of the twentieth, when boat-loads of odontoglossum were brought to England, fine varieties of *Odontoglossum crispum* sold for as much as £1,000. In today's terms, this would represent between £80,000 to £100,000 for just one plant. These varieties were much sought after and were extensively used by the pioneers of orchid hybridization.

What orchid growers refer to as the 'odontoglossum alliance' encompasses odontoglossums and several other related genera, including *Brassia, Cochlioda, Oncidium* and *Miltonia*. From this group come some of the most beautiful flowers in the world and some of the best modern hybrids. Flowers have a 3in (8cm) to 4in (10cm) spread, and are carried on spikes of up to 30 blooms. Flowers are found in every color imaginable; all sorts of patterned and spotted types are also obtainable. Many of the finest intergeneric hybrids have been bred from species of different genera in this alliance.

One of the most important species has been *Odontoglossum crispum*, which will be found in the background of numerous hybrids. Most crispums you see today are white, sometimes with purple or red spots.

*Odontoglossum luteo-purpureum, O. harryanum,* and *O. triumphans* have bred the yellow odontoglossum hybrids, while the fine red odontioda hybrids seen today have been bred from the small-flowered, brilliant-red species called *Cochlioda noezliana*.

Two other intergeneric

**The Odontoglossum Alliance**
Flowering time - various.
Orchids in the odontoglossum alliance (right) possess a wide range of colors. These are very small first-flowering seedlings. Stronger plants would produce up to 15 flowers on arching sprays.

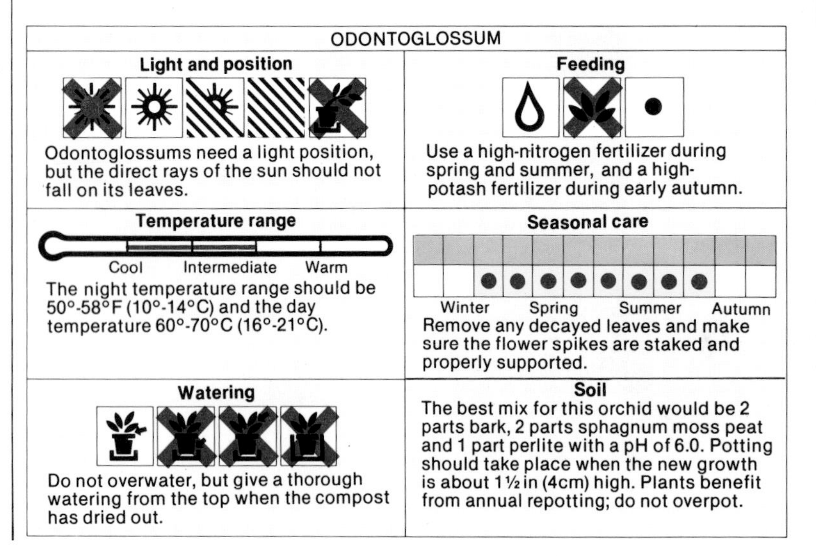

hybrids, odontoncidium (odontogloassum x oncidium) and wilsonara (odontoglossum x cochlioda x oncidium), are largely the result of the following species in the *Oncidium* genus: *O. tigrinum, O. wentworthianum, O. leucochilum* or *O. incurvum*. These species are native to Mexico and Guatemala.

Another intergeneric hybrid, vuylslekeara, has been bred from species of odontoglossum, cochlioda and miltonia. It particularly shows the influence of the latter, the 'Pansy Orchid', very clearly. The *Miltonia* genus is characterized by large flat flowers, and passes this on to its progeny. The most famous orchid in the world, certainly the one most propagated, is *Vuylstekeara Cambria var. Plush*. The quality of the flower, its ease of growth and its ability to thrive under varying conditions account for its popularity.

Plants within the odontoglossum alliance have a wide range of temperature requirements. Consequently, the 'ideal' temperature varies accordingly. Most, however, are happy at a night temperature of around 50-55°F (10-13°C). The day temperature should be controlled so that it does not rise above 80°F (27°C) if this is at all possible. Providing the plant is in good condition and well-rooted, it will tolerate temperatures as low as 40°F (4°C) and as high as 90°F (32°C). These levels of cold and heat will, however, place a certain amount of stress on the plants, so limit their exposure to such extremes as much as possible.

Watering is critical for this group of orchids. It is most important not to overwater; in fact it would be better to slightly underwater. Use rainwater if possible.

Aphids sometimes trouble plants within the odontoglossum alliance, and in recent years, there have been several instances of plants being attacked by false spider mites, which in some plants can be mistaken for virus disease. This pest can be eliminated by using an appropriate insecticide.

When potting these orchids, use a mix of 2 parts sphagnum moss peat, 2 parts Sequoia bark, 1 part perlite, with the pH adjusted to 6.0 and a base fertilizer added to the peat. Repot annually, when new growth is about 1½in (4cm) long. Ideally, odontoglossums should be in a greenhouse when not in flower. If this is not possible, place plants in a light location indoors but not in direct sun.

**Vuylstekeara Edna x Odontioda Mardley** Flowering time - various.

This fine hybrid (top) has small to medium-sized flowers carried on a semi-arching spike. The broad flat lip is the characteristic that has been inherited from the miltonia orchid in its background.

**Odontioda Le Nez Point**
(*O.* Trixon x *O.* Fremar)
Flowering time - various.

This beautifully shaped odontioda is made even more attractive by the lighter-colored margins of its sepals and petals (above).

**Odontoglossum and allied genera**
Flowering time - various.

This display of orchids and ferns in a greenhouse (left) is just one example of the many ways orchids can be used in combination with other plants to create interesting flower arrangements. The orchids shown here can flower at almost any time of the year, although there are two main peak flowering periods. These occur in autumn and the late spring.

**Odontoglossum Crutordo x Odontioda Elpheon**
Flowering time - various.

This unnamed hybrid (below left) that is referred to by its crossing is an excellent example of a heavily patterned odontioda. This first-flowering seedling bears large, well-shaped flowers. Mature plants may have a spike of up to 20 flowers.

**Odontoglossum Royal Wedding 'Cooksbridge'**
(*O.* Pancho x *O.* Ardentissimum)
Flowering time - various.

The superb hybrid (above) is bred from a line of superior odontoglossums, all of which have the albino characteristic. Flowers from this hybrid were included in the wedding bouquet of HRH The Princess of Wales. This plant is vigorous and free-flowering.

# Paphiopedilum

BEFORE THEY were re-classified, paphiopedilums used to be known as cypripediums, and many orchid-growers still use the latter name. The popular name for this orchid is Lady's Slipper because, instead of forming a lip as in most orchids, the modified third petal forms a pouch that looks somewhat similar to a lady's slipper. Species of this genus are found in the Far East, and in Southeast Asia. They encompass an immense range of sizes, shapes and colors.

Because it was valued as a cut flower, *P. insigne* was at one time the most common of all paphiopedilums. It is prominent in the background of many of today's spotted and yellow hybrids. *P. delenatii*, a delightful pink species, has produced a line of attractive pink-flowered hybrids, while *P. niveum* has produced some superb white-flowered hybrids.

Another important species used in the breeding of this genus is *P. bellatulum*. This plant is native to Burma and Thailand, and is responsible for the shape and broad petals of many of today's best paphiopedilum hybrids.

In recent years, there has been increasing interest in what is termed 'primary hybrids'. These grow and bloom easily, and are produced very quickly from seed.

Plants in this genus should have a night temperature of 58°F (14°C) and a day temperature between 65°F (18°C) and 75°F (24°C), although some growers keep their plants at lower temperatures. Try not to let temperatures rise above 85°F (29°C) for prolonged periods of time.

Pathiopedilums are low-light orchids and should not be subjected to the direct rays of the sun. Give them good light, but do not place them near the window. Repot plants directly after flowering, preferably before the end of spring, When

**Paphiopedilum Hybrids**
Flowering time — winter.

This fine group of paphiopedilums (above left) shows some of the different colors and shapes of plants in this genus. While most flower in winter, some varieties do flower at different times of the year.

**Paphiopedilum Brownstone**
(*P.* Hazella x *P.* Beedon)
Flowering time — winter.

This high-quality paphiopedilum hybrid (above right) produces some exceptional striped flowers. It is a compact plant that grows and flowers very easily, usually in December-February.

watering, be careful that water does not lie in the center of growth. This will damage buds and flowers. Provide regular feeding during the summer.

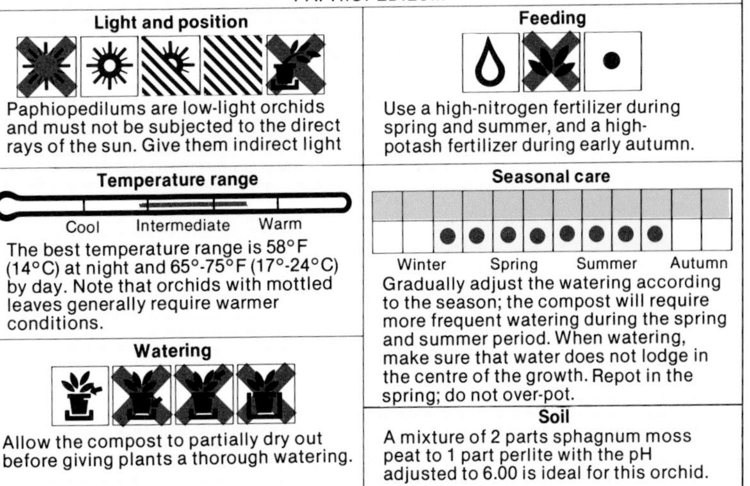

# Glossary

**Active growth**
The period when a plant puts out new leaves, increases in size and, if a flowering plant, produces flowers.

**Areoles**
The small cushion of hairs on the ribs or tubercules of cacti, from which develop spines or flowers — the growing point.

**Axil**
The point where side-shoots branch or flower stalks form.

**Bottlegarden**
A glass flagon similar to a terrarium. Because it is draught-free, moist and warm, it can be an excellent growing medium for small, slow-growing plants.

**Bract**
A modified leaf borne on a floral axis. It is often highly colored and long-lasting.

**Callus**
A cork-like seal which forms over a cut section of plant tissue.

**Calyx**
The outermost part of a flower consisting of sepals. The calyx is usually tough and green and protects the corolla within. Occasionally it is brightly colored and looks like the corolla.

**Caudex**
An enlarged tuber at the base of some plants. A swollen stem-like base.

**Caudiciform**
In the form of a caudex.

**Cephalium**
A crown of bristles that forms on some cacti and through which flowers appear, followed by seed pods.

**Compost**
A potting medium. A compost that contains soil is a soil-based or loam-based compost. A compost in which peat has been subsituted for soil is a peat-based or soil-less compost. There are many slightly differing formulas for each of the two types.

**Corolla**
The major decorative feature of a plant. Usually colorful, it may consist of separate petals or be fused in a single unit.

**Crocking**
The practice of filling a container with earthenware shards in order to promote drainage.

**Crown**
The area at the base or center of a plant from which top growth and roots emerge.

**Column**
A feature characteristic of orchids in which male and female flowers are fused together.

**Cultivar**
A variety originating in cultivation. It is the third name of a plant's name and is usually written in the vernacular rather than in Latin and appears in quotes, e.g., *Heptapleurum arboricola* 'Geisha Girl'.

**Cyathia**
Term used for the inflorescence of Euphorbia species, which consists of several unisex flowers.

**Deciduous**
A plant that loses its leaves at the end of the growing season. New leaves appear when the growth period begins.

**Dormancy**
A temporary period of inactivity when growth ceases.

**Dwarf species**
A small, slow-growing species.

**Endemic**
Native to a geographical area.

**Epidermis**
The outer layer of tissue on the body of a plant.

**Epiphyte**
Non-parasitic plants that grow on other plants or rocks.

**Evergreen**
A plant that retains its leaves throughout the year.

**Family**
The largest and most general category of botanical classification. The family name is always Latin and ends in ae, e.g., Araceae. Individual plants within a family are known by a binomial title consisting of a plant's generic and specific name.

**Feature plant**
A bold, distinctive plant that can be set out on its own. A specimen plant.

**Flower**
A blossom. The plant organ for sexual reproduction.

**Free-draining**
Describes any type of soil through which water drains quickly.

**Free-growing**
Active, quick-growing.

**Genus**
A subdivision of a plant family and the first name in a plant's binomial title, e.g., *Begonia lucerne*.

**Germinate**
To sprout or develop.

**Growing tips**
The tip of a stem where extension growth occurs.

**Growth habit**
The style in which a plant grows, e.g., upright, pendulous, spreading, low-growing or creeping.

**Habit**
The outward appearance of a plant.

**Habitat**
The natural home of a plant.

**Humus**
Well-rotted vegetative matter.

**Hybrid**
A product of cross-pollination between two dissimilar parents.

**Inflorescence**
The flowering part of a plant, a term that usually refers to a head, cluster or spike of several flowers grouped on one main stem.

**Latex**
A milky sap exuded from some species.

**Mimicry**
The resemblance of a plant to something different, e.g., conophytums resemble pebbles or stones.

**Monopodial**
A stem that grows indefinitely from a single growing point. This term usually applies to orchids.

**Monotypic**
A genus containing only one species.

**Node**
A point or joint on a stem from which leaves and sideshoots appear.

**Nomenclature**
The botanical system of naming plants.

**Offset**
A new plant that a mature plant produces, usually at its base.

**Offshoot**
See offsets.

**Pedicel**
A plant stalk.

**Petals**
Inner segments of a flower (collectively called the calyx).

**Petiole**
The leafstalk, a stem that supports the blade of a foliage leaf.

**Pinching out**
Removing the growing point of a stem to stimulate the growth of buds lower down on a stem.

**Potting on**
Transferring a plant to a larger container to provide more space for spreading roots.

**Propagation**
The creation of new plants either by asexual or sexual reproduction.
Two types of propagation are possible, either vegetative propagation (using some part of the plant, such as a leaf, stem, or offset for propagation) or propagation by seed.

**Pseudo-bulb**
A thick stem in orchids that rises from the rhizome. This swelling at its base enables the plant to store water and other nutrients.

**Rhizome**
A fleshy stem, usually horizontal and underground. It often serves as a storage organ and usually produces subterranean feeding roots as well as top growth.

**Rootball**
The embedment of plant roots and potting medium in a container.

**Rooting powder**
A powder that is applied to the cut end of a cutting to stimulate root production.

**Rootstock**
The underground part of a plant to which another plant can be grafted. Rootstock is sometimes loosely used as a synonym for rhizome.

**Rosette**
A cluster of leaves arising from the crown, either on individual stalks or in an overlapping spiral.

**Sepals**
A separate segment of a divided calyx in a flower.

**Spathe**
The large, sometimes brightly coloured bract or modified leaf that surrounds or encloses the flower spike in plants of the family Araceae.

**Species**
A category of botanical classification ranking immediately below the genus and comprising related organisms capable of interbreeding. It is designated by a binomial that consists of the name of a genus followed by a Latin name, e.g., *Acalypha hispida* is a species in the genus *Acalypha*.

**Sphagnum moss**
A type of bog moss used in potting mixtures. It is often used for orchids, which need an open, moisture-retaining material.

**Stamen**
The male pollen-bearing organ of a plant.

**Stigma**
The tip section of the female organ of the flower, the pistil.

**Style**
The stalk that links the stigma with the ovary in the pistil of a flower.

**Sympodial**
A term, often used for orchids, that refers to a stem or rhizome having successions of growths. These produce annual inflorescences. Further growth is carried on through branching.

**Taproot**
A strong root, often the main root of a plant, growing downward.

**Terrarium**
A glass or plastic sealed container used for growing plants.

**Terrestrial**
Growing in soil on the land.

**Tuber**
The fleshy root of a plant.

**Tubercles**
Projections or swellings on a plant organ. Tubercles are a characteristic feature of cacti.

**Top dressing**
A fresh layer of potting medium applied to a potted plant after the equivalent amount of old mixture has been removed. Top dressing is an alternative to repotting, and is often used when a plant has grown too large for moving on to a bigger pot.

**Variegated**
A term used to describe leaves that are striped or spotted, or patterned in a color other than green.

**Variety**
A subdivision of a species that has only trifling differences from the specific types. Botanists today use the term strictly to apply to variations that occur in the wild, but the term is sometimes used to describe cultivars, variations occurring in cultivation. When they exist, varieties form the third word of a plant's Latin name. True varieties usually have Latin names and are not enclosed in quotation marks, e.g., *Pleomele reflexa variegata*.

# Index

Page numbers in *italic* refer to captions and illustrations.

## ACKNOWLEDGEMENTS

The publishers would like to give special thanks to Clive Innes and Ray Bilton for the pictures they supplied. Mr Innes provided all the photographs that appear in the section on cacti and succulents, except for the bottom two pictures on page 105. Mr Bilton provided all the photographs that appear in the orchids chapter, except for the bottom three pictures on page 135, and the pictures on pages 137 and 138. The other pictures in this book were reproduced by courtesy of the following:

Michael Boys, page 13 (bottom three), page 16 (top two), page 64.
Pat Brindley, page 47 (bottom left), page 60 (middle), page 61 (top right), page 72 (top left), page 98 (bottom right), page 100 (left).
Eric Crichton, page 41 (all pictures), page 46 (bottom two), page 50 (bottom left), page 54 (bottom left), page 62 (top), page 66 (bottom), page 67, page 69, page 72 (right), page 77 (top), page 82 (top), page 86, page 95, page 100 (right), page 102 (right), page 103.
Spectrum Colour Library, page 46 (top), page 51 (top).
Michael Warren, page 66 (top), page 68.

All other photographs that appear are property of Quarto Publishing Ltd.

While every effort has been made to acknowledge all copyright holders, we apologize if any omissions have been made.